THE G7/G8 SYSTEM

The G8 and Global Governance Series

The G8 and Global Governance Series explores the issues, the institutions and the strategies of participants in the G8 network of global governance, as they address the challenges of shaping global order in the new millennium. Intensifying globalization is moving many once domestic issues into the international arena, requiring constant international co-operation, and demanding new collective leadership to direct the galaxy of multilateral institutions created in 1945. In response, the Group of Eight, composed of the world's major market democracies, including Russia and the European Union, is emerging as the effective source of global governance in the new era. This series focuses on the new issues at the centre of global governance, from finance, investment, and trade, through transnational threats to human security, to traditional political and security challenges. It examines the often invisible network of G8 and G7 institutions as they operate within and outside established international organizations to generate desired outcomes. It analyzes how individual G7 members and other international actors, including multinational firms and those from civil society, devise and implement strategies to secure their preferred global order.

Also in the series

The G8's Role in the New Millennium
Edited by
Michael R. Hodges, John J. Kirton and Joseph P. Daniels
ISBN 1 84014 774 1

The G7/G8 System

Evolution, role and documentation

PETER I. HAJNAL
University of Toronto

With a contribution by Sian Meikle, University of Toronto

Ashgate

Aldershot • Brookfield USA • Singapore • Sydney

Published by
Ashgate Publishing Ltd
Gower House
Croft Road
Aldershot
Hants GU11 3HR
England

Ashgate Publishing Company
Old Post Road
Brookfield
Vermont 05036
USA

British Library Cataloguing in Publication Data
Hajnal, Peter I.
  The G7/G8 system: evolution, role and documentation. -
  (The G8 and global governance)
  1. Group of Seven 2. Group of Eight 3. Group of Eight -
  History 4. International economic relations 5. Summit
  meetings
  I. Title
  337

Library of Congress Catalog Card Number: 99-72597

ISBN 1 84014 776 8
Printed and bound in Great Britain by MPG Books Ltd, Bodmin, Cornwall

Contents

List of Figures		viii
List of Tables		ix
Foreword by Sir Nicholas Bayne		x
Preface		xii
Acknowledgements		xiv
List of Abbreviations		xv
1	The G7/G8 as an International Institution	1
	Origins of the G7 Summit	4
	The Role of the Summit	5
	Summit Reform	7
2	The Summit Meetings	13
	Summit Cycles	19
3	The Players	25
	Russia's Membership	26
	Other Candidates for Membership	28
4	The G7/G8 System	35
	Ministerial Meetings	35
	Sherpa Meetings	41
	Meetings of Task Forces, Working Groups and Expert Groups	41
5	Connections with Other International Organisations and Fora	45
6	The Agenda of the Summit	57
7	Summit Results	67

8   G7/G8 Documentation   73
             Summit Documentation   73
                  The Communiqué   73
                  Preparing the Communiqué   74
                  The Political Declarations and Chairman's
                       Statements   75
                  Other Types of Leaders' Documents   79
                  Outside Communications to the Summit   80
             Documentation of Ministerial Conferences, Task
             Forces, Working Groups, and Expert Groups   81
                  Ministerial Documentation   81
                  Other Official-Level Documentation   84

9   Assessing G7/G8 Documentation   93

10   Other Sources of Information about the G7/G8   101
             Archives   101
             Writings about the G7/G8   101
             Appendix: Examples of Writings About the G7/G8   102

11   G7/G8 Information: Internet Resources   107
         Sian Meikle
             Government Sites   107
             International Organisations   109
             Other G7/G8-Related Web Sites   110
             Academic Sites   110
             University of Toronto G8 Information Centre   111
                  History, Purpose and Philosophy   111
                  Contents   112
                  Indexing and Searching of the Site   114
                  Issues of Site Maintenance   115
                  Users of the G8 Information Centre   116

12   Conclusion   125

G7/G8 Bibliography   129
             Books, Shorter Writings, and Publications in Series   130
             Chapters in Books   143
             Articles in Periodicals   148

Government Publications 171
International Organisation Publications 181
Internet Resources 185
Index 187

List of Figures

3.1   Model of a Three-tier Evolution of the G7/G8   29

11.1   Total Pages Requested from the G8 Information Centre,
by Week   117

11.2   Top 250 Pages: Subject Category by Proportion of Total,
1998   120

11.3   Top 250 Pages: Subject Category by Proportion of Use,
1998   120

11.4   Summary of Email Questions by User Category, 1998   122

11.5   Summary of Email Questions by Subject Category, 1998   122

List of Tables

2.1	G7/G8 Annual Summit Meetings, 1975-1999	14
2.2	Main Events of the 1993 Tokyo Summit	16
2.3	Main Events of the 1996 Lyon Summit	17
2.4	Main Events of the 1997 Denver Summit of the Eight	18
2.5	Main Events of the 1998 Birmingham G8 Summit	19
3.1	Real GDP Changes of the G7, the EU, Russia and China	31
4.1	The G7/G8 System	36
4.2	Main Events of the Pre-Summit Meeting of the G7/G8 Foreign and Finance Ministers, London, 8-9 May 1998	40
5.1	G7/G8 Voting Power in the IMF and the World Bank	53
7.1	Co-operative Achievements of G7/G8 Summits, 1975-1998	68
7.2	Performance Assessment of the Birmingham Summit by Issue Area	69
11.1	Most Popular Thirty Pages at G8 Information Centre	118
11.2	Summary of Email Questions Received by Country, 1998	123

Foreword

by Sir Nicholas Bayne

The G7–now G8–is an institution. It brings together the governments of the United States, Japan, Germany, France, Italy, the United Kingdom, and Canada (the original seven powers) with the European Union (Commission and Presidency) and most recently Russia. It embodies both an annual summit and a proliferation of other meetings, ministerial or official, regular or occasional, avowed or unpublicised. But it is not an organisation. It does not have a charter, a headquarters or a secretariat, let alone a cafeteria or a pension plan, both identified by the late Dr Michael Hodges as vital signs of an organisation.

Most important, the G7/G8 does not have a public relations department, an information service or a web site. Other institutions–the International Monetary Fund, the World Trade Organization, the OECD–are prodigal in the information they disseminate. The G7/G8 is secretive and unforthcoming, apart from agreed communiqués and other documents which issue from its meetings. True, each time a G8 member hosts a summit or similar meeting, it produces extensive briefing material and, these days, creates a web site. Other G8 members may do the same, even if not hosts. But all this material has national origins and–inevitably–a national bias. There is no collective information effort. Nothing is done for those curious about the G7/G8 itself, whether journalists, academic researchers, non-G8 governments or the general public. In some ways the G7/G8 has even gone backwards. Originally the G7 heads of government all took part in the concluding press conference. Now they brief separately, leaving only the host to present the final declaration.

How, then, can anyone find out about the G7/G8? Fortunately, since 1988, the University of Toronto G7, now G8, Research Group has been filling the gap left by the G7/G8 itself. Over the last ten years it has built up, with the implicit encouragement of the G7/G8 governments, a comprehensive archive in both written and electronic form and a body of analytical work accessible to scholars and the general reader alike.

Peter Hajnal is the librarian and bibliographer of the Research Group. He has an encyclopaedic command of this material. From it he has created, in this volume, the first guide-book or manual to the G7/G8. He explains how it started, who takes part and how it works. He traces its development from a single annual summit, prepared by quasi-independent sherpas, to the present intricate network of ministerial conferences, specialised meetings, working groups and task forces; from a limited list of economic themes to an agenda open to every possible international topic; from the two-page statement produced at the first summit at Rambouillet in 1975 (President Giscard resisted even this) to the hundreds of pages issued by G7/G8 meetings in 1998, even though the actual summit documents were half the length of previous years. Peter Hajnal has the skill and experience needed to guide us through this labyrinthine documentation. This extends beyond the papers issued by the G7/G8 itself to wider analytical writings about it; and his book concludes with a thorough bibliography.

Sian Meikle, the University of Toronto Library's web development co-ordinator and the author of Chapter 11 of this book, has been instrumental in designing and developing the G8 Information Centre web site in co-operation with the G8 Research Group. Her survey of internet resources of G7/G8 information, along with her thorough analysis of the patterns of use of the Information Centre, form a most valuable component of this guide.

Peter Hajnal possesses what Thomas Carlyle called "transcendent capacity of taking trouble". He has taken immense trouble to make this guide reliable and definitive. It is comprehensive in coverage, precise in accuracy, meticulous in attention to detail, judicious in interpretation. Anyone who is curious about the G7/G8, puzzled by its statements or baffled by its workings, will find this book an indispensable source of instruction.

Preface

This study is based on the assumption that the G7/G8 is one of the central international institutions of the 1990s and, potentially, of the twenty-first century. Notwithstanding serious criticism of its institutional growth, proliferating agenda and lack of representativeness, the G7/G8 has achieved more than some critics would have us believe, and has been able to secure a significant degree of compliance from its members on a number of issues. It has also served as an effective means of socialising the leaders and ministers of member states, enabling them to get well-acquainted with one another and to understand one another's domestic political and economic constraints, and providing them with a means of policy coordination. Questions remain, however, about the effectiveness of the G7/G8 in changing the behaviour of non-member states and multilateral institutions, and in improving broader global conditions.

The purpose of this work is to discuss the origins, characteristics, role and agenda of the G7/G8 system; to review its evolution; and to provide a detailed study of its complex and elusive documentation.[*]

Chapter 1 introduces the G7/G8 as an international institution, reviews its origins and role, surveys the major debates and questions about it in the scholarly literature, and discusses proposals and initiatives for reforming the G7/G8. Chapter 2 reviews the summit meetings from the inception of the G7 in 1975 through the 1998 Birmingham Summit, highlighting the milestones in summit history. Chapter 3 discusses questions of G7/G8 membership and the major players, with a more detailed treatment

---

[*] Earlier, shorter versions of this work appeared as "The G7" in *International Information: Documents, Publications and Electronic Information of International Governmental Organizations*, 2nd ed., 202-40, edited by Peter I. Hajnal (Englewood, Colo.: Libraries Unlimited, 1997); *From G7 to G8: Evolution, Role and Documentation of a Unique Institution* (New York: Columbia International Affairs Online, Columbia University Press, 1998; URL: https:/wwwc.cc.columbia.edu/sec/dlc/ciao/book/hajnal/index.html; and "The Documentation of the G7/G8 System," *G7 Governance*, No. 4 (June 1998); URL:
www.library.utoronto.ca/www/g7/governance/gov4/index.html.

of Russian membership and potential further evolution of the institution.

The subject of Chapter 4 is the larger G7/G8 system, with the increasingly complex network of ministerial meetings, the sherpas, and various task forces and expert groups. The G7/G8 system does not function in a vacuum: Chapter 5 explores the nature of its relationship with other international organisations and fora. Chapter 6 presents an overview of the changing summit agenda; and Chapter 7 is a survey of studies evaluating the results of the summits both in terms of co-operative agreements reached and compliance with summit undertakings.

Chapter 8 surveys the evolving documentation of the G7/G8 system, examining the types, characteristics, subject matter, production and dissemination of documents as well as their importance. Chapter 9 is a systematic assessment of the documentation as seen by a number of analysts and observers. Going beyond official documents, Chapter 10 discusses briefly the major sources of additional information, notably archives and writings about the G7/G8 and related issues. Chapter 11, written by Sian Meikle, examines and evaluates internet resources, with emphasis on the web site of the G8 Information Centre at the University of Toronto.

It is hoped that this study, along with the accompanying comprehensive bibliography, will add something of value to the scholarly literature and will serve as a useful work of reference for academics, government officials, the news media, libraries and the general public.

Peter I. Hajnal

Acknowledgements

I gratefully acknowledge the encouragement and suggestions of Sir Nicholas Bayne, former British High Commissioner in Canada (now with British Invisibles and the London School of Economics and Political Science); Dr Sylvia Ostry, Professor John Kirton, Professor Louis Pauly and Dr Eleonore Kokotsis of the University of Toronto; Laurette Glasgow, Michael Rooney, Janet Gompf and Kimberly Phillips of the Canadian Department of Foreign Affairs and International Trade; David Malone of the International Peace Academy (formerly with the Canadian Department of Foreign Affairs and International Trade), and Professor George M. von Furstenberg of Indiana University, Bloomington, Indiana. I am grateful to my colleague Sian Meikle, web development co-ordinator at the University of Toronto Library, for contributing an important and excellent chapter, and for her assistance in overcoming technical obstacles while preparing the text. I also thank Marc Lalonde of the University of Toronto Library for his technical help. My gratitude is due to the Centre for International Studies of the University of Toronto for providing space and many kinds of support. For their very able and dedicated research and editorial assistance I thank Edna Hajnal, Katrina Švihran, Karen Van Der Zon, Barbara Vasa and Audrey Malloch. Last but certainly not least, I thank Kirstin Howgate and her colleagues at Ashgate for encouraging and helping along the preparation of the manuscript for publication. All of them contributed significantly to making this a better book. Any omissions or inaccuracies are my sole responsibility.

Peter I. Hajnal

List of Abbreviations

AIDS	Acquired Immune Deficiency Syndrome
BIS	Bank for International Settlements
CSCE	Conference on Security and Co-operation in Europe
EBRD	European Bank for Reconstruction and Development
EC	European Community (-ies)
ECB	European Central Bank
ECOSOC	Economic and Social Council (UN)
EMU	European (Economic and) Monetary Union
EU	European Union
FAO	Food and Agriculture Organization of the United Nations
FATF	Financial Action Task Force
G5	Group of Five
G7	Group of Seven
G8	Group of Eight
G10	Group of Ten
G15	Group of Fifteen
G22	Group of Twenty-two
GAB	General Arrangements to Borrow (IMF)
GATT	General Agreement on Tariffs and Trade
GDP	Gross Domestic Product
GNP	Gross National Product
HIPC(s)	Heavily Indebted Poor Countries
HIV	Human Immunodeficiency Virus
HTML	Hypertext Markup Language
IDA	International Development Association
IFAD	International Fund for Agricultural Development
IFI(s)	International Financial Institution(s)
IGO(s)	International Governmental Organisation(s)
ILO	International Labour Organisation
IMF	International Monetary Fund
IOs	International Organisations
IOSCO	International Organization of Securities Commissions
ISPO	Information Society Project Office (EU)
MARIS	Maritime Information Society

MTCR	Missile Technology Control Regime
NAFTA	North American Free Trade Agreement
NATO	North Atlantic Treaty Organization
NBC	Nuclear, Biological and Chemical (weapons)
ODC	Overseas Development Council
OECD	Organisation for Economic Co-operation and Development
OPEC	Organization of the Petroleum Exporting Countries
OSCE	Organization for Security and Co-operation in Europe
P8	Political 8 (G7 + Russia)
PHARE	Assistance for Economic Restructuring in the Countries of Central and Eastern Europe
Quad	Trade Ministers Quadrilateral (US, Canada, Japan, EU)
SDR	Special Drawing Rights (IMF)
SIG	(G7) Support Implementation Group
SME	Small and Medium-sized Enterprises
START	Strategic Arms Reduction Treaty
TOES	The Other Economic Summit
UK	United Kingdom
UN	United Nations
UNAIDS	United Nations Programme on AIDS/HIV
UNCED	United Nations Conference on Environment and Development
UNCTAD	United Nations Conference on Trade and Development
UNDP	United Nations Development Programme
UNEP	United Nations Environment Programme
Unesco	United Nations Educational, Scientific and Cultural Organization
UNICEF	United Nations Children's Fund
UNIDO	United Nations Industrial Development Organization
US	United States of America
USSR	Union of Soviet Socialist Republics
WB	World Bank (International Bank for Reconstruction and Development)
WHO	World Health Organization
WTO	World Trade Organization

1 The G7/G8 as an International Institution

The Group of Seven/Group of Eight (G7/G8) is an unorthodox international institution. To place it in context, it is useful to recall that the authoritative *Yearbook of International Organizations* defines international governmental organisations (IGOs) as bodies that are "based on a formal instrument of agreement between the governments of nation states; ... includ[e] three or more nation states as parties to the agreement; ... [and have] a permanent secretariat performing ongoing tasks".[1] The G7/G8 is a less structured international arrangement; it was not established by formal international agreement, and it has no secretariat. The British government, prior to hosting the 1998 Birmingham Summit, characterised the G8 as "an informal organisation, with no rules or permanent Secretariat staff".[2] The group's relative informality and the fact that it is relatively unencumbered by bureaucracy have enabled the leaders of these countries to get to know one another and to understand one another's domestic political and economic constraints. It has also given them a forum and venue for policy co-ordination.

Occasional proposals to establish some form of permanent, continuing machinery have met with stiff resistance from at least some members. Nonetheless, the G7/G8 has become a most important actor on the international scene and has evolved into what may be termed the G7/G8 system. The best-known part of that system is the series of annual meetings of heads of state or government. These annual summit meetings are covered in great detail–albeit unevenly–by the news media and increasingly by scholarly and other specialised writing, but the resulting documentation is not widely understood. This work explores the context and the nature of that documentation.

The term G7, and now G8, has come to predominate as the name of the annual series of summit meetings. Earlier it was called the economic summit, the summit of industrialised countries, the Western economic summit, and the seven-power summit. None of these names is totally accurate:

1

- The summit is no longer just economic; political questions and various global issues have taken on increasing importance for a number of years.
- With the exception of the 1976 summit, it has not been strictly a summit of the seven; the first summit had six participants, only the second had seven, and subsequent meetings had seven countries plus the European Union (EU; formerly European Community, EC); beginning with the 1994 Naples Summit (following post-summit meetings with the USSR in 1991 and then Russia in 1992 and 1993), Russia has been directly associated with the political aspects of the summit which, for this purpose, came to be referred to as the P8 (or "political G8"). In 1997, Russia became associated with the G7 even more closely, forming the "Summit of the Eight", leaving only financial and certain other economic issues to the core G7; in Birmingham in 1998, the G7 became officially the G8, with Russia as a full member, although the G7 configuration not only survives but thrives alongside the G8, especially for financial and other economic matters. Because of the continued participation of the EU, the "G8" is not precisely the G8, either.
- It is not completely Western, at least in a geographic sense: Japan is a charter member and Russia is an Asian as well as a European state.
- Not all the–prospectively or arguably–major industrialised countries participate; conversely, Russia's status as a major modern industrialised country is open to question.

Several scholars affirm the unique character and growing importance of the G7/G8 in the post-Cold War world. John J. Kirton states that "the G7 system of institutions is the late twentieth century global equivalent of the Concert of Europe that helped produce peace among the great powers, and prosperity more widely, from 1818 to 1914". He argues that "the G7 Summit system has become the effective centre of global governance, replacing the order earlier provided by the 1919-1945 [League of Nations and] United Nations and 1947 Atlantic family of institutions, and recurrently creating consensus and inducing compliance among its members and other states and international institutions".[3] Cesare Merlini, on the other hand, expresses the view that the G7 "is not an international institution in the real sense of the term ... . [It is] a quasi institutional structure ... semi-personal and at the same time semi-institutional". The French view, according to Philippe Moreau Defarges, is that "the G-7 summit cannot and must not be a Western council". Michael R. Hodges gives the British view that the G7 "is a forum rather than an institution".[4] In a speech he gave just before the 1998 Birmingham Summit, Hodges remarked that "an institution has a cafeteria and a pension plan" and the G8 has neither.

Andrea de Guttry, viewing the dynamic development of the institutionalisation of the summit, notes "the total absence of a fixed summit structure or any kind of administrative/bureaucratic support" at the summit's beginnings, and the gradual process whereby, over the years, "the structure of the summit has slowly, almost unconsciously, become more complicated".[5] Nicholas Bayne and Robert D. Putnam contrast the "stand-alone" G7 summit with other kinds of summits that have become common in recent years and that depend on a parent international organisation for their existence, such as the United Nations (UN) "Earth Summit" in 1992, or the periodic summit meetings of the EU, the Commonwealth and the Francophonie.[6] G. R. Berridge lists G7 summits among the category of "serial summits", in contrast with *ad hoc* (usually one-time only) summits and with a third type, high-level exchanges of views.[7] Bayne observes that "[t]he G7 Summit is at the same time an institution and an anti-institution. This ... may be the secret of its survival".[8]

The 1991 London Summit, important for the development of the summit as an institution, emphasised officially that the summit had a chairman, rotating each calendar year, in the person of the host leader for that year. (A study team of the Group of Thirty, a Washington-based think tank, made several recommendations in a report released on the eve of the 1991 Summit. The main proposals were: setting a new core agenda for future summits; sharing responsibility systematically and comprehensively; and improving follow-up arrangements for summit initiatives.)[9] The 1993 Tokyo Summit also addressed the question of the summit as an institution, and stated the leaders' wish that "summits should be less ceremonial, with fewer people, documents and declarations, and with more time devoted to informal discussion".[10] As a further indication of institutional development, Canada, as chair of the G7 in 1995, issued a report, *1995, Canada's Year As G7 Chair: The Halifax Summit Legacy*, in February 1996.[11] The British hosts of the 1998 Birmingham Summit released a background brief commenting on the annual rotation of G8 presidency among the member states, outlined the British presidency's proposals to change the style of the summit and set a focused agenda for Birmingham.[12]

Origins of the G7 Summit

The G7/G8 Summit takes its origin from several major events in the early 1970s that had a profound effect on the world economic system:

- "The collapse of the Bretton Woods monetary system" based on fixed exchange rates and on the United States dollar's convertibility into gold. The two Bretton Woods institutions, the International Monetary Fund (IMF) and the World Bank–known formally as International Bank for Reconstruction and Development–tried to set up the necessary reforms, but were not successful in this effort.[13]
- The first enlargement of the EC in 1972, with Britain, Denmark and Ireland joining the original six members.
- The first oil crisis, when the Organization of the Petroleum Exporting Countries (OPEC) placed an embargo on oil supplies following the October 1973 Yom Kippur war. Western countries disagreed about how to respond to the embargo and to the resulting sharp price increases.
- The 1974 economic recession in Organisation for Economic Co-operation and Development (OECD) countries, in which inflation and unemployment rates rose sharply.

With these developments, "the traditional organs of international co-operation were no longer able to reconcile the differences among the leading Western powers or to give them a sense of common purpose".[14]

It was in this evolving context that the finance ministers of the US, Germany, Britain and France, meeting on 25 March 1973 in the White House library, formed the "Library Group". Later joined by Japan, the group met periodically for a number of years and came to be known as the Group of Five finance ministers (G5). The governors of the central banks of the Five sometimes joined the finance ministers at these meetings. Some two years after the initial get-together of the Library Group,

> thirty-five heads of state and government gathered in Helsinki to sign the Final Act of the Conference on Security and Co-operation in Europe. The leaders of the four Western powers met for lunch at the British Embassy in Helsinki on 31 July, together with their foreign ministers. Those present were Gerald Ford and Henry Kissinger; Valéry Giscard d'Estaing and Jean Sauvagnargues; Helmut Schmidt and Hans-Dietrich Genscher; Harold Wilson and

James Callaghan. They discussed President Giscard's proposal that they should meet later that year, together with Japan, to address economic and monetary problems. This was the genesis of the summits.[15]

It is worth noting that Giscard d'Estaing and Helmut Schmidt were former finance ministers who understood monetary and other economic issues well and were eager to discuss such issues with their opposite numbers from other major industrialised countries. The subsequent generation of G7 leaders did not share this background; some of them were, therefore, more inclined to broaden the scope of their discussions to political and other non-economic topics and to entrust economic issues to their finance ministers. More recently, especially in the situation of widespread financial turmoil, the leaders' concentration on economic issues is on the rise again, though in increasingly greater collaboration with their finance ministers.

The Role of the Summit

Perhaps the central role of the G7, according to Kirton, is "to create consensus among its members, at the highest political level, on the major global issues of the moment. It does so ... through the G7's *deliberative* function of forcing the leaders to get acquainted, listen and learn about one another's national constraints, priorities and goals ... [leading] to effective ongoing relationships ...[;] the *directional* function of setting the agenda [and] defining the priorities ... [and] the *decisional* function of reaching concrete agreements on specific subjects ... ".[16] Merlini, in contrast, holds that "[t]he summit is not a decision-making forum ... . [It] does not play; it conducts the orchestra, interpreting the score, assigning the instruments and giving the starting note".[17]

Joe Clark, a prominent former summit participant (first as prime minister and later as foreign minister of Canada) remarks that

> summits are extremely constructive. They focus the attention of governments and leaders and often allow breakthroughs that would not occur in the more cumbersome traditional system. Precisely because heads of government are so busy now, they can become locked into patterns of dealing only with the most urgent issues and the most familiar allies. Summits free leaders of those patterns and allow both a wider experience of international issues

and a real opportunity for initiative and co-operation. They rescue multilateralism from its inherent bureaucracy and caution.[18]

A study by the Atlantic Council highlights the G7 function "to link together political, economic and security issues which might otherwise be dealt with in highly compartmentalized contexts, without any overall strategy or set of objectives".[19] Hisashi Owada distinguishes three major purposes of the summit: "[p]olicy convergence through the process of an exchange of views and discussion ...; [p]olicy cooperation through the process of agreeing to a common strategy ...; [and p]olicy coordination through the process of concerted action undertaken ... ".[20]

Kirton endorses the G7 with special enthusiasm:

> the G7 possesses a decisive advantage over the competing United Nations-Bretton Woods system .... [Its] ability to effectively deliberate, set policy directions for the global community, and reach and respect ambitious, timely and well tailored agreements rests on four fundamental features: concerted power ...[,] restricted participation, common purpose, and political control by democratically and popularly elected leaders.[21]

In a similar vein, Wendy Dobson observes that

> Summit participants are quick to note two enduring values of Summits that are next to impossible to quantify. First, there is great value in leaders meeting for the purpose of getting to know one another and one another's views on current issues .... Second, the complexity and range of issues with which leaders must deal is such that Summits provide opportunities to identify issues where cooperative action might be possible, delegate authority to analyze and respond, and provide for accountability by the delegates. In effect, Summits are less and less forums for initiatives, and more and more forums for issue identification and delegation.[22]

The evolving role of the G7/G8 continues to occupy the attention of the academic community, government officials and the news media. A new book, based on the proceedings of two conferences (one an academic symposium, the other a public policy conference) held in London the week before the 1998 Birmingham Summit and edited by Michael R. Hodges, John J. Kirton and Joseph P. Daniels, analyses the institution's role in the new millennium, exploring challenges, capacities, commitments and effectiveness.[23]

Summit Reform

Former British Prime Minister John Major has stated his conviction, perhaps more emphatically than his G7 peers, "that the summits have lost their original personal character, becoming institutional (or at least bureaucratic) and [he has invoked] a return to their origins. His proposal seems to have met with consensus from his colleagues ... ".[24] His letter of August 1992, detailing his concerns to other G7 heads of state or government, has not been released to the public but a summary of it appeared in the *Financial Times* of London.[25] The fact that his proposals have indeed found resonance with the other heads is shown by the 1993 Tokyo communiqué, and the more informal, leader-oriented summits of Naples, Halifax, Lyon, and especially Birmingham.

Others have proposed various courses of action for the G7, ranging from abolition to institutional strengthening. W. R. Smyser states that although the G7 became "for a time one of the most influential institutions of the twentieth century ... , it ... [later] evolved in ways that could not be foreseen and that no longer serve its original purpose". Because he considers that the "G-7 mechanism now receives a failing score ... [and] is not functioning as originally conceived ... , [he asks whether] the G-7 structure, including the ministerials and especially the summits, should be discontinued". Nevertheless, he then acknowledges the continuing reasons for some type of summit: the usefulness of informal talks among leaders, the need to discuss post-Cold War problems on the highest level, and the need for agreement of the most important states in order to build "a successful world order"; and goes on to suggest a different format and agenda, and a cabinet-level working committee to replace the sherpas.[26]

William E. Whyman, on the other hand, asserts that the summit has a future but must be strengthened. He presents two "trajectories" of summit evolution: (1) a revitalized G7 process that would refocus the agenda on core macroeconomic issues, keep membership small but develop associations with other countries or groups of countries and make the summit process simple and flexible, with closer ties with finance ministers; and (2) an incremental process that would expand the summit agenda to include more political and global issues, result in larger membership as well as association relationships, and increase the complexity of the process, with "creeping institutionalism". Staking out a middle ground between summit optimists and pessimists, Whyman concludes that the "incremental" scenario is the more realistic one.[27]

Flora Lewis, writing about the summit in the early 1990s, is rather optimistic about the state of the institution, but suggests a greater role for Russia.[28] Kuniko Inoguchi is very supportive of the summits in the post-Cold War era, stating that "periodic meetings of the leaders of major nations to discuss international problems are becoming the most realistic means of overseeing the world order and building consensus on new directions. In a sense, this format can be seen as laying the groundwork for joint management of the post-hegemonic international politics of the twenty-first century".[29]

De Guttry envisions a greater degree of bureaucratic institutionalisation; she suggests a secretariat for the G7 (either by creating one within the G7 or by using the OECD for this purpose). G. John Ikenberry goes even further, calling for a G7 secretariat and a G7 council of ministers, composed of foreign and treasury ministers, with varying membership according to topic. Hanns W. Maull, by contrast, states that from a German perspective "the answer to the idea of a G-7 secretariat is an unequivocal 'no'" and that Germany would rather see other international organisations–the OECD, the IMF, the World Bank, the EBRD–assume follow-up and monitoring of summit undertakings. Writing about ideas of radical summit reform, Putnam points out that "neither Smyser's recommendation to 'abolish it' nor Ikenberry's advice to 'institutionalize it' has significant official support".[30]

As indicated earlier, the Birmingham G8 Summit produced several innovations in format, agenda and participation, thus taking major steps in summit reform. It had a more focused agenda than previous summits. It was a leaders-only summit, with foreign and finance ministers meeting separately in London a week before the Summit, on 8-9 May, to prepare for the summit agenda and to deal with issues not on the agenda of the summit itself. This format made it possible to achieve greater informality than was possible in previous summit history, enabling the leaders to spend considerable time together and to focus personally on topics that they wished to discuss. And Birmingham officially integrated Russia into the club, making it the G8.

There is a continuing need for G7/G8 reform, and there is no shortage of reform proposals. The G7/G8 has proven itself to be a flexible, adaptable institution, which bodes well for its future evolution.

Notes

1   *Yearbook of International Organizations*, 1992/93, 29th ed., Vol. 1, p. 1649. More recent editions have simplified the definition: "An organization is intergovernmental if it is established by signature of an agreement engendering obligations between governments, whether or not that agreement is eventually published". *Yearbook of International Organizations*, 1997/98, 34th ed., Vol. 1, p. 1755.

2   "G8 Structure: An Informal Club", Great Britain, Foreign and Commonwealth Office, [*Birmingham G8 Summit Web Site*]. URL: http://birmingham. g8summit.gov.uk/brief0398/what.is.g8.shtml.

3   John J. Kirton, "The Diplomacy of Concert: Canada, the G7 and the Halifax Summit", *Canadian Foreign Policy* 3, No. 1 (Spring 1995), pp. 64-65. See also his "Economic Cooperation: Summitry, Institutions, and Structural Change", Paper prepared for a conference on "Structural Change and Co-operation in the Global Economy". Center for International Business Education and Center for Global Change and Governance, Rutgers University, New Brunswick, NJ, May 19-20, 1997. URL: www.library.utoronto.ca/www/g7/scholar/rutcon.htm.   Will appear in *Structural Change and Co-operation in the Global Economy*, edited by John Dunning and Gavin Boyd (London: Edward Elgar, forthcoming, 1999).

4   Cesare Merlini, "The G-7 and the Need for Reform", in *The Future of the G-7 Summits*, p. 5 (*The International Spectator* 29, No. 2; April/June 1994, Special Issue); Philippe Moreau Defarges, "The French Viewpoint on the Future of the G-7", in *The Future of the G-7 Summits*, p. 182; and Michael R. Hodges, "More Efficiency, Less Dignity: British Perspectives on the Future Role and Working of the G-7", in *The Future of the G-7 Summits*, p. 155.

5   Andrea de Guttry, "The Institutional Configuration of the G-7 in the New International Scenario", in *The Future of the G-7 Summits*, p. 68.

6   Nicholas Bayne and Robert D. Putnam, "Introduction: The G-7 Summit Comes of Age" in *The Halifax G-7 Summit: Issues on the Table*, eds. Sylvia Ostry and Gilbert R. Wynham (Halifax: Centre for Foreign Policy Studies, Dalhousie University, 1995), pp. 1-2.

7   G. R. Berridge, *Diplomacy: Theory and Practice* (London; New York: Prentice Hall/Harvester Wheatsheaf, 1995), pp. 83-84.

8   Nicholas Bayne, "The G7 Summit and the Reform of Global Institutions", *Government and Opposition* 30, No. 4 (Autumn 1995), p. 494.

9   Group of Thirty, *The Summit Process and Collective Security: Future Responsibility Sharing* (Washington, DC: Group of Thirty, 1991).

10   "Tokyo Economic Declaration", July 9, 1993, para. 16, in *The Twenty G-7*

Summits (Rome: Adnkronos Libri in Collaboration with Istituto Affari Internazionali, 1994), p. 251. Hodges notes that this "paragraph had reportedly been square bracketed in the preparatory sherpa meetings ... [,] designed to reflect the personal opinion of the heads and the natural reluctance of the sherpas to anticipate their conclusions". Hodges, "More Efficiency, Less Dignity: British Perspectives on the Future Role and Working of the G-7", p. 146. (Sherpas are personal representatives of leaders of summit countries and of EU leaders participating in summits.)

11   Canada, Department of Foreign Affairs and International Trade, *1995, Canada's Year As G7 Chair: The Halifax Summit Legacy* (Ottawa: DFAIT, 1996). See also the Department's web site at www.dfait-maeci.gc.ca/english/g7summit/hfax2.htm.

12   Great Britain, Foreign and Commonwealth Office, *G8 Birmingham Summit, May 1998: Background Brief* (London: FCO, March 1998). URL: http://files.fco.gov.uk/info/briefs/g8summit.pdf.

13   Robert D. Putnam and Nicholas Bayne, *Hanging Together: Cooperation and Conflict in the Seven-Power Summits*, rev. ed. (Cambridge, Mass.: Harvard University Press, 1987), p. 25.

14   *Ibid.*, p. 27.

15   *Ibid.*, p. 25.

16   Kirton, "The Diplomacy of Concert: Canada, the G7 and the Halifax Summit", p. 66.

17   Merlini, "The G-7 and the Need for Reform", p. 22.

18   Joe Clark, "The PM [Prime Minister] and the SSEA [Secretary of State for External Affairs]: Comment 2", *International Journal* 50, No. 1 (Winter 1994/1995), p. 215.

19   *Summit Meetings and Collective Leadership in the 1980's*, Charles Robinson and William C. Turner, co-chairmen; Harald B. Malmgren, rapporteur (Atlantic Council of the United States Policy Papers; Washington, DC: Working Group on Political Affairs, Atlantic Council of the United States, 1980), pp. 38-39. Cited in Stefano Silvestri, "Between Globalism and Regionalism: The Role and Composition of the G-7", in *The Future of the G-7 Summits*, pp. 28-29.

20   Hisashi Owada, "A Japanese Perspective on the Role and Future of the G-7", in *The Future of the G-7 Summits*, p. 96.

21   John J. Kirton, "Economic Cooperation: Summitry, Institutions, and Structural Change".

22   Wendy Dobson, "Summitry and the International Monetary System: The Past as Prologue", *Canadian Foreign Policy* 3, No. 1 (Spring 1995), p. 6.

23   Michael R. Hodges, John J. Kirton, and Joseph P. Daniels, eds., *The G8: Its Role in the New Millennium* (Aldershot; Brookfield USA; Singapore; Sydney: Ashgate; forthcoming, 1999).

24   Merlini, "The G-7 and the Need for Reform", p. 6; Hodges, "More

Efficiency, Less Dignity", p. 146.

25   Philip Stephens, "Major Calls for Overhaul of G7 Summits". *Financial Times* (London), September 10, 1992, p. 1.

26   W. R. Smyser, "Goodbye, G-7", *The Washington Quarterly* 16, No. 1 (Winter 1993), pp. 16, 23, 26.

27   William E. Whyman, "We Can't Go On Meeting Like This: Revitalizing the G-7 Process", *The Washington Quarterly* 18, No. 3 (Summer 1995), pp. 149-63.

28   Flora Lewis, "The 'G-7½' Directorate", *Foreign Policy*, No. 85 (Winter 1991-92), pp. 25-40.

29   Kuniko Inoguchi, "The Changing Significance of the G-7 Summits", *Japan Review of International Affairs* 8, No. 1 (Winter 1994), p. 23.

30   De Guttry, "The Institutional Configuration of the G-7 in the New International Scenario", p. 76; G. John Ikenberry, "Salvaging the G-7", *Foreign Affairs* 72, No. 2 (Spring 1993), pp. 136-38.; Hanns W. Maull, "Germany at the Summit", in *The Future of the G-7 Summits*, p. 135; Robert D. Putnam, "Western Summitry in the 1990s: American Perspectives", in *The Future of the G-7 Summits*, p. 86.

2 The Summit Meetings

The first summit was held in Rambouillet, France, on 15-17 November 1975. The participants were the Five (France, the US, the UK, Germany, and Japan) plus Italy. The Rambouillet meeting was originally intended by some of the participants–and presented by all of them–as a one-time get-together of the leaders, but US President Gerald Ford decided to call another such conference the following year. That summit, with Canada joining for the first time, met in San Juan, Puerto Rico, on 27-28 June 1976. With San Juan, the summit became a regular annual event, taking place in strictly determined rotation among the Group of Seven (G7) countries: France, US, UK, Germany, Japan, Italy, Canada. The 1977 London Summit saw the European Community (EC) become a participant (then and still a less-than equal one). The complex issue of Russian participation is discussed in Chapter 3. Table 2.1 shows the places and dates of the twenty-four annual summit meetings held from 1975 to 1998 as well as the 1999 summit.

In addition to the regular annual summits, there have been two special summit meetings: in 1985 and 1996. The 1985 special G6 summit took place in New York, without France. US President Ronald Reagan used the occasion to discuss arms-control proposals in preparation for the first US-USSR superpower summit.[1] The 1991 London Summit held out the possibility of convening an extraordinary summit meeting later that year, if necessary, to boost the chances of a successful conclusion of the Uruguay Round. That extraordinary summit was not called, even though the Uruguay Round failed to be concluded by the end of 1991.

A special Nuclear Safety and Security Summit was held in Moscow on 19-20 April 1996, at the "political G8" (P8) level; that is, with the full participation of Russia. Discussion focused on the safety of civilian nuclear reactors, the question of nuclear liability, energy-sector strategies in countries in transition to a market economy, nuclear-waste management, the security of nuclear material and the prevention of illicit trafficking in nuclear material, the control and physical protection of–and accounting for–nuclear material, and the safe and effective management of weapons-grade fissile material designated as no longer required for defence purposes.

Following the G7 finance ministers' and central bank governors' meeting on 14 September 1998 that promised concerted action to respond to

Table 2.1   G7/G8 Annual Summit Meetings, 1975-1999

Rambouillet, France (G6)	15-17 November 1975
San Juan, Puerto Rico, US	27-28 June 1976
London, United Kingdom ("London I")	7-8 May 1977
Bonn, West Germany ("Bonn I")	16-17 July 1978
Tokyo, Japan ("Tokyo I")	28-29 June 1979
Venice, Italy ("Venice I")	22-23 June 1980
Ottawa (Montebello), Canada	20-21 July 1981
Versailles, France	4-6 June 1982
Williamsburg, Virginia, US	28-30 May 1983
London, United Kingdom ("London II")	7-9 June 1984
Bonn, West Germany ("Bonn II")	2-4 May 1985
Tokyo, Japan ("Tokyo II")	4-6 May 1986
Venice, Italy ("Venice II")	8-10 June 1987
Toronto, Canada	19-21 June 1988
Paris, France ("Summit of the Arch")	14-16 July 1989
Houston, Texas, US	9-11 July 1990
London, United Kingdom ("London III")	15-17 July 1991
Munich, Germany	6-8 July 1992
Tokyo, Japan ("Tokyo III")	7-9 July 1993
Naples, Italy	8-10 July 1994
Halifax, Canada	15-17 June 1995
Lyon, France	27-29 June 1996
Denver, Colorado, US ("Summit of the Eight")	20-22 June 1997
Birmingham, United Kingdom (G8)	15-17 May 1998
Köln, Germany	18-20 June 1999

the worldwide financial turmoil, British Prime Minister Tony Blair floated the idea of calling an emergency G7 or G8 summit in late October on the financial crisis in Russia, Asia and Latin America. It was reported that the decision on whether or not to call the special summit would be made in light of a report by G7 officials to be submitted to the G7 leaders.[2] On 30 October 1998 the G7 leaders, having consulted one another without meeting for a summit, issued a *G7 Leaders' Statement on the World Economy*.[3] According to the *Financial Times*, "the finishing touches to the leaders' statement were apparently made in a series of phone calls between President Clinton and German Chancellor Gerhard Schröder".[4] This action obviated the need for a special summit.

The special summit held by the US, Germany, the UK and France in Guadeloupe on 5-6 January 1979 was not part of the regular G7 cycle but rather a legacy of past Atlanticism. The four participants discussed missiles in Europe and arms-control negotiations with the USSR, as well as the situation in Iran.[5] G7 members Japan, Italy and Canada, as well as some other countries, resented not being invited. The Guadeloupe meeting gave those three "a strong incentive to develop the economic summit as a more formal and visible vehicle for political discussions, going beyond spontaneous exchanges over meals. This would ensure that they would not be excluded from high-level political decisions in future".[6]

At the Denver Summit of the Eight, the Russians participated from the beginning of the summit but with time set aside for the G7 to consider financial and other economic questions. This contrasts with the 1994 Naples Summit, the 1995 Halifax Summit and the 1996 Lyon Summit, each of which had two quite distinct phases: these summits were G7 events up to and including the release of the communiqué but then turned themselves into P8 for the rest of the summits.

In Birmingham in 1998, the G7 became officially the G8, with Russia as a full member. Tables 2.2, 2.3, 2.4 and 2.5 summarise the main events, respectively, of the 1993, 1996, 1997 and 1998 summits, as a comparative illustration of the recent evolution of the institution: Table 2.2 details the summit programme as it unfolded prior to the official participation of Russia as summit partner, appearing on the scene only after the ending of the summit; Table 2.3 shows the 1996 programme–that year, as in 1994 and 1995, the Russians joined at the end of the summit, after the release of the economic communiqué, for the political discussions; Table 2.4 shows the programme of the 1997 Denver Summit of the Eight when Russia, for the first time, participated from the beginning, except for a 90-minute meeting of the G7 heads; and Table 2.5 shows the Birmingham programme in which the Russians were full participants.

Nonetheless, the G7, after Birmingham, remains very much alive. In fact, not only did the finance ministers meet at the G7 level in London the week before the summit, but the G7 heads themselves had their own meeting in Birmingham for half a day, before the official start of the G8 summit.[7] And, as the year 1998 draws to a close, a very active G7 is much more in evidence than the G8: during and after the Fall 1998 meetings of the International Monetary Fund (IMF) and the World Bank, the G7–both at the finance ministers' and at the leaders' level–produced important and high-profile initiatives (these are described in more detail in Chapter 5).

Table 2.2   Main Events of the 1993 Tokyo Summit

5-6 July	arrival of delegations
7 July	
1:45-2:15 PM	welcoming reception
2:15-2:25 PM	group photograph
2:30-5:30 PM	separate sessions: heads of delegation, foreign ministers, finance ministers
7:30-9:30 PM	working dinner of heads of delegation
7:40-9:40 PM	foreign ministers' working dinner
7:50-9:50 PM	finance ministers' working dinner
8 July	
9:15-10 AM	work session of heads of delegation and foreign ministers
10:15 AM-12:30 PM	work session of heads of delegation
11:00 AM	announcement of political declaration by the foreign minister of Japan
12:45-2:30 PM	separate working luncheons: heads of delegation, foreign ministers, finance ministers
3:00-5:30 PM	plenary session
7:30-10:00 PM	court banquet at the Imperial Palace
9 July	
9:15-10:15 AM	plenary session
10:20-11:20 AM	work session of heads of delegation
11:25-11:35 AM	announcement of economic declaration by the Prime Minister of Japan
END OF SUMMIT MEETING	
	National press conferences
2:45 PM	arrival of Russian President Yeltsin
2:52-2:54 PM	group photograph with President Yeltsin
3:00-6:00 PM	meeting of heads of delegation with President Yeltsin
6:30-7:00 PM	joint press conference of the Prime Minister of Japan and President Yeltsin

Source: Adapted from media information released at the Tokyo Summit.

Table 2.3   Main Events of the 1996 Lyon Summit

27 June	arrival of heads of delegation
7:45 PM	reception for heads of delegation, hosted by French President Chirac
8:00 PM	working dinner for the 7 heads of delegation
28 June	
9:15-9:30 AM	another reception for heads of delegation, given by the French President
9:30 AM-12:15 PM	first work session of heads of delegation
12:30 PM	plenary session with finance and foreign ministers
1:30 PM	working luncheon for heads of delegation
1:30 PM	official photograph of heads of delegation
3:00 PM	announcement, followed by the release, of the communiqué; chairman's press conference
4:15 PM	reception for head of Russia's delegation, given by the French President
5:00-6:30 PM	work session of the 7 heads with the head of Russia's delegation (Russia is included in the rest of the programme)
8:00 PM	dinner for heads of delegation
10:30 PM	evening of entertainment
29 June	
9:00 AM	work session of the heads of delegation and foreign ministers
9:40 AM	work session of the foreign ministers
10:15 AM	host leader announces release of chairman's statement
10:45 AM	work session of the 8 heads of delegation with the UN Secretary-General, the President of the World Bank, the IMF Managing Director, and the Director-General of the World Trade Organization
12:00 noon	luncheon of heads of delegation with the 4 invited heads of IGOs, followed by official photograph
1:45 PM	press conference of the host head, with the 4 invited heads of IGOs

Source: Adapted from media information released at the Lyon Summit.

Table 2.4   **Main Events of the 1997 Denver Summit of the Eight**
[**G7** heads held a 90-minute meeting–without Russia–
during the Denver Summit]

19-20 June	arrival of heads of delegation
20 June	
5:30 PM	leaders' welcoming reception, hosted by US President Clinton, the Governor of Colorado and the Mayor of Denver
7:30 PM	leaders' dinner, hosted by the US President
8:00 PM	foreign ministers' dinner, hosted by US Secretary of State Madeleine Albright
8:30 PM	finance ministers' working dinner, hosted by US Secretary of the Treasury Robert Rubin
21 June	
8:30-9:00 AM	the US President greets guest leaders
9:00-11:00 AM	leaders' meeting, session I
9:30 AM-12 noon	foreign ministers' meeting
9:30 AM-12:15 PM	finance ministers' working meeting
11:30 AM-12:30 PM	leaders' meeting, session II
12:30-1:30 PM	foreign ministers' working lunch, hosted by the US Secretary of State
12:30-2:00 PM	finance ministers' informal lunch, hosted by the US Secretary of the Treasury
1:00-2:30 PM	leaders' lunch, hosted by the US President
2:00-3:30 PM	foreign ministers' afternoon meeting
3:00-4:00 PM	leaders' afternoon meeting
6:00 PM	ministers' dinner, hosted by the US Secretary of State and Secretary of the Treasury
6:50-7:30 PM	President and Mrs Clinton greet guest leaders and spouses
7:30 PM	leaders' dinner
9:30 PM	Saturday night at the Summit (entertainment hosted by the Denver host committee)
22 June	
10:15 AM-12 noon	leaders' meeting
12:50 PM	presentation of the final communiqué

Source: Adapted from media information released at the Denver Summit.

Table 2.5   Main Events of the 1998 Birmingham G8 Summit

15 May   arrival of delegations
[half-day meeting of **G7** heads– without Russia–before official opening of the G8
         Summit]
6:00 PM   opening reception, hosted by the Lord Mayor of Birmingham,
                     Councillor Mrs Sybil Spence (Council House,
                     Birmingham)
7:30 PM   reception for heads of delegations, spouses and sherpas, hosted by
                     the UK Prime Minister and Mrs Blair (Birmingham
                     Museum and Art Gallery)
16 May
9:40 AM   arrivals at the retreat venue (Weston Park estate)
                     official photo session
                     G8 meeting
7:30 PM   social dinner for heads of delegation and spouses, hosted by the
                     Prime Minister and Mrs Blair (Birmingham Botanical
                     Gardens)
9:30 PM   entertainment (International Convention Centre and Symphony
                     Hall)

17 May
8:45 AM   arrivals (International Convention Centre)
9:00 AM   G8 meeting (International Convention Centre)
11:00 AM   press conference of the Presidency (UK Prime Minister) and
                     presentation of the final communiqué
11:00 AM   national press conferences by heads of delegations

Source: Adapted from media information released at the Birmingham Summit.

Summit Cycles

Chronologically, the summit meetings–until the full inclusion of Russia–can
be viewed in septennial cycles defined by hosting rotation, but there are a
number of other ways of viewing summit history. Nicholas Bayne, writing
in May 1997, distinguishes four cycles by rhythm and pace of activity: the
first, 1975-1980, had summits that "were very ambitious in economic
policies, arguably too ambitious". The second, 1981-1988, saw summits
paying "much more attention ... to non-economic foreign policy issues". The
third, 1989-1994, was the first post-Cold War cycle, focusing on Central and
Eastern Europe and the USSR, then Russia, but with lively activity "on trade

and debt issues; and new work on transnational issues, especially the environment, drugs and money laundering". The fourth cycle started with the 1995 Halifax Summit, whose "key feature [was] the focus on reforming international institutions".[8]

In terms of institutional development, summit history may be divided into three cycles: the first, 1975-1981–as John J. Kirton notes–"consisted solely of the annual meeting of leaders, accompanied by their ministers of foreign affairs and finance"; the second, 1982-1988, "added regular stand-alone meetings of ministers of trade starting in 1982, foreign affairs in 1984, and finance in 1986, as well as a special Summit (absent France) in 1985. The third cycle from 1989 to 1995 saw the birth in 1991 of the annual G7 post-Summit meeting with the USSR and then Russia, the emergence of environment ministers' meetings in 1992, and a flurry of *ad hoc* ministerial meetings from 1993 onward dealing with assistance to Russia and Ukraine and the microeconomic issues of jobs and the information highway".[9]

From the perspective of successful summit performance, Kirton–writing in 1989–notes "a threefold progression–from effectiveness in the period 1975-1980, to reduced effectiveness in the period 1981-1984, to a renaissance in effectiveness in the period 1985-1988".[10] By contrast, C. Fred Bergsten and C. Randall Henning, writing on the eve of the 1996 Lyon Summit, present quite a pessimistic assessment of G7 performance, though focused on the G7 finance ministers rather than the summit itself. They remark that "[t]he G-7's effectiveness has declined sharply over the last decade ... [and] that this recent paralysis is the strongest indictment of the contemporary G-7".[11] Kirton notes that this criticism "comes from those who conceive the G7's central purpose as producing large package deals, embracing macroeconomic, trade and energy policy, through which governments can optimize economic performance through direct, collective intervention".[12]

Guido Garavoglia and Pier Carlo Padoan, writing in 1994, distinguish four summit periods in terms of economic issues[13]:

- 1975-1979–a period of strong economic growth accompanied by high inflation and balance-of-payments problems. Macroeconomic co-ordination, especially in Bonn in 1978, was a major summit preoccupation;
- 1980-1984 was a time of economic recession during which the summit emphasised microeconomic issues and anti-inflationary measures;

- 1985-1989, during which macroeconomic aspects were re-emphasised, and so was economic development. This phase saw the Plaza (1985) and Louvre (1987) accords;
- 1990-, another recessionary cycle, during which summit interest shifted again to microeconomics and structural problems.

Hanns W. Maull–also in 1994–states that

> [d]uring the 1970s, the summits were primarily concerned with management of international economics ... [:] the future of the international monetary order; ... the enhancement of international economic growth through further liberalisation of world trade, macroeconomic policy coordination among the major industrialised countries and measures to alleviate the situation of the poor developing countries; and ... the containment of oil insecurity and instability. During the second cycle of summitry from 1982 to 1988, the emphasis shifted away from economic policy coordination ... towards broader political issues and transnational problems such as the global environment, international terrorism and drugs.[14]

As to the evolution of the political agenda of the summit, Garavoglia and Padoan identify three periods:[15]

- 1975-1981, when France opposed the extension of political and security discussions beyond itself, Great Britain and the US, and when Japan remained reluctant to commit itself in what had traditionally been the competence of the Atlantic Alliance;
- 1982-1988, when political and other non-economic issues became increasingly important for the summits; and
- from 1989 onward, with the emergence of global issues such as democratisation, the environment, drugs and terrorism.

Notes

1   John J. Kirton, "The Diplomacy of Concert: Canada, the G7 and the Halifax Summit", *Canadian Foreign Policy* 3, No. 1 (Spring 1995), p. 66.
2   "World Leaders Back Joint Action in Face of Financial Turmoil", *Financial Times*, 15 September 1998, p. 1; "Report on Russian Crisis Prepared for G7", *Financial Times*, 15 September 1998, p. 2.

3   *G7 Leaders' Statement on the World Economy*, 30 October 1998. URL: www.number-10.gov.uk/public/news/uktoday/uktoday_right.asp?id=248 and www.library.utoronto.ca/www/g7/g7_103098.html.

4   Gerard Baker, "G7 Attempts to Restore Calm to World Finance", *Financial Times*, 31 October/1 November 1998, p. 2.

5   Valéry Giscard d'Estaing, *Le pouvoir et la vie (Power and Life)* ([sl.:] Compagnie 12, 1988), pp. 109-11.

6   Robert D. Putnam and Nicholas Bayne, *Hanging Together: Cooperation and Conflict in the Seven-Power Summits*, rev. ed. (Cambridge, Mass.: Harvard University Press, 1987), p. 105.

7   The Russians professed indifference to meetings at the G7 level before and at Birmingham, saying that this was of no interest to them because the meetings had taken place before the summit proper.   On the other hand, they were quick to offer to host a G8 summit in Russia in 2000–which would displace Japan, the scheduled host of the event that year. This issue remained unresolved in Birmingham.

8   Nicholas Bayne, "Changing Patterns at the G7 Summit", *G7 Governance*, No. 1 (May 1997), p. 1. URL: www.library.utoronto.ca/ www/g7/ governance/ g7gove1.htm.

9   Kirton, "The Diplomacy of Concert: Canada, the G7 and the Halifax Summit", p. 66.

10   John J. Kirton, "Contemporary Concert Diplomacy: The Seven-Power Summit and the Management of International Order" (Paper prepared for the annual meeting of the International Studies Association and the British International Studies Association, London, March 29-April 1, 1989; unpublished in print), p. 3.   Text available at URL: www.library.utoronto.ca/www/g7/kirtoc.htm.

11   C. Fred Bergsten and C. Randall Henning, *Global Economic Leadership and the Group of Seven* (Washington, DC: Institute for International Economics, 1996), pp. 3-4.

12   John J. Kirton, "Economic Cooperation: Summitry, Institutions, and Structural Change", Paper prepared for a conference on "Structural Change and Co-operation in the Global Economy".   Center for International Business Education and Center for Global Change and Governance, Rutgers University, New Brunswick, NJ, May 19-20, 1997. URL: www.library. utoronto.ca/ www/g7/scholar/rutcon.htm.   Will appear in *Structural Change and Co-operation in the Global Economy*, edited by John Dunning and Gavin Boyd (London: Edward Elgar, forthcoming, 1999).

13   Guido Garavoglia, and Pier Carlo Padoan, "The G-7 Agenda: Old and New Issues", in *The Future of the G-7 Summits*, p. 50 (*The International Spectator* 29, No. 2; April/June 1994, Special Issue).

14   Hanns W. Maull, "Germany at the Summit", in *The Future of the G-7 Summits*, p. 120.
15   Garavoglia and Padoan, "The G-7 Agenda: Old and New Issues", pp. 50-53.

3 The Players

Up to and including the 1997 Denver Summit of the Eight, delegations of each summit country included the head of state or government, the foreign minister, the finance minister, and the "sherpa", a term that originates from the name (or, rather, nationality) of the mountain guides in the Himalayas and denotes the senior official who is the leader's personal representative. There are some variations: France, the US and Russia are the only three G8 countries that are represented at the level of head of state (although at the 1996 Lyon Summit Russia was represented in President Boris Yeltsin's absence by Prime Minister Viktor Chernomyrdin); Germany and Japan, traditionally with coalition governments, have sent the minister of economy (in Germany's case) and minister of international trade and industry (for Japan), in addition to their foreign and finance ministers; and France, during its period of "cohabitation" (1986-87) sent both its president (then François Mitterrand) and its prime minister (then Jacques Chirac)–during the current "cohabitation" that began in June 1997, Prime Minister Lionel Jospin has chosen not to accompany President Chirac. The EU is represented by the president of the Commission, the vice-presidents for external relations and for economic and financial affairs, and the president's personal representative. The president of the European Council is also represented in years when that office is held by a non-G7 European country. This has occurred thus far in 1982 (Belgium), 1986 (Netherlands), 1987 (Belgium), 1991 (Netherlands) and 1997 (Netherlands).

The 1998 Birmingham G8 Summit changed this pattern: Birmingham was a leaders-only summit, with foreign and finance ministers meeting separately in London a week before the Summit, on 8-9 May, to prepare for the leaders' agenda and to deal with issues not on the agenda of the summit itself. This format made it possible to achieve a long-desired but never-before-fulfilled informality, enabling the leaders to spend considerable time together and to focus personally on topics that they wished to discuss. This was further enhanced by an all-day retreat at the beautiful, secluded seventeenth-century Weston Park estate on the border of Staffordshire and Shropshire, away not only from bureaucrats but, more importantly, from the prying eyes of the media. At the end of the summit, the leaders expressed great satisfaction with this format, and Germany, the host of the next summit

–in Köln on 18-20 June 1999–has expressed its intention to follow the same arrangement.

Russia's Membership

On 14 July 1989, former Soviet President Mikhail Gorbachev sent a letter to President Mitterrand expressing the Soviet Union's wish to be associated with the summits. Although that did not happen immediately, Russia has played an increasingly important role since that time. The event that dominated the 1991 Summit was Gorbachev's historic visit to London. He did not attend the Summit *per se* but met with G7 leaders individually and collectively, and discussed in detail his government's plans for Soviet economic and political reform. Although attitudes among the G7 varied about how and how much to help the Soviet Union, the leaders "all agreed to work together to promote the integration of the Soviet Union into the world economy".[1] It was at their meeting in London on 17 July 1991 that presidents Gorbachev and George Bush solved the last impediment to the Strategic Arms Reduction Treaty (START). They subsequently signed the treaty on 31 July 1991, during their bilateral summit meeting held in Moscow. But then, the unsuccessful coup that took place a month after the Summit led to the demise of the Soviet Union and the end of Gorbachev as leader of his country.

The following year, President Yeltsin's visit to Munich took the spotlight. Although formally outside the summit framework, he held bilateral meetings as well as joint sessions with the G7 leaders, and returned home not only with a greater show of goodwill but also a more concrete aid package (some US$4.5 billion) than had his predecessor. The idea was even floated by Bush (but not taken up then by other summit leaders) of turning the G7 into a G8 with the formal participation of Russia. However, it was only at the 1994 Naples Summit that Russia participated for the first time as a full partner in the political discussions. Russia itself referred to a new "political G8", but the preferred Western term, at least until the 1997 Denver Summit, was P8. At Denver, Russia joined the G7 (except for certain financial and other economic issues), to form the Summit of the Eight.[2] In Birmingham in 1998, the G7 became officially the G8, with Russia as a full member, although–as noted earlier–the G7 continues to exist as well, both at the summit and ministerial levels. G7 leaders met in Birmingham for half a day on 15 May, before the official start of the G8 summit. Ironically, just as the leader of the USSR and then Russia had been invited to meet with the G7 heads after the official ending of the 1991, 1992 and 1993 summits, in Birmingham it was the G7 that met outside of the G8 summit, as it had at the Denver Summit of the Eight.

Russia's full membership has changed the institution. The G8 is more representative than the G7, and reflects greater diversity. At the Denver Summit of the Eight in 1997 the host leader, President Bill Clinton stated: "we believe we are stronger because we now have Russia as a partner ...–evidence of Russia's emergence as a full member of the community of democracies".[3]   Going one step further, Prime Minister Tony Blair, the chairman of the 1998 Birmingham G8 Summit, affirmed: "The contribution that Russia has made to the G8 has already been very evident ... we appreciate very well that without the voice of Russia being heard in the G8 councils, it is far more difficult for us to deal with the serious international issues that confront us". [4] Blair cited nuclear energy and the millennium bug as examples of areas where Russia had contributed.

Russia's new-found democratic credentials, economic reforms and commitment to free markets were cited prior to Birmingham as justification for its full G8 membership. One must, however, wonder–especially in light of the chaotic Russian economy and politics in late 1998–how much Russia can now contribute to economic policy co-ordination, notwithstanding its contributions in respect of other issues–and how strong its democracy really is. It seems more likely that the decision to integrate Russia was driven to a large extent by geopolitical, strategic considerations rather than by recognition of Russia's status as an advanced democracy and a major market-based industrial power. The stated desire of the G7 to integrate Russia into political, global and other areas of co-ordination as much as possible has to be accompanied by the recognition of a strong *quid pro quo* element; it would be too much of a coincidence that Russia's acquiescence (after earlier strenuous opposition) to North Atlantic Treaty Organization (NATO) enlargement was followed very closely by its admission to the G7 and the Paris Club of creditor nations, as well as promises of early admission to the Organisation for Economic Co-operation and Development (OECD) and possibly the World Trade Organization (WTO).

Other Candidates for Membership

Other, unsuccessful, candidates for membership "have included Belgium and the Netherlands in the early years, Australia in the late 1970s and early 1980s, ... Spain in 1992 and Indonesia in 1993" as well as India and the other major developing countries whose leaders were invited to dinner by French President Mitterrand on the eve of the 1989 Summit that he hosted (not, it must be added, with the intention of enlarging the G7.)[5] As noted above, however, Belgium was represented at the summits of 1982 and 1987 and the Netherlands at the summits of 1986, 1991 and 1997 by virtue of holding the presidency of the European Council when those summits met. The fifteen developing countries whose leaders dined in 1989 with President Mitterrand subsequently formed their own Group of 15 (G15). Indonesia, as chair of the nonaligned movement, was invited to a 1993 pre-summit dinner in Tokyo by Japan and the US. Ukraine was represented at the Moscow Nuclear Safety and Security Summit in 1996. The administrative heads of four major international organisations–the Secretary-General of the UN, the Managing Director of the IMF, the President of the World Bank and the Director-General of the WTO–had a working session and lunch with the eight summit leaders in Lyon in 1996. The IMF Managing Director, the World Bank President and the WTO Director-General participated in the pre-summit joint meeting of G7/G8 finance and foreign ministers on 8-9 May 1998 in London. Thus, there has been occasional wider participation in and around summits.

A former government official, previously closely involved with summits, observes that there is a mismatch between current summit structure and real economic geography, and that this will have to be faced. Another former high official argues "that the G7 is no longer representative of the range of countries active in the international system. In particular, large, populous countries, like China, India, Mexico and Brazil, deserve more weight as they open up their large, internal markets", but then cites the counterargument that the "present G7 membership provides the best opportunity for exerting reciprocal pressure between the highly developed countries of Europe, North America and Japan, which would be lost if the composition were changed".[6]

Writing on the eve of the 1996 Lyon Summit, Zbigniew Brzezinski notes that "the very concept of the Group of Seven not only has become compromised but distorts global realities". He adds that "the group's membership is no longer representative of power or of principle, and it needs to be expanded. Russia ... cannot now be excluded. ... China, India and Brazil are as entitled to participation as Russia, and in some respects much more so". Acknowledging the need to limit membership, he thus advocates a Group of Eleven.[7]

In Jeffrey Sachs's view, time has come for a G16 instead of a G8. This would consist of the G8 and eight major countries of the developing world, all satisfying the common standard of democratic governance. Sachs sees Brazil, India, South Korea and South Africa as the four core developing-country members in the G16, soon to be joined by a more democratic Nigeria, as well as "[s]maller democratic countries that carry disproportionate credibility in the world, such as Chile and Costa Rica". He does not indicate which country might be the sixteenth member.[8]

One possible model of an expanded G8 may be visualised as three concentric circles, illustrated by Figure 3.1.[*] The innermost one is the core G3: the US, Japan and Germany which, together, are capable of exercising leadership and crisis management–these are still the most powerful countries, Japan's current financial difficulties notwithstanding. This tight

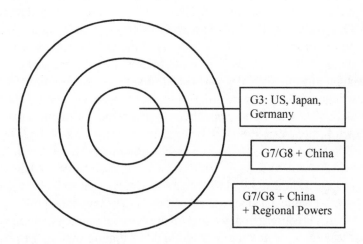

G3: US, Japan, Germany

G7/G8 + China

G7/G8 + China + Regional Powers

Figure 3.1 Model of a Three-tier Evolution of the G7/G8

---

*   I am grateful to Dr Sylvia Ostry for suggesting this model.

group combines power with responsibility and flexibility. The middle circle consists of the present G7/G8, possibly with the addition of China which would be the logical partner at this level. This group could deal with geopolitical, security and other global issues. The outer circle, representing a more widely representative institution, would embrace major regional powers that could play an appropriate role in their own right and as representatives of their regions. An example is Brazil, a potential regional leader. India, Australia and South Africa or a more democratic Nigeria would be other possible candidates.

China merits further comment as a plausible future candidate. It is a potentially major economic power, although its lack of commitment to democracy and human rights places it outside the small circle of like-minded major democratic countries with advanced, primarily market-based economies that has comprised the G7. With the advent of the G8, China is the only one of the five permanent members of the UN Security Council that remains outside the "club"; a curious anomaly when one considers that earlier the G7 membership of Japan and Germany ensured a full global-governance role for those two strong powers not part of the Permanent Five, giving them a strong voice along with the Five. It is significant that many economic indicators place China as close as or closer than Russia to G7 countries; for example, in 1997 China's Gross Domestic Product (GDP) was US$902 billion while Russia's was only 463 billion.[9] Table 3.1 shows the economic growth (real GDP changes) of the G7, the EU, Russia and China for the period 1991-1999. It should be noted that in the wake of the 1998 financial turmoil, the IMF, the OECD and others have revised 1998 and 1999 growth projections downward, sometimes sharply downward. The October 1998 IMF *World Economic Outlook* gives the following projected GDP growth figures for 1998–and, when available, for 1999: US: 3.5 (1998), 2.0 (1999); Japan: -2.5 (1998), 0.5 (1999); Germany: 2.6 (1998), 2.5 (1999); France: 3.1 (1998), 2.8 (1999); Italy: 2.1 (1998), 2.5 (1999); UK: 2.3 (1998), 1.2 (1999); Canada: 3.0 (1998), 2.5 (1999); Russia: -6.0 (1998); China: 5.5 (1998).[10] (Table 3.1 does not reflect these late revisions.)

C. Fred Bergsten, writing on the eve of President Clinton's June 1998 visit to China, notes the World Bank's estimate that "China has already passed Germany to become the third-largest economy on the globe" and adds that "China will obviously play an increasingly central role in the world economy. Hence, it must also play a central role in global economic management.... [It] should shortly begin participating in the 'finance G-7', the

Table 3.1   **Real GDP Changes of the G7, the EU, Russia and China**
(percentage changes from previous period)

	1991	1992	1993	1994	1995	1996	1997	1998	1999
USA	-0.9	2.7	2.3	3.5	2.0	2.8	3.8	2.7*	2.1*
Japn	3.8	1.0	0.3	0.6	1.5	3.9	0.9	-0.3*	1.03*
Ger	5.0	2.2	-1.2	2.7	1.8	1.4	2.2	2.7*	2.9*
Fran	0.8	1.2	-1.3	2.8	2.1	1.5	2.4	2.9*	2.8*
Italy	1.1	0.6	-1.2	2.2	2.9	0.7	1.5	2.4*	2.7*
UK	-2.0	-0.5	2.1	4.3	2.7	2.2	3.3	1.7*	1.8*
Can	-1.9	0.9	2.5	3.9	2.2	1.2	3.8	3.3*	3.0*
EU	1.6	1.0	-0.5	2.9	2.5	1.7	2.6	2.7*	2.8*
Rus	-5.0	-14.5	-8.7	-12.7	-4.1	-4.9	0.4^a	0.5^b	3.0^b
Chi	7.0	12.0	13.5	12.6	10.5	9.7	8.8^c	6.7^b	7.6^b

* OECD projections
[a] EIU estimates
[b] EIU forecasts
[c] Official figure quoted in press reports

Note: Due to the 1998 financial turmoil, 1998 and 1999 projections have been revised downward. This table does not reflect these late revisions.

Source for the G7 and the EU: OECD, *OECD Economic Outlook*, June 1998.
Source for Russia: *EIU Country Report: Russia*, 4th Quarter 1996 (for 1991), 4th Quarter 1997 (for 1992),   2nd Quarter 1998 (for 1993-99).
Source for China: *EIU Country Report: China, Mongolia*, 4th Quarter 1996 (for 1991), 4th Quarter 1997 (for 1992), 2nd Quarter 1998 (for 1993-99).

club of finance ministers and central bank governors of the seven largest industrial democracies". Bergsten acknowledges, however, that "[i]n light of China's continued failure to democratize, its inclusion in the G-7 summits ... would ... be premature". *The Economist* agrees: "China seems to some to be an island of stability, perhaps a new economic leader in the region, worthy of a seat at the G7's top financial table".[11]   Hodges adds that "China is a major player, not only in the regional context of the 1997-8 Asian crisis, but also in the world economy as a whole. China may not be a suitable candidate for membership in a new G9.   However, it may be useful to extend formalised links between the G7 or G8 and China, given the growing importance of China to the global economy".[12]

There is an additional perspective on the dynamics of the G7.   The four European members–France, Germany, the UK, and Italy–interact regularly within the EU, just as Canada and the US have interacted, even before the Canada-US Free Trade Agreement and then the North American Free Trade Agreement (NAFTA). In some ways, therefore, the G7 is a forum for what is often a three-way dialogue among North America, Europe, and Japan.   In fact, Bergsten and C. Randall Henning–writing about the G7 finance ministers' group rather than the larger G7–express the view that "the G-7 should streamline its own membership by becoming a G-3 as soon as the progression of monetary union in Europe permits that region to be represented by a single spokesperson on macroeconomic policy".[13] John J. Kirton echoes that possibility: "Institutionally, the prospect of EMU as an accomplished reality, with a European Central Bank, suggests the G7 may be replaced by a G3, with Canada and perhaps Britain excluded".[14] It should be added, however, that evolution along such lines is more likely to occur in the finance ministers' forum rather than in the G7/G8 as a whole.

Notes

1   "Transcript of Joint Press Conference Given by the Prime Minister, Mr John Major, and the Soviet President, Mr Mikhael [sic] Gorbachev, in London on 17 July 1991" (unpublished; released at the London Economic Summit, 17 July 1991), p. 3. Also available at URL: www.library.utoronto.ca/www/g7/91joint.htm.

2   Chrystia Freeland and Matthew Kaminski, "Helsinki Talks Reach Nuclear Breakthrough", *Financial Times* (March 22-23, 1997), p. 1.

3   United States, White House, Office of the Press Secretary, *Press Conference of the President* (Denver, Colorado, 22 June 1997), pp. 1-2.

URL: www.library.utoronto.ca/www/g7/denver/clint22.htm.

4   Great Britain, Prime Minister's Office, *Press Conference Given by the Prime Minister, Mr Tony Blair, In Birmingham, on Sunday, 17 May 1998.* Available at URL:
www.library.utoronto.ca/www/g7/birmingham/blaira.html and
www.library.utoronto.ca/www/g7/birmingham/blairb.html.

5   John J. Kirton, "The Diplomacy of Concert: Canada, the G7 and the Halifax Summit", *Canadian Foreign Policy* 3, No. 1 (Spring 1995), p. 65.

6   Nicholas Bayne, "The G7 Summit and the Reform of Global Institutions", *Government and Opposition* 30, No. 4 (Autumn 1995), p. 497.

7   Zbigniew Brzezinski, "Let's Add to the G-7", *The New York Times*, 25 June 1996, p. A11.

8   Jeffrey Sachs, "Global Capitalism: Making It Work", *The Economist* 348, No. 8085 (September 12, 1998), pp. 23-25.

9   Institute for International Finance, quoted in *The New York Times*, October 18, 1998, p. Y10.

10   International Monetary Fund, *World Economic Outlook*, October 1998 (Washington, DC: 1998), p. 25 (Table 2.2), p. 31 (Table 2.4), p. 32 (Table 2.5).

11   C. Fred Bergsten, "The New Agenda with China", *International Economics Policy Briefs*, No. 98-2 (May 1998), pp. 1-2; "Welcome to China, Mr Clinton", *The Economist* 347, No. 8074 (June 27, 1998), p. 17.

12   Michael R. Hodges, "The G8 and the New Political Economy", in *The G8's Role in the New Millennium*, edited by Michael R. Hodges, John J. Kirton, and Joseph P. Daniels (Aldershot; Brookfield USA; Singapore; Sydney: Ashgate, forthcoming, 1999).

13   C. Fred Bergsten and C. Randall Henning, *Global Economic Leadership and the Group of Seven* (Washington, DC: Institute for International Economics, 1996), pp. 139-40.

14   John J. Kirton, "Economic Cooperation: Summitry, Institutions, and Structural Change, Paper prepared for a conference on "Structural Change and Co-operation in the Global Economy". Center for International Business Education and Center for Global Change and Governance, Rutgers University, New Brunswick, NJ, May 19-20, 1997. URL: www.library.utoronto.ca/www/g7/scholar/rutcon.htm. Will appear in *Structural Change and Co-operation in the Global Economy*, edited by John Dunning and Gavin Boyd (London: Edward Elgar, forthcoming, 1999).

4   The G7/G8 System

Over the years, an elaborate system has evolved around, and in addition to, the annual summit meetings of the Group of 7/Group of 8 (G7/G8) that form the basis of the institution. Related meetings take place several times during the year to discuss and make decisions on issues of concern to the G7/G8. The leaders' summits are at the apex of the G7/G8 system. The second layer consists of the progressively intensifying and increasingly widespread meetings of ministers. Several of these ministerial meetings take place on a regular basis, while others are *ad hoc* affairs. In addition, the G7/G8 system has a third component consisting of the leaders' personal representatives or sherpas, who meet several times a year as part of their function to prepare for each summit.   As well, an intricate network of task forces, working groups and expert groups has been established by the G7/G8 leaders. Table 4.1 is a partial list of component bodies of the G7/G8 system.

Ministerial Meetings

G7 *trade ministers* met at the 1978 and 1993 summits, and the 1981 Ottawa Summit created the Trade Ministers' Quadrilateral ("the Quad") which brings together ministers from the US, Canada, Japan and the European Union (EU). Starting in 1982, the Quad has generally met three or four times per year. The Quad meeting held just before the 1993 Tokyo Summit was especially important because it hammered out an agreement on market access to manufactured goods–an agreement that was a catalyst for the completion of the stalled Uruguay Round of multilateral trade negotiations.

   Finance ministers of the G7 have met annually at the summit site since 1975, and the 1986 Tokyo Summit officially set up the G7 finance ministers' group as a separate entity that meets four or more times a year, usually attended also by the chairmen of the central banks of the Seven and often by the Managing Director of the IMF. An even more exclusive club was the "Group of Five" (G5) finance ministers (the Seven minus Italy and Canada), dating back to the Library Group and its aftermath and first running parallel with, then subsumed by, the G7 finance ministers. The Plaza Accord of 22 September 1985, which began the "managed floating" of exchange

Table 4.1   The G7/G8 System (partial list)

Annual Summit Meetings of Leaders: 1975-
Special Summit Meetings of Leaders: New York 1985 (G6), Moscow 1996 (G8)

Regular Ministerial Meetings:
Finance: G5: irregular, 1973-1986; G7: annual on summit site, 1975-1997; 3-4 or
        more times a year as stand-alone meeting, 1986-; a G3 finance ministers'
        forum is also reported to exist
Foreign affairs: annual on summit site, 1975-1997; annual as stand-alone meeting,
        1984-
Trade Ministers' Quadrilateral ("the Quad"): on summit site, 1978, 1993 and 1995;
        3-4 times a year as stand-alone meeting, 1982-
Environment: 1992; annual, 1994-
Employment: 1994; annual, 1996-
Global Information Society: 1995 (G7), 1996 (40 countries and 18 international
        organisations)
Terrorism: 1995, 1996
Finance and foreign ministers' pre-summit meeting: 1998- (in 1998, included a brief
        G8 finance ministers' meeting)

Ad Hoc **Ministerial Meetings:**
Aid to the Russia (finance and foreign ministers): 1993
Economic Aid to Ukraine: 1994
Global Marketplace for *Small and Medium-size Enterprises*: 1997
Crime: 1997
Energy: 1998

Sherpa Meetings: 4-5 times a year, 1975-

Other G7/G8 Bodies and Meetings:
International Nuclear Fuel Cycle Evaluation Group, 1977-
International Energy Technology Group, 1979-
Expert Group on Aid to Sub-Saharan Africa, 1985
Financial Action Task Force, 1989- (broader than G7/G8; secretariat provided by
        OECD)
Chemical Action Task Force, 1990-1992 (broader than G7/G8)
Permanent Working Group on Assistance to Russia, 1990-
Nuclear Safety Working Group,1992-
Counterterrorism Experts' Group, 1995-
Senior Experts' Group on Transnational Organized Crime ("Lyon Group"), 1995-
Expert Group on Financial Crime, 1997-

Table 4.1 (continued)

Group of Experts on the Prevention and Treatment of AIDS, 199--
Group of Experts on Export Controls To Prevent Proliferation of Weapons of Mass
     Destruction, 199--

G7-inspired Institutions:
London Suppliers' Group on Nuclear Materials, 1977-
International Ethics Committee on AIDS, 1987-
Missile Technology Control Regime (MTCR), 1989-
G-24, 1989-
Assistance for Economic Restructuring in the Countries of Central and Eastern
     Europe (PHARE), 1989-
Brazil Pilot Program on Tropical Forests, 1990-
European Bank for Reconstruction and Development (EBRD), 1991-
GEF Working Group of Experts, 1992
Support Implementation Group (SIG; with "non-institutional secretariat"), 1993-97

Compiled by Peter I. Hajnal, with contributions by John J. Kirton and Eleonore Kokotsis.

rates, was a notable achievement of the Group of Five. The Louvre Accord
of 22 February 1987, aimed at further stabilisation of exchange rates, was the
result of a meeting of the G6 (G7 minus Italy) finance ministers. The finance
and foreign ministers' joint pre-summit meeting that took place for the first
time in 1998 will be discussed in more detail later in this chapter. The G7
finance ministers' and central bank governors' meetings on 3 and 30 October
1998 (especially the latter) developed a series of far-reaching proposals to
deal with the financial crisis and to enable the Bretton Woods institutions to
play a greater role in addressing this crisis and preventing or mitigating
future ones. (See Chapter 5 for more detail on the October 1998 meetings.)

     With the creation of the European Central Bank (ECB) and the
launching of the common currency, the euro on 1 January 1999, there is a
strong possibility of the G7 finance ministers' meetings changing into a
format similar to that of the Trade Ministers' Quadrilateral. The EU speaks
with one voice in trade matters; the European Economic and Monetary Union
(EMU) will lead to a similar phenomenon in monetary and exchange rate
matters, with representation of the US, Canada, Japan, and the EU, as well
as G7 member UK which has opted out of EMU for the time being. It would
be interesting if this were to lead to a new G5. An early indication of
evolution in this process is that President Willem Duisenberg of the ECB

participated for the first time in the 3 October 1998 Washington meeting of the G7 finance ministers and central bank governors.

It has been reported that a G3 of the US, Germany and Japan exists as well. It meets as needed, and fulfils important crisis-management and other functions; for example, in the Indonesian crisis of 1998. The G3 is understood to act intensively together under such circumstances.

G7 (now G8) *foreign ministers* also met annually at the summit site from 1975 to 1997. In addition, they have, since 1984, met annually for a working dinner in New York in September, around the time of the opening of the United Nations (UN) General Assembly. The foreign and finance ministers' joint pre-summit meeting that took place for the first time in 1998 will be discussed in more detail later in this chapter.

The impetus for the G7 (now G8) *environment ministers* to form their own forum began around the time of the United Nations Conference on Environment and Development (UNCED, or the Earth Summit) in 1992. The ministers first met formally in Germany just before the 1992 Munich Summit, then in Florence, Italy on 12-13 March 1994, in Hamilton, Canada on 30 April-1 May 1995, in Cabourg, France on 9-10 May 1996, in Miami, Florida, US on 5-6 May 1997, and in Kent, UK on 3-5 April 1998.

The *employment ministers'* first meeting was the "Jobs Summit" in Detroit on 14-15 March 1994 (not truly a summit; the participants were ministers of labour, industry, trade and finance). Subsequent employment ministerial meetings took place in Lille, France on 1-2 April 1996; Kobe, Japan on 28-29 November 1997; and London on 21-22 February 1998 ("G8 Conference on Growth, Employability and Inclusion"), bringing together ministers for economic, financial and employment issues.

A G7 ministerial conference on the "*global information society*" took place in Brussels on 24-26 February 1995, with the participation of relevant ministers; for example, Canada was represented by the ministers of industry and of heritage, and the Secretary of State for Science, Research and Development; the US delegation was led by the Secretary of Commerce, but the Vice-President delivered the keynote speech. For the first time in a G7 meeting, industrial leaders participated alongside government representatives. The conference adopted eight core policy principles and set out several pilot projects. The 1995 Halifax Summit welcomed these results and the proposal that a follow-up information society conference be held in South Africa in the spring of 1996.[1] This "Information Society and Development Conference" met in Midrand, South Africa on 13-15 May 1996, but as a much larger gathering, with representatives from forty countries as well as the EU and seventeen other international organisations.

Ministerial meetings on *terrorism* took place in Ottawa, Canada, on 19 December 1995 and in Paris, France, on 30 July 1996. A related G8 conference on land-transportation anti-terrorism measures met in Washington, DC on 22-23 April 1997.

A G8 *foreign and finance ministers' pre-summit meeting* was held in London a week before the 1998 Birmingham Summit to prepare for the summit agenda and to deal with issues not on the agenda of this "heads only" summit. This formula is likely to be used again in Germany in 1999, making the new configuration an annual event. The details of this complex set of meetings are discussed in Chapter 8, under "Documentation of Ministerial Conferences, Task Forces, Working Groups, and Expert Groups". Table 4.2 illustrates the main events of the 1998 foreign/finance ministers' joint meeting.

Besides these regularly scheduled G7/G8 ministerial meetings, several *ad hoc* meetings have been and will likely continue to be held. Some *ad hoc* meetings become a regular series. Here are some examples:

- G7 foreign and finance ministers, with Russia also present, assembled in Tokyo on 15 April 1993 in preparation for the 1993 Tokyo Summit, to discuss support for reform in Russia.
- G7 foreign ministers, with Russian participation, held a Conference on "Partnership for Economic Transformation in Ukraine"in Winnipeg, Canada on 27 October 1994.
- A conference on the global marketplace for small and medium-sized enterprises (SMEs) took place in Bonn, Germany, on 7-9 April 1997. A related regional conference was held in Manchester, UK, on 8-9 September 1998, and an "EU-US SMEs' partnering event" is scheduled to take place in Dallas, Texas, USA on 14-16 April 1999.
- A G8 justice ministers' meeting on crime was held in Washington, DC on 10 December 1997, and the 1998 G8 Birmingham communiqué refers to a proposal to hold another ministerial meeting on transnational crime in Moscow in 1999.[2]
- A G8 energy ministers' meeting took place in Moscow on 31 March-1 April 1998.
- A special meeting of G8 foreign ministers and the EU representative took place on 12 June 1998 in London to discuss the recent Indian and Pakistani nuclear tests. This resulted in a collective commitment of the G8 to use their votes in the international financial institutions

to block loans to India and Pakistan.[3]   Having talked since 9:30 that morning, at 11:30 the meeting transformed itself, unusually, into a (non-G8) Contact Group meeting on the Kosovo crisis. In addition to Contact Group members US, UK, France, Germany, Russia and Italy, the meeting, on that occasion, also included Canada and Japan

Table 4.2	Main Events of the Pre-Summit Meeting of the G7/G8 Foreign and Finance Ministers, London, 8-9 May 1998

8 May

3:30 PM	arrival of **G7** finance ministers
4:00 PM	arrival of **G8** foreign ministers
4:30 PM	**G7** finance ministers' working session
4:30 PM	**G8** foreign ministers' working session
7:30 PM	**G7** finance ministers' working dinner, with the IMF Managing Director and the World Bank President, hosted by the British Chancellor of the Exchequer
7:30 PM	**G8** foreign ministers' working dinner, hosted by the British Foreign Secretary

9 May

8:30 AM	press conference of the Chancellor of the Exchequer on **G7** issues, and release of the *Conclusions of G7 Finance Ministers*; briefings by other **G7** finance ministers
9:15 AM	Foreign Secretary's press conference; briefings by other **G8** foreign ministers
10:00 AM	**G8** finance ministers' working session
10:00 AM	**G8** foreign ministers' working session, followed by release of the *Conclusions of G8 Foreign Ministers*
11:30 AM	**G8** foreign and finance ministers' joint plenary
1:00 PM	**G8** foreign and finance ministers' working lunch with the IMF Managing Director, the World Bank President and the WTO Director-General
3:00 PM	joint Presidency press conference, and release of the *Conclusions of the Joint Meeting of G8 Foreign and Finance Ministers*
3:30 PM	press conferences by other **G8** foreign and finance ministers

Source: Adapted from media information released at the G7/G8 Foreign and Finance Ministers' Meeting, London, 8-9 May 1998.

–presumably due to the vagaries of timing rather than a decision to expand the Contact Group. At 2 PM there was an informal lunch that–again unusually–included representatives of Argentina, Brazil, China, the Philippines, South Africa, and Ukraine, in addition to ministers and representatives of the Contact Group plus Canada and Japan.

Sherpa Meetings

In addition to the leaders' summit meetings and the various ministerial meetings, the G7/G8 system has a third component: sherpas meet several times a year as part of their function to prepare for the forthcoming summit, and sometimes to follow up on the past summit. National sherpa teams generally include, in addition to the sherpa, two sous-sherpas (one for finance, the other for foreign affairs) and a political director from each foreign ministry. Between Denver and Birmingham, for example, the following sherpa meetings took place:

- Follow-up sherpa meeting, Washington, DC, 30-31 October 1997
- First sherpa meeting, Chevening, UK, 16-17 January 1998
- Foreign affairs sous-sherpa meeting, London, 13-14 February 1998
- Finance sous-sherpa meeting, London, 22 February 1998
- Second sherpa meeting, London, 27-28 February 1998
- Sherpa plenary meeting, London, 25-26 April 1998.

Sherpa activity is not necessarily confined to summit preparation or technical follow-up of past summits. The G7 leaders' consultation process in September and October 1998 (culminating in the 30 October *G7 Leaders' Statement on the World Economy*, described in Chapters 2 and 5) was conducted principally through the sherpa network, beginning with the year's sherpa chairman (the British sherpa, since 1998 was the UK's turn to chair the G7/G8) contacting his counterparts in other G7 countries each of whom, in turn, consulted his leader.

Meetings of Task Forces, Working Groups and Expert Groups

Regular and *ad hoc* task forces and working groups are also part of the

G7/G8 system. Over the years, the summits have established a number of such groups (see Table 4.1 for a more extensive list). Here are some examples:

- The 1977 London Summit created the International Nuclear Fuel Cycle Evaluation Group.
- The 1979 Tokyo Summit set up the International Energy Technology Group.
- The 1989 Paris Summit established a Financial Action Task Force to co-ordinate efforts to fight drug-related money laundering (FATF) whose membership has since become broader than the G7/G8. The 1998 pre-summit meeting of G7 finance ministers (8-9 May, London) supported the extension of FATF's mandate by a further five years as well as a further extension of its membership.
- The 1990 Houston Summit mandated the Chemical Action Task Force to monitor the movement of chemical precursors used in the manufacturing of drugs.
- The Nuclear Safety Working Group was established in 1992.
- The 1995 Halifax Summit established the Senior Experts' Group on Transnational Organized Crime which after the 1996 Lyon Summit became known as the "Lyon Group".
- The 1997 Denver Summit of the Eight set up an expert group on financial crime.

Official G7/G8 groups or G7/G8-inspired groups include, among others, the Missile Technology Control Regime (MTCR, established in 1989), the London Suppliers' Group on Nuclear Materials (established in 1977), the International Ethics Committee on AIDS (established in 1987), the Group of 24 or G24 (established in 1989), and the European Bank for Reconstruction and Development (EBRD, established in 1991).   Recent meetings of another entity, the Counterterrorism Experts' Group (sometimes referred to as the Terrorism Experts' Group) took place on 14-15 April 1997 and 5-6 March 1998.

A more recent creation is the Group of 22 or G22–also known as the Willard Group, after the Washington hotel where representatives first met in April 1998 to prepare the ministerial meeting at US initiative.   The G22–which characterises itself as "Finance Ministers and Central Bank Governors from a number of systemically significant economies"–brings together those officials from the G7 plus Argentina, Australia, Brazil, China,

Hong Kong, India, Indonesia, Korea, Malaysia, Mexico, Poland, Russia, Singapore, South Africa and Thailand.[4] Originally conceived as a one-time meeting, it was given an extension, and duly met for the second time on 5 October 1998, on the margins of the Fall 1998 meetings of World Bank and the IMF. At that second meeting, four more countries joined the group. It remains to be seen whether the G22 will continue to exist now that it has submitted its three reports, prepared by G22 working groups, to the IMF and the World Bank.

An interesting institutional development was the establishment, by the 1993 Tokyo Summit, of the Support Implementation Group (SIG) on assistance to Russia. Japan chaired the SIG briefly and temporarily, and was then succeeded by the US as chair of the group, located in Moscow. The group's mandate was troubleshooting rather than administering actual aid programmes.[5] SIG facilitated the implementation of G7 assistance to Russia through information sharing and co-ordination among the G7, and through consultation with Russian organisations, international financial institutions and non-G7 countries. SIG had a secretariat whose role was to co-ordinate G7 action concerning taxation aspects of assistance; to serve as an information source on external assistance to Russia; to be a research centre on problems of assistance implementation; and to facilitate the co-ordination of assistance, bringing together Russians and external donors.[6] On 31 December 1997, SIG ceased functioning as a secretariat to G7 embassies on assistance to Russia.[7]

Not everyone sees the G7 institution as a true system. According to W. R. Smyser, "[d]uring the 1980s, the G-7 system split into two separate structures related more in name than in reality ... . The summits became political and representational. Economic coordination moved back to the finance ministers". Hodges concurs, stating that "[t]he summit is perceived in the UK as separate from the finance ministers' process ... ". De Guttry, on the other hand, comments that "the degree of institutionalization, bureaucratization and formalization of ... [the G7 system's] new structures is ... higher and more sophisticated than that of the summit itself".[8] The SIG Secretariat, however, carefully characterised itself as a "flexible non-institutional technical secretariat".[9]

The advent of a new, leaders-only summit format in 1998 (see Chapter 1 for more detail) has again brought the relationship between G7 leaders and finance ministers closer together. The latter, along with G8 foreign ministers, met separately a week before the Birmingham Summit and their deliberations fed directly into the summit itself. And the 30 October

1998 *Declaration of G7 Finance Ministers and Central Bank Governors* was endorsed simultaneously and in a co-ordinated fashion by the leaders in their *G7 Leaders' Statement on the World Economy.*

Notes

1   *Halifax Summit Communiqué*, paragraph 10. In United States, Department of State, Bureau of Public Affairs, *US Department of State Dispatch* 6, Supplement No. 4 (July 1995), p. 6. See also the University of Toronto G8 Information Centre at URL:
www.library.utoronto.ca/www/g7/95grow.htm.

2   Birmingham Summit, 1998, *G8 Birmingham Summit Communiqué*, para. 21. URL:
www.library.utoronto.ca/www/g7/birmingham/finalcom.htm.

3   "G8 To Step Up Pressure on India and Pakistan", *Financial Times*, 13 -14 June 1998, p. 3.

4   G22, *Summary of Reports on the International Financial Architecture* (Washington, DC, October 1998), p. 1. URL:
www.imf.org/external/np/g22/summry.pdf.

5   Michael R. Hodges, "More Efficiency, Less Dignity: British Perspectives on the Future Role and Working of the G-7", in *The Future of the G-7 Summits*, p. 156 (*The International Spectator* 29, No. 2; April/June 1994, Special Issue).

6   G7 Support Implementation Group, web site. URL: www.g7sig.org/.

7   G7 Support Implementation Group, web site. URL:
www.g7sig.org/html/announce/announce.htm.

8   W. R. Smyser, "Goodbye, G-7", *The Washington Quarterly* 16, No. 1 (Winter 1993), p. 20; Hodges, "More Efficiency, Less Dignity, p. 142; Andrea de Guttry, "The Institutional Configuration of the G-7 in the New International Scenario", in *The Future of the G-7 Summits*, p. 72.

9   G7 Support Implementation Group, web site. URL:
www.g7sig.org/html/SIG/SIGRole.htm.

5 Connections with Other International Organisations and Fora

The G7/G8 system does not and could not exist in isolation from other international events and organisations. The summits have made it clear from their beginning that "the G7 intends to make use of existing [international organisations] to achieve certain objectives, but absolutely does not intend to replace them".[1] Andrea De Guttry noted in 1994 that

> [t]he G-7 is cautious toward universal IOs [international organisations] (United Nations ..., GATT ..., etc.) in which it has little decisional weight ..., [although s]ince 1989 ... the G-7 has become much more enterprising, going so far as to urge reforms of the UN charter or parts of it ... . Towards IOs in which it has some weight ... (e.g., in the IMF ... or ... the OECD) ... the G-7 has made precise attempts to orient important decisions and to establish what relations among them should be like ... . The G-7 has an almost hierarchical relationship with ... the OECD, which the G-7 often rather peremptorily asks to carry out certain activities ... . [I]n a very limited number of cases, the G-7 has worked out concrete proposals for the establishment of new international organizations ... .[2]

Since this was written, the G7/G8–and especially the G7–has taken an increasingly more activist role in its relations with international governmental organisations (IGOs), particularly with international financial institutions. Summit documents often refer to the activities of the International Monetary Fund (IMF), the Organisation for Economic Co-operation and Development (OECD), the General Agreement on Tariffs and Trade (GATT) and its successor the World Trade Organization (WTO), the United Nations Environment Programme (UNEP), and other international institutions, including the European Union (EU). Conversely, traditional international organisations sometimes produce official publications instigated by the summit. Here are some examples:

- The 1990 Houston summit requested studies on the Soviet economy; accordingly, one was prepared jointly by the IMF, the World Bank, the OECD and the European Bank for Reconstruction and Development (EBRD), the other by the European Community (EC).[3]
- The 1993 Tokyo Summit requested the OECD to prepare a "jobs study"; the result was duly released in time for the 1994 Naples Summit.[4]
- The 1995 Halifax Summit welcomed OECD's initiative to prepare a review of each member country's structural and employment policies. It also asked G7 finance ministers "to commission studies and analysis from the international organizations responsible for banking and securities regulations and to report on the adequacy of current arrangements ... at the next Summit".[5] Accordingly, at the 1996 Lyon Summit, the G7 finance ministers reported the December 1995 publication of the "Basle Committee capital adequacy standards for banks' exposure to market risk" and welcomed the "Basle and IOSCO [International Organization of Securities Commissions] Committees' reports on prudential regulation and supervisory cooperation" as well as the report of the "G-10 Working Party on the Resolution of Sovereign Liquidity Crises".[6]

The Halifax Summit went further than its predecessors in proposing a number of concrete steps in the review and reform of international institutions. These proposals range from delineating the respective roles of the UN and the Bretton Woods institutions and clarifying the mandates of some UN agencies, through urging IGOs to focus their programmes more sharply, eliminate duplication and improve their working methods, to supporting the establishment of new institutions (for example, a new institution and financing mechanism for regional co-operation in the Middle East, and a new emergency financing mechanism within the IMF). In the area of direct G7 relations with IGOs, the Halifax Summit endorsed enhanced consultations of G7 ministers with the IMF.[7] Louis W. Pauly notes that "in recent years the [IMF] managing director has been invited to provide finance ministers at G-7 meetings with a summary of the Fund's current views on the condition of the international system and the requirements for stability. Over time, the ministers and their deputies have relied on the senior staff of the Fund for an increasing amount of technical assistance, particularly related to the use of comparable economic indicators to monitor and evaluate policy trends across the G-7".[8]

The Halifax Summit also made a commitment that the G7 "will contribute to the OSCE [Organization for Security and Co-operation in Europe] study into a security model for Europe for the 21st century".[9] This serves to illustrate the growing reach of the G7 in the security area.

In its broad programme of reforming international institutions, the Halifax Summit concentrated mostly on "international financial issues [emphasis removed], especially the work of the IMF and the World Bank ... and the United Nations family [emphasis removed], especially its humanitarian, development and other related activities".[10] Nicholas Bayne comments that in undertaking the institutional review, "[f]or the first time, the leaders decided to work not from outside international institutions but from inside them".[11]

The Lyon Summit welcomed the progress in the implementation of the Halifax proposals, noting that the "surveillance capacities of the IMF have been enhanced, standards for the provision of economic and financial information to the markets have been established and an emergency financing mechanism has been created". The Lyon Summit also welcomed the agreement on the doubling of IMF resources under the General Arrangements to Borrow (GAB). The G7 leaders at Lyon moved further toward giving direct guidance to IGOs: "[T]he IMF should remain an institution based on quotas providing the [necessary] resources ... . The IMF should continue to reflect on the role of Special Drawing Rights within the international monetary system ... . We strongly urge the OECD to vigorously pursue its work ... aimed at establishing a multilateral approach" in limiting tax competition between States.[12]

The leaders at Lyon noted progress achieved since the Halifax Summit in the reform not only of international financial institutions but also of the UN itself. They commented favourably on the ninth session of the United Nations Conference on Trade and Development (UNCTAD) which had laid the groundwork for "a thorough reform" of the UN economic and social sector. The Lyon communiqué sets out what the G7 leaders see as the UN's priorities: "reduction of poverty, employment, housing, the provision of essential services ... especially those relating to health and education, the advancement of women and protection of children, and humanitarian assistance ... [,] the promotion of democracy, human rights and the rule of law, protection of the environment, emergency relief and post-conflict stabilization, and technical assistance to ... the poorest" countries.[13]

The Lyon communiqué states categorically that the "UN must clarify its role and comparative advantages ... must enhance the efficiency of its

Secretariat and operational framework ... [and must] ensure genuine coordination". The communiqué then gives detailed guidance on the central points of UN reform efforts, down to the role of the Economic and Social Council (ECOSOC) and the proposed Under-Secretary-General for Development.[14]

The Chairman's Statement of the Lyon Summit, issued on behalf of the P8 and thus reflecting the views of the G7 and Russia, includes, as a Halifax Summit follow-up, a review of UN reforms in the economic and social fields. The review deals with:

- system wide UN issues involving ECOSOC, the World Food Programme, the UN Efficiency Board, the UN Office of Internal Oversight Services, and a number of other UN bodies;
- budgeting for the UN, Food and Agriculture Organization of the United Nations (FAO), World Health Organization (WHO), International Labour Organisation (ILO), International Fund for Agricultural Development (IFAD), the World Food Programme, and United Nations Development Programme (UNDP);
- humanitarian relief;
- review of the FAO, United Nations Educational, Scientific and Cultural Organization (Unesco), WHO and the United Nations Industrial Development Organization (UNIDO);
- reforms and other developments in the United Nations Children's Fund (UNICEF), the World Food Programme, UNEP and UNDP;
- review of the UN regional economic commissions; and
- the evolution of the UN "Agenda for Development".[15]

The leaders at the Denver Summit of the Eight noted progress in economic and social fields since Lyon, welcomed UN Secretary-General Kofi Annan's reform proposals, and expressed continuing commitment to work with all UN members to accomplish these and other proposed UN reforms. The Denver communiqué states that "financial reform should proceed together with necessary reform measures in other areas ... the UN system must be placed on a firm financial footing ... [and affirms that] robust oversight mechanisms and sound personnel policies are essential for success". The eight leaders emphasise the need for the UN to streamline its subsidiary bodies and improve its working relationship with international financial institutions and the WTO. The communiqué calls for "a thorough and urgent review of the UN's funds and programs, as well as a system-wide review of the roles and mandates of specialized agencies and commissions". It reaffirms the necessity for improving the UN's ability in conflict prevention and resolution.[16]

The eight foreign ministers, reporting at the Denver Summit, welcome progress already achieved in UN reform. They "anticipate ... the prompt implementation of responsive measures during ... 1998-99 ... [to] ensure that the United Nations is fully able to meet the challenges of the new century as the premier international organization responsible for peace, security and the promotion of human welfare and sustainable development in all its aspects".[17]

In their statement issued at the G7 rather than G8 level, the leaders at Denver reaffirm their support for reform of the international financial institutions, and welcome the IMF's progress in strengthening surveillance and improving transparency, as well as the World Bank's "Strategic Compact". They call for amending the IMF Articles of Agreement to allow for capital account liberalisations, and "urge the IMF and the World Bank to finalize governance policies, consisting of principles and guidelines on best governance practices". They recognise the G7's duty to ensure that international financial institutions have the necessary support and resources to fulfil their responsibilities.[18]

The 1998 Birmingham *G7 Chairman's Statement* endorses the report of the G7 Finance Ministers, entitled *Strengthening the Architecture of the Global Financial System*. This report deals with proposed further reforms of the IMF, the World Bank, the Bank for International Settlements (BIS) and other international financial institutions. Among other initiatives, the G7 heads at Birmingham

- encourage the IMF to consider adopting a code of good practice on transparency in fiscal policy;
- encourage the IMF to publish more information about its members and their policies and about its own decision-making;
- urge the IMF to examine ways to monitor effectively capital flows, to provide information and promote market stability;
- ask the IMF to signal its preparedness, in the event of a financial crisis, to consider lending to countries in arrears; and
- ask their finance ministers "to consider further how the existing global discussion fora, particularly the IMF's Interim Committee, could be developed to permit a deeper and more effective dialogue".[19]

In the *G8 Birmingham Summit Communiqué*, the G8 leaders:

- express confidence in the ability of IMF programmes to restore stability in countries affected by the financial crisis in Asia, but they also recognise the impact of the crisis on the poorest and most vulnerable sectors of society, and point to the need to protect these groups with the support of the World Bank, the Asian Development Bank and bilateral donors;
- reaffirm their commitment to trade and investment liberalisation within the multilateral framework of the WTO;
- express strong support for widening WTO's membership and encourage greater transparency in the WTO and in other international organisations;
- agree to negotiate an adequate replenishment of the International Development Association (IDA 12) and to provide adequate resources for IMF's Enhanced Structural Adjustment Facility and for the African Development Fund;
- endorse the Heavily Indebted Poor Countries (HIPC) initiative on debt relief, agreed by international financial institutions, stating that they "expect the World Bank to join the future financial effort to help the African Development Bank finance its contribution to the HIPC initiative";
- support the WHO initiative to "Roll Back Malaria" by 2010 as well as the continuing efforts to fight AIDS, including support for the United Nations Programme on AIDS/HIV (UNAIDS);
- state their willingness to share their principles and experiences with other members of the ILO, OECD and the international financial institutions in matters of growth, employability and inclusion;
- agree to wide-ranging action on transnational organised crime, including negotiating a UN convention;
- welcome the UN General Assembly special session on the world drug problem and the work of the UN International Drug Control Programme on eliminating or reducing illicit drug production; and
- express willingness to work together in the World Bank, the OECD and other international organisations to help solve the Millennium Bug problem.[20]

In late September 1998 Prime Minister Blair, as 1998 chairman of the G7, called for major reforms of the Bretton Woods institutions, including better supervision and regulation of the world's financial system, greater transparency and accountability of the World Bank and the IMF and possibly even a partial merger of those two institutions.   In criticising the Bretton Woods institutions he stated: "The existing system has not served us terribly well" in the current financial crisis.[21]   Around the same time, President Clinton presented his initiative to step up World Bank aid to Asia, to create an IMF emergency fund to combat economic contagion in Latin America, to establish an emergency line of credit and to adopt other robust international measures to develop a new international financial architecture.[22] G7 member France also floated its own proposals to address the financial crisis, calling for a "new Bretton Woods".[23]

During the annual meetings of the World Bank and the IMF held in Washington on 6-8 October 1998 (plus related meetings that began on 29 September) the financial crisis dominated the agenda. The flurry of meetings engaged not only the IMF Interim Committee, the Development Committee–which is a joint forum of the IMF and the World Bank–and other bodies of the two institutions but other groups as well, including a meeting on 3 October of the G7 finance ministers, a meeting of the Group of 10 and a meeting of the Intergovernmental Group of Twenty-Four on International Monetary Affairs. Although the meetings addressed many aspects of the financial crisis, the G7 was dissatisfied with the way the results reflected or failed to reflect G7 understandings that had already been reached. Hence the two statements issued on 30 October by the G7: *Declaration of G7 Finance Ministers and Central Bank Governors*, and *G7 Leaders' Statement on the World Economy*.[24]   The IMF and the World Bank, both much criticised in the media in September 1998 for their handling (some said mishandling) of the financial crisis, were given detailed guidelines by the G7.

The finance ministers and central bank governors took steps to address the situation at hand, and specified detailed reforms of the international financial system in general and the international financial institutions in particular. The G7 set these specific goals:

- to increase the transparency and openness of the international financial system;
- to identify and disseminate international principles, standards and codes of best practice;
- to strengthen incentives to meet these international standards; and
- to strengthen official assistance to help developing countries reinforce their economic and financial infrastructures.

These are longer-term goals, fleshed out by a G7 call on the IMF: to monitor the implementation of the new codes and standards; to publish systematically and in a timely fashion a transparency report showing the results of its surveillance of member countries' compliance with transparency and disclosure codes and standards; to work together with the World Bank and the OECD as well as international regulatory and supervisory organisations to provide advice and assistance to countries in meeting these standards and codes. They further call upon the IMF to develop a formal mechanism for systematic evaluation, with external input, of the effectiveness of its operations, programmes, policies and procedures. In addition, the G7 agreed on concrete steps to strengthen the international financial system; for example, prudential regulation of financial systems in industrial countries as well as in emerging-market economies, and greater participation by the private sector in crisis containment and crisis resolution. The ministers committed themselves to monitor progress and to meet as necessary to develop further measures.

The 30 October 1998 statement of the G7 heads of state and government not only endorsed the work of their finance ministers but also welcomed such specific developments as: the agreement to increase IMF quotas and "New Arrangements to Borrow", yielding additional IMF resources of US$90 billion; and the reduction of interest rates in the US, Japan, Canada, the UK, Italy and other countries; and the progress made in several Asian countries for economic recovery. Among the most important direct results of G7 initiatives was the agreement to establish an IMF precautionary line of credit to be made available to countries that follow strong IMF-approved policies, so that those countries can avoid financial crises; and the agreement to establish a new World Bank emergency facility to provide support to the most vulnerable groups in times of crisis. The leaders also referred specifically to their willingness to support Brazil, in co-operation with the broader international community. (On 13 November 1998 the IMF announced a $42 billion rescue package for Brazil.[25])

The *Financial Times* commented editorially that the set of the 30 October G7 initiatives "was, in effect, an agenda to avert future financial crises" and that the longer-term proposals were intended to tackle the problems of uneven financial risk-taking, and of the "obscurity of corporate accounting and national financial statistics in some emerging countries". An early measure of the potential success of these recent G7 initiatives was the fact that "shares in New York and London rose again in response to the G7 announcement".[26]

As an indication of the seriousness of G7 commitments concerning the IMF, the representatives of the seven countries in the IMF Executive Board sent a memorandum, also dated 30 October 1998, to the IMF Managing Director and to members of the Executive Board, entitled "Work Program on Strengthening the Architecture of the International Monetary System". The memorandum proposes a number of priority reforms in light of the G7 leaders' and finance ministers' statements. These reforms embrace standards and codes of good practice, transparency and accountability, and terms and conditions of IMF loans.[27]

It is clear from the foregoing discussion that the G7/G8 is continually widening and deepening its links with international organisations. That the G8, but especially the G7, has a very large measure of influence in the international financial institutions is not surprising when one considers that the G7/G8 collectively wields about one half of all votes in the IMF and the World Bank, as illustrated by Table 5.1.

Table 5.1   G7/G8 Voting Power in the IMF and the World Bank

Country	% of IMF Votes	% of World Bank Votes
United States	7.78	16.68
Japan	5.53	8.00
Germany	5.53	4.57
France	4.98	4.38
United Kingdom	4.98	4.38
Italy*	4.02	3.47
Canada*	3.72	3.91
G7 TOTAL	**46.54**	**45.39**
Russia	2.90	2.83
G8 TOTAL	**49.44**	**48.22**

* Includes a small number of votes cast on behalf of other countries.
Source: Based on IMF, *Annual Report of the Executive Board for the Financial Year Ended April 30, 1998*; and World Bank, *The World Bank Annual Report, 1998.*

Notes

1   Andrea de Guttry, "The Institutional Configuration of the G-7 in the New
        International Scenario", in *The Future of the G-7 Summits*, p. 73 (*The
        International Spectator* 29, No. 2; April/June 1994, Special Issue).
2   *Ibid.*, p. 74.
3   *The Economy of the USSR: Summary and Recommendations* (Washington,
        DC: World Bank, 1990); "Stabilization, Liberalization and Devolution:
        Assessment of the Economic Situation and Reform Process in the Soviet
        Union", *European Economy*, No. 45 (December 1990).
4   Organisation for Economic Co-operation and Development, *The OECD
        Jobs Study, Vol. 1: Facts, Analysis, Strategies*; *Vol. 2, Evidence and
        Explanations* (Paris: OECD, 1994).
5   *Halifax Summit Communiqué*, para. 7, 22. In United States, Department of
        State, Bureau of Public Affairs, *US Department of State Dispatch* 6,
        Supplement No. 4 (July 1995), pp. 6-7. See also URL:
        www.library.utoronto.ca/www/g7/95grow.htm; and
        www.library.utoronto.ca/www/g7/95meet.htm..
6   Lyon Summit, 1996, *Finance Ministers' Report to the Heads of State and
        Government on International Monetary Stability*, 28 June 1996. URL:
        www.library.utoronto.ca/www/g7/96financ.htm.
7   *Halifax Summit Communiqué*, para. 13. In United States, Department of
        State, Bureau of Public Affairs, *US Department of State Dispatch* 6,
        Supplement No. 4 (July 1995), p. 6. See also URL:
        www.library.utoronto.ca/www/g7/95meet.htm.
8   Louis W. Pauly, *Who Elected the Bankers? Surveillance and Control in the
        World Economy* (Ithaca; London: Cornell University Press, 1997), pp. 129-
        30.
9   Halifax Summit, 1995, *Chairman's Statement*, June 17, 1995, para. 11. In
        United States, Department of State, Bureau of Public Affairs, *US
        Department of State Dispatch* 6, Supplement No. 4 (July 1995), p. 10. See
        also URL: www.library.utoronto.ca/www/g7/95chair.htm.
10   Nicholas Bayne, "The G7 Summit and the Reform of Global Institutions",
        Government and Opposition 30, No. 4 (Autumn 1995), pp. 501-2.
11   *Ibid.*, p. 508.
12   Lyon Summit, 1996, *Economic Communiqué*, paras. 12, 13, 16. Lyon, 28
        June 1996. URL: www.library.utoronto.ca/www/g7/96eco1.htm.
13   *Ibid.*, paras. 40-41. URL: www.library.utoronto.ca/www/g7/96eco5.htm.
14   *Ibid.*, paras. 42-43.
15   Lyon Summit, 1996, *Chairman's Statement*. Lyon, 29 June 1996. URL:
        www.library.utoronto.ca/www/g7/96poli.htm.
16   Denver Summit of the Eight, 1997, *Communiqué*, paras. 49-53. Denver, 22

June 1997. URL: www.library.utoronto.ca/www/g7/denver/g8final.htm.

17 Denver Summit of the Eight, 1997, *Foreign Ministers' Progress Report*. Denver, 21 June 1997. URL: www.library.utoronto.ca/www/g7/denver/formin.htm.

18 Denver Summit of the Eight, 1997, *Confronting Global Economic and Financial Challenges: Denver Summit Statement by Seven*, Denver, 21 June 1997), paras. 15-19. URL: www.library.utoronto.ca/www/g7/denver/confront.htm.

19 *G7 Chairman's Statement* (Birmingham, 1998), paras. 8-9. URL: www.library.utoronto.ca/www/g7/birmingham/chair.htm.

20 Birmingham Summit, 1998, *G8 Birmingham Summit Communiqué*, paras. 4, 5, 7, 17, 21, 23 and 25. URL: www.library.utoronto.ca/www/g7/birmingham/finalcom.htm.

21 Robert Peston, "Blair To Urge Full Overhaul of IMF and WB", *Financial Times*, 21 September 1998, p. 1.

22 David E. Sanger, "Clinton Presents Strategy To Quell Economic Threat", *The New York Times*, 15 September 1998, pp. A1, A16.

23 "Message de Monsieur Jacques Chirac, Président de la République, aux membres du G7 à la suite des déclarations sur le renforcement du système financier mondial", 24 septembre 1998. URL: www.elysee.fr/plweb-cgi/fastweb?getdoc+site_francais+discours+909+2 7+wAAA+%28g7%29.

24 *Declaration of G7 Finance Ministers and Central Bank Governors*, 30 October 1998. URL: www.hm-treasury.gov.uk/pub/html/docs/g7dec.html and www.library.utoronto.ca/www/g7/finance/fm103098.htm.; *G7 Leaders' Statement on the World Economy*, 30 October 1998. URL: www.number-10.gov.uk/public/news/uktoday/uktoday_right.asp?id=248 and www.library.utoronto.ca/www/g7/g7_103098.html.

25 David A. Sanger, "Brazil Is To Get I.M.F. Package for $42 Billion,", *The New York Times*, 13 November 1998, p. A1.

26 "The G7 Lays Its Plans", *Financial Times*, 31 October/1 November 1998, p. 6.

27 International Monetary Fund, "Work Program on Strengthening the Architecture of the International Monetary System" (Office Memorandum), 30 October 1998. URL: www.imf.org/external/np/g7/103098ed.htm.

6   The Agenda of the Summit

Macroeconomic policy co-ordination, international trade and North-South relations have been of concern to the G7/G8 from the beginning. East-West economic issues, energy and terrorism have also been recurrent preoccupations. Later additions have included microeconomic topics such as employment and the global information infrastructure; other global, transnational issues such as the environment, crime, drugs, and AIDS; and political and security issues such as human rights, migration, regional security, arms control, terrorism, and nuclear safety.

The main topics at Rambouillet in 1975 were monetary reform (in the area of inflation and exchange rates), economic growth, oil prices and supplies, unemployment, and trade including the Tokyo Round of General Agreement on Tariffs and Trade (GATT) negotiations. The final communiqué–known as the Declaration of Rambouillet–reflected these concerns. The San Juan Summit in 1976 added to the agenda balance-of-payments problems and reaffirmed the G7 commitment to the completion of the Tokyo Round. Energy–especially the use of nuclear energy–and North-South relations were added to the summit agenda in London in 1977. The key issues of the 1978 Bonn Summit were economic growth, energy, and trade. A non-economic issue, aircraft hijacking, entered the agenda as well.

Energy was the paramount concern of Tokyo I in 1979. The final communiqué included specific undertakings by summit countries to curb their oil imports. Hijackings and Indochinese refugees were also discussed. Energy continued to be at the top of the agenda in Venice in 1980, with Afghanistan and the occupation of the US Embassy in Tehran as additional issues. The 1981 Ottawa Summit (also known as the Summit of Montebello where, in the "world's largest log cabin", the delegations held their meetings away from the media waiting for news in Ottawa and Canadian Prime Minister Pierre Elliot Trudeau, as summit chair, flew back to Ottawa by helicopter to brief journalists following each afternoon session) discussed trade and other economic issues, along with aid to developing countries, East-West economic relations, and terrorism. The Versailles Summit of 1982 reviewed the whole gamut of economic concerns, concentrating on East-West trade and setting the stage for more effective multilateral surveillance of monetary policies and exchange rates, to be co-ordinated by the International

Monetary Fund (IMF).   The Israeli invasion of Lebanon also received attention.   At Williamsburg, Virginia in 1983 the summit participants again discussed economic issues, including the growing debt crisis, but the principal subject was arms control and the stationing of US cruise and Pershing II missiles in Europe ("Euromissiles"), and this was reflected in the political declaration.   Debt was again a central concern at "London II" in 1984.   Democratic values, terrorism, East-West security relations, and the Iran-Iraq conflict were discussed as well.

The most important issue at Bonn in 1985 was trade, but that summit failed to agree on a starting date for the Uruguay Round of multilateral negotiations, thereby earning the lowest mark in Robert D. Putnam and Nicholas Bayne's ranking of summits by result.[1]   Bonn II was, however, notable for introducing the topic of the environment to the summit agenda. It also commemorated the fortieth anniversary of the end of the Second World War.   "Tokyo II" in 1986, considered to be one of the more successful summits, called for an overhaul of agricultural policies of summit countries, established the Group of Seven finance ministers, and agreed to launch (through GATT) the Uruguay Round.   Action against terrorism–following the US raid on Libya–was a key issue of Tokyo II which also concerned itself with the Chernobyl nuclear-reactor accident.   Terrorism, the Iran-Iraq war, AIDS, and narcotic drugs were the non-economic agenda items in Venice in 1987.

The 1988 Toronto Summit produced the so-called "Toronto terms" for relieving the debt burden of the poorest developing countries.[2]   Toronto also reaffirmed the Uruguay Round, and discussed the Middle East, South Africa and Cambodia.   Debt relief also played an important part in the "Summit of the Arch" of 1989, with the adoption of the Brady Plan.   Other topics included the environment, the strengthening of GATT, and economic efficiency, as well as human rights, China and the Tiananmen Square massacre, democratisation in Eastern and Central Europe and help for that region, money laundering, and terrorism.

The 1990 Houston Summit addressed not only the usual range of economic issues but also a number of specific environmental problems; democratisation in Europe and elsewhere in the world; Soviet economic reforms; liberalisation of export controls; drug abuse; and the non-proliferation of nuclear, biological, and chemical weapons.   The most contentious issues at Houston were agricultural trade subsidies, aid to the Soviet Union, and global warming or climate change.

Help for the USSR (involving a post-summit meeting with Mikhail Gorbachev) was the main preoccupation of the London Summit of 1991 which had as its official theme "building world partnership and strengthening the international order". British Prime Minister John Major, the host leader, highlighted eight particular achievements: proposals to strengthen the United Nations (UN) in the areas of peace-keeping, peace-making and response to emergencies; proposals to ensure better regulation and control of conventional arms sales by means of a UN arms register; commitment to sustained economic recovery and price stability; personal commitment of the leaders to work for the conclusion of the Uruguay Round of trade negotiations by the end of 1991;[3] support for political and economic reform in Central and East European countries; financial and technical assistance to developing countries, including debt relief to the poorest beyond the Toronto terms; support for the June 1992 United Nations Conference on Environment and Development (UNCED); and stepping up the fight against drug abuse and drug trafficking.[4]

The theme of the 1992 Munich Summit, reflected in the title of the final communiqué, was "working together for growth and a safer world". The communiqué noted the end of the East-West conflict and the spirit of partnership of the former antagonists. It covered the world economy, with the recurrent subjects of growth, interest rates, unemployment, and trade, and gave another boost (but on a lower key than had the previous two summits) to the stalled Uruguay Round. It praised the Earth Summit as a landmark event; welcomed progress and noted problems in developing countries; and devoted special sections to Central and Eastern Europe, the new independent states of the former Soviet Union, and the problems of safety of nuclear power plants in those two parts of the world. In addition, the leaders at Munich concentrated on specific economic, political and security areas of the new partnership with Central and Eastern European countries and the new independent states of the former Soviet Union, nuclear non-proliferation, and the further strengthening of the UN.

"Tokyo III" of 1993 set out as its main economic theme "a strengthened commitment to jobs and growth". The final communiqué addressed problems of the world economy, especially the level of unemployment and insufficient economic growth. The communiqué incorporated various economic commitments by the Seven, although these were "soft" rather than specific "hard" commitments. The document also confirmed a $3 billion fund to aid Russian privatisation. Perhaps the major achievement was the agreement (actually reached on the eve of Tokyo III by the US, Canada, Japan, and the European Community (EC) trade ministers' quadrilateral meeting) on market access to manufactured goods–an agreement that proved to be a catalyst for the completion of the Uruguay Round. Concerning those negotiations, the communiqué again states: "our highest priority is a successful conclusion to the Uruguay Round".[5] (The deadline for the completion of the Uruguay Round was finally met by the end of 1993.)

The involvement of Russia in the P8 (see Chapter 3) was the most important issue for the 1994 Naples Summit. The rest of the Naples agenda included jobs and economic growth; trade, including a call for ratification of the Uruguay Round agreements and the establishment of the World Trade Organization (WTO) by January 1, 1995 (this indeed took place by the new deadline); the environment; progress in developing countries; nuclear safety in Central and Eastern Europe and the former Soviet Union; the economic and security situation in Ukraine, and aid to that country; political and economic reform in Russia; countries in transition, particularly in Central and Eastern Europe; and transnational crime and money laundering. All these issues were reflected in the Naples communiqué, this time actually called the "Summit Communiqué". The communiqué included–at Canada's initiative–a call for a conference on Ukraine. That conference took place in Winnipeg on 27 October 1994. The Naples communiqué also provided for the development of a worldwide information infrastructure, or Global Information Society. A follow-up ministerial conference on that topic met in Brussels in February 1995.[6] As noted in Chapter 4, a wider "Information Society and Development Conference" met in Midrand, South Africa in May 1996.

The Naples Summit set out the centrepiece of the agenda for the following year's Halifax Summit; namely, the role of international financial and economic institutions. The communiqué defined the question as follows: "What framework of institutions will be required to meet these challenges [sustainable development with good prosperity and well-being of the peoples ... of the world] in the 21st century? How can we adapt existing institutions and build new institutions to ensure the future prosperity and security of our people?"[7] Further, the leaders in Naples forecast "an even more flexible and less formal summit" in Halifax.[8] Writing on the eve of the 1995 Halifax Summit, Bayne and Putnam stated that "inaugurating a review of the international system ... is intended to give new momentum to the summit process as it enters its fourth seven-year cycle".[9]

Participants and many observers of the Halifax Summit agree that its objectives were largely achieved: the leaders had more time for informal, unstructured discussion than they had had for many years, and the centrality of the reform of international institutions was evident in the deliberations and documentation. The review of international institutions (the Bretton Woods institutions and the UN system in general–especially the United Nations Conference on Trade and Development (UNCTAD) and the United Nations Industrial Development Organization (UNIDO)–as well as the regional development banks) was the main item on the agenda, but Halifax also dealt with growth and employment, strengthening the global economy, creating opportunities through open markets, economies in transition, and nuclear safety.[10] A separate background document set out details of the desired review of international financial institutions, incorporating a number of specific proposals and including a call for co-ordination among the WTO, the IMF, the World Bank, the Organisation for Economic Co-operation and Development (OECD), and trade-related UN bodies.[11] The political agenda at Halifax ranged from Bosnia and the Israeli-Palestinian agreement through North Korea and Rwanda to the role of the UN and the Conference on Security and Co-operation in Europe (CSCE).

The main theme of the 1996 Lyon Summit, set out in the title of the communiqué, was "making a success of globalization for the benefit of all".[12] The G7 communiqué noted the pervasiveness of globalisation with the resultant expansion of prosperity as well as the challenges that globalisation posed to societies and economies, and the need for increased international co-operation. The Lyon agenda included the strengthening of economic and monetary co-operation; non-inflationary growth; the growth of trade and investment; problems of employment and unemployment; global partnership of developing countries, developed countries and multilateral institutions; the provision of multilateral support for development; and the integration of Russia and the countries of Central and Eastern Europe into the world economy. Building on the Halifax initiatives of the previous year, the Lyon Summit called for enhancing the effectiveness of the UN, the international financial institutions, the regional development banks, and the WTO.

The political and global-issue agenda of the Lyon Summit centred on security and stability, and encompassed the strengthening and further reform of the UN system; human rights, democratisation, and humanitarian emergencies; nonproliferation of weapons, arms control and disarmament; nuclear safety and security; environmental protection; the information society; the "Human Frontier Science Program": HIV/AIDS and other infectious diseases; illegal drugs; transnational organised crime; regional security and stability in various parts of the world including Central and Eastern Europe, the Middle East, Iran, Iraq, Libya, and the two Koreas.

The 1997 Denver Summit of the Eight had on its agenda a number of economic and social issues including globalisation and its effects, aging populations, and the prospects and problems of small and medium-size enterprises. Global issues discussed ranged from environmental topics (climate change, forests, access to fresh water, the protection of oceans, environmental standards for export credit agencies, children's environmental health, and international environmental institutions, including the role of the UN General Assembly special session on the fifth anniversary of UNCED) to infectious diseases; nuclear safety; transnational organised crime; illicit drugs; terrorism; UN reform; and a partnership for development in Africa. Political issues of concern at Denver were the growth of democracy and the protection of human rights; nuclear nonproliferation, arms control and disarmament; and potential or actual problem areas (Hong Kong, the Middle East, Cyprus, and Albania).

Several observers have noted that the Denver Summit of the Eight was not one of the more successful summits. Bayne, for example, stated that "Denver was a summit of promise rather than achievement, more interesting for what it started than what it completed". He saw greater Russian involvement as a positive development and the treatment of Africa as a useful innovation.[13]

The agenda of the 1998 Birmingham G8 Summit centred on three themes: promoting sustainable growth in the global economy; employability and social inclusion; and combatting drug trafficking and other forms of transnational crime. The communiqué issued by the G8 on 17 May 1998, at the conclusion of the Summit, addresses concerns and sets out tasks related to these three major areas.[14]

Commenting on growth in the global economy, the G8 welcomed the European Union's 2 May decision on establishing the European Economic and Monetary Union. Addressing the financial crisis in Asia, the G8 leaders expressed confidence in the ability of IMF programmes to restore stability, but they also recognised the impact of the crisis on the poorest and most vulnerable sectors of society, and pointed to the need to protect these groups with the support of the World Bank, the Asian Development Bank and bilateral donors. The leaders, looking ahead to WTO's celebration of the 50th anniversary of GATT, reaffirmed their commitment to trade and investment liberalisation and called upon all countries to resist protectionism.

They also confirmed their wish to see developing and emerging economies participate fully in the multilateral trading system; and made a commitment to provide more duty-free access for the goods of these countries. The G8 pledged support for developing countries to build democracy and good governance. They agreed to negotiate an adequate replenishment of the International Development Association (IDA 12) and to provide adequate resources for IMF's Enhanced Structural Adjustment Facility and for the African Development Fund.

On debt relief, the G8 endorsed the Heavily Indebted Poor Countries (HIPC) initiative, declaring six countries already eligible and two more to qualify soon. This fell far short of the expectations of over 50,000 demonstrators (some forming a human chain around the summit site, others rowing small coracles along Birmingham's canals) during the summit who presented a "Jubilee 2000 petition" urging complete debt forgiveness for all poor countries by the year 2000. Prime Minister Tony Blair, on behalf of the G8 leaders, responded to the petition in a separate document.[15]

The eight leaders supported the World Health Organization (WHO) initiative to "Roll Back Malaria" by 2010 as well as the continuing efforts to fight AIDS, including support for the United Nations Programme on AIDS/HIV (UNAIDS). On the energy, the Eight committed themselves to encourage the development of energy markets and to work for establishing appropriate legislative and regulatory frameworks. They reaffirmed their support for enhancing the safety of nuclear power plants. On climate change, the Birmingham Summit simply reiterated its endorsement of the 1997 Kyoto Protocol to reduce greenhouse gas emissions.

On the second agenda item, "Growth, employability and inclusion", the leaders endorsed earlier work by G8 ministers, notably the eight individual national action plans to advance these aims.[16] They stated their willingness to share their principles and experiences with other members of the International Labour Organisation (ILO), OECD and the international financial institutions.

The third item, drugs and international crime, comprised the drug trade, trafficking in weapons, smuggling of human beings, money laundering, and the abuse of new technologies by criminals. Discussion of this topic included a lively briefing, with a video presentation, by the head of the UK National Crime Squad. In one of the more successful results of this summit, the leaders agreed to wide-ranging action, including negotiating a UN convention against transnational organised crime; supporting a ten-point action plan on high-tech crime; and instituting joint law enforcement.

Remaining G8 issues were nonproliferation of weapons of mass destruction and the Millennium Bug. As had happened at several previous summits, sudden, unexpected developments imposed themselves, forcing the leaders to discuss them. Two such major events in 1998 were the Indian nuclear tests (which the leaders condemned but were unable to agree on collective sanctions against India at the Summit) and the political crisis in Indonesia. There were separate G8 statements on these issues, and another one on Northern Ireland that supported the Good Friday agreement to end sectarian violence. Additional regional issues touched upon were Kosovo, Bosnia/Herzegovina, and the Middle East peace process.[17]

G7 issues at Birmingham included economic policies of the seven countries as well as proposals for further reform of the IMF, the World Bank and other international financial institutions. The latter represents an advance over the initiatives of the 1995 Halifax Summit to reform international institutions.

The global financial turmoil of the second half of 1998, following the crisis that began in 1997 in East Asia and spread in August 1998 to Russia, then threatened to engulf South America, has naturally had an impact on the agenda of the G7. In September and October of 1998, financial and other economic issues once again took centre stage for the world's leading industrialised countries.

Notes

1   Robert D. Putnam and Nicholas Bayne, *Hanging Together: Cooperation and Conflict in the Seven-Power Summits*, rev. ed. (Cambridge, Mass.: Harvard University Press, 1987), Table 11.1, p. 270.

2   The "Toronto terms" called for a one-third reduction of the official debt (debt owed to governments) of the poorest developing countries.

3   Despite this "personal commitment", the Uruguay Round was concluded successfully and ratified only at the end of 1994.

4   Based on "Transcript of Press Conference Given by the Prime Minister, Mr John Major, at the Economic Summit in London on Wednesday, 17 July 1991" (unpublished; released at the London Economic Summit, 17 July 1991). URL: www.library.utoronto.ca/www/g7/91press1.htm.

5   Tokyo Summit, 1993, *Economic Declaration: A Strengthened Commitment to Jobs and Growth*, para. 7. URL: www.library.utoronto.ca/www/g7/93trade.htm.

6   Naples Summit, 1994, *Naples Summit Communiqué*, p. 2. In United States, Department of State, Bureau of Public Affairs, *US Department of State*

Dispatch 5, Supplement No. 6 (July 1994), pp. 4-6. See also URL: www.library.utoronto.ca/www/g7/94com.htm.

7   Naples Summit, 1994, *Naples Summit Communiqué*, p. 1. In United States, Department of State, Bureau of Public Affairs, *US Department of State Dispatch*, Vol. 5, Supplement No. 6 (July 1994), pp. 4-6. See also URL: www.library.utoronto.ca/www/g7/94com.htm.

8   Naples Summit, 1994, *Naples Summit Communiqué*, p. 9. In United States, Department of State, Bureau of Public Affairs, *US Department of State Dispatch* (July 1994), pp. 4-6. See also URL: www.library.utoronto.ca/www/g7/94com.htm.

9   Nicholas Bayne and Robert D. Putnam, "Introduction: The G-7 Summit Comes of Age", in *The Halifax G-7 Summit: Issues on the Table*, p. 4; eds. Sylvia Ostry and Gilbert R. Wynham (Halifax: Centre for Foreign Policy Studies, Dalhousie University, 1995).

10   Halifax Summit, 1995, *Halifax Summit Communiqué*. In United States, Department of State, Bureau of Public Affairs, *US Department of State Dispatch* 6, Supplement 4 (July 1995), pp. 5-9. See also URL: www.library.utoronto.ca/www/g7/95halifax.htm.

11   Halifax Summit, 1995, *The Halifax Summit Review of International Financial Institutions; Background Document*. URL: www.library.utoronto.ca/www/g7/95financ.htm.

12   Lyon Summit, 1996, *Economic Communiqué: Making a Success of Globalization for the Benefit of All*. URL: www.library.utoronto.ca/www/g7/96eco.htm.

13   Nicholas Bayne, *Impressions of the Denver Summit* (Toronto, University of Toronto G7 Research Group, 22 June 1997). URL: www.library.utoronto.ca/www/g7/evaluations/forepol.htm.

14   Birmingham Summit, 1998, *G8 Birmingham Summit Communiqué*. URL: www.library.utoronto.ca/www/g7/birmingham/finalcom.htm.

15   Birmingham Summit, 1998, *Response by the Presidency on Behalf of the G8 to the Jubilee 2000 Petition*. URL: www.library.utoronto.ca/www/g7/birmingham/2000.htm.

16   "G8 Employability Action Plans", 1988. URL: www.library.utoronto.ca/www/g7/employment/actionplans/index.html.

17   Birmingham Summit, 1998, *[Political Statement: Regional Issues]*, 15 May 1998. URL: www.library.utoronto.ca/www/g7/birmingham/regional.htm#top; Birmingham Summit, 1998, *Northern Ireland*. URL: www.library.utoronto.ca/www/g7/birmingham/ireland.htm.

7   Summit Results

Throughout their history, the G7/G8 summits have performed in an uneven manner. John J. Kirton characterises the first cycle of summits, 1975-1981, as high-performance; the second cycle, 1982-1988, as low-performances; and the third cycle, 1989-1995, as medium-performance.[1]

Several analysts have graded the degree of success of summit meetings and compliance with summit decisions. These evaluations fall into two main classes: Robert D. Putnam and Nicholas Bayne, and Kirton–see (1) and (2) below–rate summits on the basis of agreements aimed at co-ordination or co-operation; George M. von Furstenberg and Joseph P. Daniels (3), Eleonore Kokotsis and Kirton (4) and the University of Toronto G8 Research Group (5) evaluate members' compliance with measurable or verifiable commitments by the summits.

(1) In their grading of the 1975-1986 summits, Putnam and Bayne award the highest mark, "A", to Bonn I (1978) on growth, energy and trade. Bonn II (1985) receives the lowest mark, "E", with the note that it achieved "nothing significant" in terms of co-operation.[2] Writing in 1997, Bayne remarks that "an updating of the Putnam scale ... reveals higher marks for the Summits of the third cycle [1989-1994] than the second [1981-1988], though still below the first [1975-1980]" and adds that the "first two Summits of the fourth cycle [1995 and 1996] also score well".[3] Subsequently, Bayne updated and revised the score to cover the years 1975 through 1998, giving Birmingham a "B+" grade (see Table 7.1). Table 7.2 presents a performance assessment of the Birmingham Summit by issue area.

(2) Kirton ranks 1988-1994 summits, mostly on the basis of editorials of the Toronto newspaper *The Globe and Mail*, as follows: 1988, "A"; 1989, "A"; 1990, "B+"; 1991, "C"; 1992, "B-"; 1993, "B"; and 1994, "B-".[4] Apart from quantitative assessments, it may be noted that reports by the news media generally show growing disenchantment with the summits, although there are some exceptions.

Michael R. Hodges comments that "[o]verall the G-7 summits are considered to be a worthwhile endeavour, although individual meetings have been of variable utility. Munich was ... not worth the time invested; Tokyo [1993] was perceived as more successful".[5]

Table 7.1   **Co-operative Achievements of G7/G8 Summits, 1975-1998**

Year	Summit	Grade	Achievements
1975	Rambouillet	A-	Monetary reform
1976	San Juan, Puerto Rico	D	Nothing significant
1977	London I	B-	Trade, growth, nuclear power
1978	Bonn I	A	Growth, energy, trade
1979	Tokyo I	B+	Energy
1980	Venice I	C+	Afghanistan, energy
1981	Ottawa	C	Trade ministers' quadrilateral
1982	Versailles	C	East-West trade, surveillance
1983	Williamsburg	B	Euromissiles
1984	London II	C-	Debt
1985	Bonn II	E	Nothing significant
1986	Tokyo II	B+	Terrorism, surveillance, G7 finance ministers
1987	Venice II	D	Nothing significant
1988	Toronto	C-	Debt relief for the poorest
1989	Paris	B+	Helping Eastern Europe, environment, debt
1990	Houston	D	Nothing significant
1991	London III	B-	Helping USSR
1992	Munich	D	Nothing significant
1993	Tokyo III	C+	Trade
1994	Naples	C	Russia into P8
1995	Halifax	B+	Institutional review, IMF, UN reform
1996	Lyon	B+	Trade, macroeconomic issues
1997	Denver	C-	Russian participation, Africa
1998	Birmingham	B+	Economic policy, crime, debt, new financial architecture

Source: Based on Robert D. Putnam and Nicholas Bayne, *Hanging Together,* rev. ed. (1987), p. 270 (for 1975-1987), and a note from Nicholas Bayne revising and updating the grades for 1975-1998.

(3) Von Furstenberg and Daniels, writing in 1991 and 1992, examine the degree of compliance with 209 verifiable undertakings of fifteen summits (1975-1989), primarily in the areas of inflation, unemployment, economic growth, fiscal imbalances, interest rates, exchange rates, and energy policy.[6]

Table 7.2   Performance Assessment of the Birmingham Summit by Issue Area

Issue	Grade
New International Financial Architecture	B+
Macroeconomics (Japan)	A-
Employability	A-
Trade	B-
Development (HIPC 2000)	B+
Health	B+
Environment (Climate Change)	B
Crime and Drugs	A-
Nuclear Safety (Chernobyl to Kursk)	B+
Indian Nuclear Explosion	B
Indonesian Crisis	B+
Process Reforms	A
OVERALL SCORE	B+

Source: Nicholas Bayne and John Kirton, "Performance Assessment of the 1998 Birmingham G8 Summit by Issue Area," G8 Information Centre. URL: www.library.utoronto.ca/www/g7/evaluations/birmingham/issues/birmperf.htm.

They give a combined score of 0.317 (simple average) or 0.280 (weighted average); that is, these undertakings were honoured only one-fourth to one-third. Their findings show wide variation in compliance among summit countries (with Canada and the UK scoring higher than France and the US) as well as different rates from issue to issue. Writing in 1995 about implementation of summit commitments (based on these data), Kirton remarks that "[c]ompliance is very high in the fields of international trade and in energy (a category which has now broadened to include the global environment), very low in the monetary policy areas of foreign exchange, inflation and interest rates, and somewhat better in the Keynesian fundamentals of demand composition, fiscal adjustments, official development assistance, and Gross National Product (GNP) growth".[7] Von Furstenberg and Daniels conclude:

> the fact that undertakings remain largely unfulfilled means that the process has as yet acquired little binding force and that fuzziness and credibility have not been supporting each other in this regard.

Rather, the low level of credibility may have made fuzziness indicative of a lack of commitment. If ... the economic declarations are the main institutional product of the summit process, the product has yet to prove itself as deserving of much credit with the public.[8]

(4) Kokotsis and Kirton, in 1997 and 1998, explore compliance with G7 commitments in the areas of environment and development from 1988 to 1995.[9] Analysing the record of the US and Canada, they examine 83 commitments in four issue areas: climate change, biodiversity, the debt of developing countries, and assistance to the USSR/Russia. They give the overall compliance score of 43%, with Canada scoring 53% and the US, 34%. On assistance to Russia, the Kokotsis/Kirton score is a high 81%; on developing-country debt, 73%, on climate change, 34%, and on biodiversity a negative record, -13%.

(5) The University of Toronto G7 (now G8) Research Group evaluated compliance with commitments of the 1996 Lyon Summit by the time of the 1997 Denver Summit of the Eight.[10] The Research Group's study focused on the record of all G7 countries on compliance with undertakings in the following nineteen issue areas: macroeconomics, trade, micro-economics, development, IFI (international financial institutions) reform, terrorism, United Nations (UN) reform I (UNCTAD IX, the 9th UN Conference on Trade and Development), UN reform II (financial contributions by G7 countries), human rights, arms control, proliferation (land mines), nuclear safety, environment, the Global Information Society, crime, East/West relations, Middle East, Asia, and conflict in Europe. The Group arrived at the overall score of 0.36 (that is, commitments 36% fulfilled). In time for the Birmingham Summit, the Research Group completed a similar study of compliance with six key commitments made at the Denver Summit: transnational organised crime (combatting trafficking in illegal firearms), development (focusing on Africa, especially the heavily indebted poor countries or HIPCs), employment (labour market, education and training, structural changes), environment (climate change and greenhouse gas emission targets in follow-up of the 1997 Kyoto conference), anti-personnel land mines, and early Russian accession to the World Trade Organization (WTO).

The fact that each of these studies starts from different premises and each measures or evaluates different aspects of the subject makes them difficult to compare. Nonetheless, these studies cover the period from the inception of the summits (1975) to 1998, yielding evaluations over a twenty-four-year time span. They reveal relatively high success rates on certain issues and by some summit countries, and lower rates (in some cases, negative values) for other issues and countries. They do, however, make a good case that, overall, there has been a fairly significant degree of compliance with summit undertakings.

Notes

1   John J. Kirton, "The Diplomacy of Concert: Canada, the G7 and the Halifax Summit", *Canadian Foreign Policy* 3, No. 1 (Spring 1995), p. 66.

2   Robert D. Putnam and Nicholas Bayne, *Hanging Together: Cooperation and Conflict in the Seven-Power Summits*, rev. ed., (Cambridge, Mass.: Harvard University Press, 1987), Table 11.1, p. 270.

3   Nicholas Bayne, "Changing Patterns at the G7 Summit", *G7 Governance*, No. 1 (May 1997), p. 1. URL: www.library.utoronto.ca/www/g7/governance/gov1sum.htm.

4   John J. Kirton, "The Diplomacy of Concert: Canada, the G7 and the Halifax Summit", p. 66 (footnote 11), and John J. Kirton, "Contemporary Concert Diplomacy: The Seven-Power Summit and the Management of International Order" (Paper prepared for the annual meeting of the International Studies Association and the British International Studies Association, London, March 29-April 1, 1989; unpublished in print). Text available at URL: www.library.utoronto.ca/www/g7/kirtoc.htm.

5   Michael R. Hodges, "More Efficiency, Less Dignity: British Perspectives on the Future Role and Working of the G-7", in *The Future of the G-7 Summits*, p. 149 (*The International Spectator* 29, No. 2; April/June 1994, Special Issue).

6   George M. von Furstenberg, and Joseph P. Daniels, "Policy Undertakings by the Seven 'Summit' Countries: Ascertaining the Degree of Compliance". *Carnegie-Rochester Conference Series on Public Policy* 35 (Autumn 1991), pp. 267-308; George M. Von Furstenberg, and Joseph P. Daniels, *Economic Summit Declarations, 1975-1989: Examining the Written Record of International Cooperation*. Princeton Studies in International Finance, No. 72 (Princeton, NJ: International Finance Section, Dept. of Economics, Princeton University, 1992).

7   Kirton, "The Diplomacy of Concert: Canada, the G7 and the Halifax Summit", p. 67.

8   Von Furstenberg and Daniels, *Economic Summit Declarations, 1975-1989: Examining the Written Record of International Cooperation*, p. 43.

9   Eleonore Kokotsis, *National Compliance with G7 Environment and Development Commitments, 1988-1995*. PhD dissertation (Toronto:

University of Toronto, 1998. Unpublished); Eleonore Kokotsis, *Promises Kept* (New York; London: Garland Publishing, forthcoming, 1999); Eleonore Kokotsis and John J. Kirton, "National Compliance with Environmental Regimes: The Case of the G7, 1988-1995", paper prepared for the Annual Convention of the International Studies Association, Toronto, 18-22 March 1997. Unpublished.

10   University of Toronto G8 Research Group, *Compliance with G7 Commitments: From Lyon 1996 to Denver 1997*. URL: www.library.utoronto.ca/www/g7/evaluations/compnew.htm.

8   G7/G8 Documentation

The G7/G8 system has generated a great deal of varied and often significant documents in the course of its work. Because this documentation is the principal primary source of information about the G7/G8 and its activities, and because of the absence of a G7/G8 secretariat to pull together, disseminate and analyse the document output, there is a clear need for a detailed survey as well as careful, systematic assessment of this source material.

Summit Documentation

The two main broad types of G7/G8 summit documents are economic and political. From the outset of the G7, summits have always issued a single communiqué covering a whole gamut of economic subjects and supported at times by an annex (as in London in 1977 and in Williamsburg in 1983) or a background document (as in Halifax in 1995.) The political declarations and other types of leaders' documents have, by contrast, been much less consistent and uniform.

The Communiqué

The *communiqué* is the principal document of each summit. Prior to Naples 1994 it was called *final communiqué*) and has often been entitled *declaration* or *economic declaration*. The subjects of the communiqué range from exchange rates, interest rates, inflation, unemployment and economic growth to North-South and East-West relations, the environment and sustainable development, Third World debt, international organisations, and any other issue on the agenda. Philippe Moreau Defarges comments that "[f]inal declarations resemble Jacques Prévert's inventories or Jorge Luis Borges' lists: they can include the whole world".[1] William E. Whyman, too, notes that "[t]he communiqué has grown into a long, unwieldy 'Christmas tree' with each country adding its cherished special interest 'ornament'".[2] In earlier years, the text of the communiqué was often carried in full in *The New York Times* and other newspapers of record, but this practice was discontinued, partly because the communiqués had grown progressively longer, and partly because the media lost interest in transmitting the documents *in extenso*.[3] On the other hand, with the ever-expanding use of the internet, several web sites publish full texts of communiqués and other G7/G8 documents; see Chapter 10, Appendix for examples.

Andrea De Guttry, analysing summit communiqués from an international-law point of view, isolates the following types of formulations the communiqués contain: "international obligations for the participant states ..., [r]ecommendations to the G-7 member states ..., [s]imple invitations to international organizations ... [and] acts relative to international organizations". Instruments available to the G7 to achieve implementation include direct formulation of recommendations, invitations to member states, delegation of various tasks to other organisations, and the establishment of new international bodies.[4]

Preparing the Communiqué

The preparation of the communiqué is a long, involved process occurring during the lead-up to each summit. The sherpas (personal representatives of the head of state or government of each summit country) play a crucial role in the production of this document. They meet several times during the year –beginning usually in January–preparing the agenda and developing the draft of the communiqué for the forthcoming summit. For example, as noted in Chapter 4, the sherpas met four times between the 1997 Denver and 1998 Birmingham summits, first for a follow-up of the Denver Summit of the Eight, then starting with a discussion of the priorities and political constraints of their leaders, and moving on to shape the structure and preliminary agenda of the summit, isolating specific issues for discussion at the summit, beginning the draft of the communiqué and, at their final pre-summit meeting, completing the "thematic paper" that closely resembles the final draft. In Michael R. Hodges's words, the thematic paper "simply serves as a quarry for the preparation of the final communiqués".[5]

The actual final draft usually involves feverish last-minute preparations, well into the last night of the summit–and beginning with 1994, the night before the release of the communiqué; in Naples (1994), Halifax (1995), and Lyon (1996), the communiqué was released on the second day rather than at the end of the summit, in order to allow the last day to be devoted to "Political 8" (P8) discussions with the Russians. This pattern changed with the Denver "Summit of the Eight" when the communiqué was again released at the end of the summit, this time reflecting the consensus of the Eight. In Naples the sherpas stayed up until 5:30 AM to complete the final draft. The communiqué (which, according to a French viewpoint articulated by Defarges, "reflects a soft consensus", contrasted with Whyman's characterisation of it as "a fully negotiated, binding statement"[6]) is presented by the leader of the host country with considerable ceremony. In a departure from the practice at earlier summits where the host leader had read out the full text, at Houston in 1990 President George Bush simply summarised it (with the evident approval of the guest leaders assembled on the stage) while the full text was being distributed to the media. This simplified procedure seems to have taken hold following Tokyo III (1993) where the leaders had signalled their intention to have more informal meetings and to produce shorter documents once again.

It is instructive to compare the summit communiqué with the communiqué issued by the Organisation for Economic Co-operation and Development (OECD) ministerial meeting usually held about a month before the summit. Hisashi Owada remarks that "each year the communiqué of the OECD ministerial meeting offers a reference model for preparation of the summit's economic declaration".[7] For example, the communiqué of the OECD ministerial meeting held on 26-27 May 1997 raised many of the economic and political concerns that figure prominently in the Denver communiqué. The 27-28 April 1998 OECD ministerial communiqué, in its discussion of the effects of the Asian financial crisis, the multilateral trading system, harmful tax competition and other issues, again foreshadows topics covered by the Birmingham G7 and G8 documents.[8]

An interesting development occurred before the 1995 Halifax Summit when, on 6 June, Canadian New Democratic Party Member of Parliament Nelson Riis released to the press a draft communiqué dated 27 May 1995.[9] Comparing the missing sections and especially the square-bracketed passages in the leaked draft with the appropriate parts of the agreed communiqué throws additional light on the preparatory process and the role of the leaders in working out final agreement on the main document of the Summit. There are earlier as well as subsequent instances of leaked draft communiqués; some of these attracted more attention than others.[10]

The Political Declarations and Chairman's Statements

The *political* or other non-economic *declaration* was, through 1993, the primary document "[r]anking second in the hierarchy of summit scripture".[11]

The first such declaration was issued by the 1978 Bonn Summit, on the subject of the hijacking of aircraft. Prior to that time, because of initial French opposition to wider political and security discussions and Japanese reluctance to engage in those areas, "final declarations contained no political statements".[12] Tokyo I (1979) also deplored air hijackings and issued a special statement on Indochinese refugees. Declarations, which have subsequently proliferated in number, have ranged in subject from refugees and terrorism through East-West security concerns to drug trafficking and human rights. "In order to preserve the [essentially] economic nature of the [final] communiqué, these political statements have been issued as separate documents".[13] This changed with the Denver Summit of the Eight and with the Birmingham G8 Summit.

The non-economic concerns of Venice I (1980), expressed in special statements, were Afghanistan and the occupation of the US Embassy in Teheran. In Ottawa (1981) there was a separate statement on terrorism. The main political statement of the 1982 Versailles Summit addressed the situation in Lebanon after the Israeli invasion. The 1983 *Statement at Williamsburg [Declaration on Security]*, an important first summit initiative in this area, called for arms control and greater co-operation in that field between the Soviet Union and the G7; it also covered the stationing of US missiles in Europe. In London (1984) there were declarations on democratic values, terrorism, and East-West security relations, as well as a statement on the Iran-Iraq conflict.

The 1985 Bonn Summit produced a political declaration commemorating the fortieth anniversary of the end of World War II. One of the political declarations at Tokyo in 1986 commented on the Chernobyl nuclear accident. Venice II (1987) brought forward statements on East-West relations, terrorism, the Iran-Iraq war, AIDS, and narcotic drugs. The Paris (1989) Summit of the Arch also issued declarations on human rights (to commemorate the bicentennial of the Rights of Man and of the Citizen), on China (following the Tiananmen Square massacre of June 1989), on East-West relations (especially in connection with post-Cold War democratisation in Eastern and Central Europe), and on terrorism. The 1991 London Summit produced a *Political Declaration* subtitled *Strengthening the International Order*, a separate *Declaration on Conventional Arms Transfers and NBC [nuclear, biological and chemical] Non-proliferation* and a *Chairman's Statement (As Prepared)* in which British Foreign Secretary Douglas Hurd commented on the first two documents.

In 1992 in Munich the political declaration, with the subtitle *Shaping the New Partnership*, dealt with specific economic, political and security areas of the new partnership with countries of Central and Eastern Europe and the new independent states of the former Soviet Union, nuclear non-proliferation, and the further strengthening of the United Nations (UN). In addition, there was a separate declaration on the crisis in the former Yugoslavia, and a *Chairman's Statement* (from German Foreign Minister Klaus Kinkel) on problems and developments in the Nagorno-Karabakh region, the Baltic States, the Middle East, Iraq, Korea, China, the Mediterranean, Africa and Latin America, as well as questions of drugs and terrorism. The 1993 Tokyo political declaration, issued as usual during the second day of the summit, was entitled *Striving for a More Secure and Humane World*. The declaration condemns Serbia and Croatia for their aggression in Bosnia and affirms human rights and nuclear nonproliferation, among other points.

Writing in early 1994, Robert D. Putnam pointed out that the formerly "largely autonomous process of preparation of the summit 'political declarations' has been taken over by the 'G-7 political directors' in foreign offices outside the purview of the sherpas themselves".[14] Soon afterward, starting with Naples in 1994, the political declaration was replaced by the *chairman's statement*, a type of summit document issued that year by the host leader on behalf of the P8, indicating Russia's increased role in the political discussion and drafted with Russian participation. This kind of statement was released also in 1995 and 1996 at the end of the summit, a day after rather than a day before the summit communiqué as had been the previous practice. The chairman's statement may not need to be as completely a consensus document as the summit communiqué.

The 1994 Naples *Chairman's Statement [Political]* dealt with a number of issues ranging from Bosnia and the Israeli-Palestinian agreement, through North Korea and Rwanda, to the role of the UN and of the Conference on Security and Co-operation in Europe (CSCE). Following the pattern set at Naples, the 1995 Halifax Summit–at its conclusion and at the P8 level–issued a *Chairman's Statement* reaffirming the commitment of the P8 to multilateral engagement, to arms control and disarmament, to new approaches in dealing with environmental and other global challenges, and to fighting terrorism and other international crime. It also reviewed European achievements (the advance of democracy and market economy) and problems (especially Bosnia); the situation in the Middle East and Africa; the Asia-Pacific region; and the Americas. The main feature of the

Halifax *Chairman's Statement*, though, was a thematic, generic approach to conflict prevention and resolution, rather than a regional focus.[15]

The 1996 Lyon Summit's *Chairman's Statement* covered a broad range of global and regional issues. It also included a long supplementary section reviewing UN reforms since Halifax, with a catalogue of achievements and a commitment by the Eight to "continue and reinforce our efforts to improve the functioning of the UN in the economic and social fields and its impact on development ... [and to] continue to work in partnership with other members to complete processes underway ... and initiate further processes as required".[16]

In addition to the communiqué and the chairman's statement, the Lyon Summit issued the following four documents:

- A declaration on terrorism, produced on the first evening of the Summit (27 June 1996), in response to the terrorist attack against a US military base in Dhahran, Saudi Arabia, which occurred just before the summit.
- *Decisions Concerning Bosnia and Herzegovina*, a P8 document issued on 29 June 1996 that dealt with elections and institutions; the International War Crimes Tribunal; a plan for civilian consolidation; reconstruction; refugees and the rule of law; and regional and security issues.
- *A New Partnership for Development*, a document issued on 29 June 1996 jointly by the P8 and the four invited heads of international organisations (the Secretary-General of the UN, the Managing Director of the International Monetary Fund (IMF), the President of the World Bank and the Director-General of the World Trade Organization (WTO).
- A report by the G7 finance ministers to the heads of delegations, dated 28 June 1996, on international monetary stability.

With the advent of the G8 in Birmingham in 1998, accompanied nonetheless by the continuing survival of the parallel G7, the *chairman's statement* reappeared as *G7 Chairman's Statement*. In it, the G7 leaders and the President of the European Commission covered economic policies of the Seven and the proposed "New Financial Architecture".[17]

Other Types of Leaders' Documents

The *chairman's summary* of earlier summits, not to be confused with the *chairman's statement* discussed above, had, for a number of years, been another important document in which the host leader summed up his or her views or impressions of the achievements of the summit. It was in the form of an oral statement, a prepared written document, or an agreed collective statement read by the host leader. An example is the 1981 Ottawa Summit where the host leader, Canadian Prime Minister Pierre Elliot Trudeau, presented a summary of political issues. At he 1988 Toronto Summit Canadian Prime Minister Brian Mulroney issued a chairman's summary on the Middle East, South Africa, and Cambodia. The *chairman's summary* was not issued at every summit.

An example of yet another type of summit document is the *communiqué de la Présidence* (*Statement from the Chair*) issued during the 1989 Paris Summit by President François Mitterrand, in his capacity as summit chairman, on the Arab-Israeli conflict, Southern Africa, Central America, Panama, Cambodia, and Lebanon. Other examples include host leader Italian Prime Minister Amintore Fanfani's statements on AIDS and narcotic drugs at the 1987 Venice Summit. The 1995 Halifax Summit saw Canadian host Prime Minister Jean Chrétien deliver a statement on Bosnia–unusual in that it was done in the first evening of the summit before Russian President Boris Yeltsin's arrival. This indicated that the Halifax Summit was more of a "leaders' summit" of the Seven, contrasted with many previous summits at which the initial working dinner of the heads had largely confined its agenda to previously prepared economic issues. The 1998 G8 Birmingham Summit produced another document in this category, entitled *Response By the Presidency on Behalf of the G8 to the Jubilee 2000 Petition.*[18] This last-mentioned item has been characterised as a "consulted" rather than a "consensus" document.

A very interesting leaders' document of a new kind is the *G7 Leaders' Statement on the World Economy*, issued on 30 October 1998 without a formal summit meeting. In it, the leaders welcome the declaration made on the same day by their finance ministers and central bank governors, and announce their agreement on further reforms needed to create a stronger financial architecture.[19] The significance of this document is discussed in more detail in Chapter 5.

At a level below the agreed public documents of the summits –described earlier–*transcripts of press conferences* constitute another important category of document. Many press conferences and briefings are held throughout the summits. Each summit country, as well as the European Union (EU), goes to great lengths to present its own initiatives and positions on various issues to the world news media so as to reflect itself in the best possible light internationally as well as back home. Hodges notes that "the press does not know what really goes on in the summit meetings and relies heavily on briefings from the press secretaries of the various heads. Each of these briefings gives a different idea of who succeeded".[20] Because the press (and whatever else the summits are, they are also big media events, with thousands of print, radio and television journalists covering the scene) cannot attend the actual meetings of the leaders (or the ministers at their conferences), journalists must depend on briefings and press conferences. Even though they tend to be self-serving, news conferences allow media representatives to ask probing questions of government officials including leaders. The press conference given at the conclusion of each summit by the leader of the host country is particularly important because it allows the host to present not only his or her evaluation of the summit but also a summation in his or her capacity as president of the summit. Examples are US President Bill Clinton's news conference at the conclusion of the Denver Summit of the Eight and UK Prime Minister Tony Blair's press conference marking the end of the Birmingham G8 Summit.[21] Press conferences of other leaders at the end of each summit are good sources of evaluation of the summit reflecting the position of each G8 country and the EU.

Outside Communications to the Summit

Although not summit documents in the strict sense, *outside communications* to the summit are important related documents. Especially significant are President Mikhail Gorbachev's 14 July 1989 letter to President Mitterrand expressing the Soviet Union's wish to be associated with the summits; and Gorbachev's letter to US President Bush, received a few days before the 1990 Houston Summit.[22] Gorbachev's letter was discussed and commented on by the leaders and reflected in Summit documents, although the text was not released to the public. Gorbachev's twenty-three page message (together with a 31-page annex) to the leaders at the 1991 London Summit, delivered by Yevgeni Primakov on 12 July, caused a flurry of journalistic speculation and comment even though its text was not officially released. The message–a synthesis of the Yavlinski reform plan and the Soviet government's plan for economic reform–was discussed intensively by the G7, although the personal dialogue, made possible by the Gorbachev visit to London, eclipsed the written communication.

Another example of an outside communication is a press release that was issued just before the 1989 Paris Summit by four Third World leaders: Hosni Mubarak of Egypt, Rajiv Gandhi of India, Abdou Diouf of Senegal, and Carlos Andrés Pérez of Venezuela. The four, in the name of the fifteen major developing countries, wished to initiate regular consultations with the developed world at the summit level. The fifteen later formed their own Group of Fifteen (G15). One might mention in the same category the co-ordinated but separate letters addressed to the 1991 London Summit by the President of Poland, the Prime Minister of Hungary, and the President of Czechoslovakia. These letters (whose text has not been released) expressed concern about the collapse of those countries' trade with the Soviet Union, and about their access to Western markets.[23] Yet another example of this type of communication is an address to the seven heads of summit delegations, dated 26 June 1992, from the Council of the Baltic States, dealing with the continued presence of Russian forces in Estonia, Latvia, and Lithuania.

Documentation of Ministerial Conferences, Task Forces, Working Groups, and Expert Groups

Ministerial Documentation

Documentation of G7/G8 ministerial meetings varies greatly. *Finance ministers* usually issue a chairman's summary or other statement at the end of their meetings, but there have also been meetings without public statements and, conversely, statements without formal meetings. Hodges remarks that "the G-7 finance ministers did not issue a communiqué after their 1993 Washington meeting, and indicated to the heads at Tokyo that they too were striving to make their meetings more substantive and informal ... ".[24] A good source in which to find published statements of the G7 finance ministers is the *IMF Survey*.[25] An example of a recent communiqué issued at the conclusion of a meeting is the *Statement of G7 Finance Ministers and Central Bank Governors*, 3 October 1998; an example of a statement issued by the finance ministers without a meeting is the *Declaration of G7 Finance Ministers and Central Bank Governors*, 30 October 1998.[26]

The *Trade Ministers' Quadrilateral* rarely released public communiqués in the past, but more recently has tended to issue them; for example, a *Chair's Statement* was released after its 30 April-2 May 1997 meeting in Toronto, Canada.[27] G7/G8 *environment ministers* generally release documents; for example, the "Environment Leaders' Summit of the Eight" meeting in Miami, Florida, on 5-6 May 1997 issued a *Chair's Summary* as well as a *Declaration of the Environment Leaders of the Eight on Children's Environmental Health*, and the 3-5 April 1998 G8 Environment Ministers' Meeting held in Leeds Castle, Kent, England issued a *Communiqué*.[28]

All the G7/G8 *employment ministerial* conferences have issued public documents. The most recent such meeting, the G8 Conference on Growth, Employability and Inclusion, held in London on 21-22 February 1998, released *Chairman's Conclusions*. The October 1994 Winnipeg conference on *assistance to Ukraine*–an *ad hoc* ministerial meeting–issued a *Chairman's Summary*.[29]

The P8 ministerial meeting on *terrorism* resulted in the *Ottawa Ministerial Declaration on Countering Terrorism* of 12 December 1995; the 30 July 1996 Paris Ministerial Meeting on Terrorism released its agreement on twenty-five measures to fight terrorism; and the French President's office released a G7/P8 communiqué on 28 December 1996 on the Peruvian hostage incident. Certain *task forces* and *working groups* produce public releases and reports, in addition to confidential documents; the deliberations of others remain secret. An example of available documents is the 40-point *Recommendations* released by the P8 Group of Senior Experts on Transnational Organized Crime on 12 April 1996. On a related topic, the G8 justice and interior ministers' meeting on crime, held in Washington, DC on 10 December 1997, reviewed the work of the Senior Experts' Group on Transnational Organized Crime. The results of this ministerial meeting were summarised in a statement by US Attorney-General Janet Reno.[30]

The February 1995 Brussels *"information society"* conference generated a fair amount of documentation, including *Chair's Conclusions*, a thematic paper, and other releases. Access to this material is provided on the internet by the EU Information Society Project Office.[31] The first annual meeting of the G7 Conference on *Global Marketplace for Small and Medium-sized Enterprises* took place in Bonn, Germany, on 7-9 April 1997 and produced several documents.[32]

G7 *foreign ministers* do not issue public statements on their September annual meetings, but one can trace indirectly some of their other reports; for example, their *Report on Aid to Africa* was submitted to the 1986 Tokyo Summit which called for implementation of the recommended measures.[33] Other documents, however, are available from meetings attended–sometimes with holders of other portfolios–by foreign ministers; for example, the G7 foreign and finance ministers' meeting in Tokyo on 15 April 1993 in preparation for the 1993 Tokyo Summit (with partial Russian participation), issued a *G-7 Chairman's Statement on Support for Russian Reform*; and the October 1994 Winnipeg G8 foreign ministers' Conference on Partnership for Economic Transformation in Ukraine released a *Chairman's Summary*.[34] The special meeting of the G8 foreign ministers held in London on 12 June 1998 issued a *G8 Foreign Ministers Communiqué on Indian and Pakistani Nuclear Tests*.[35]

The London *joint meeting of G7/G8 finance and foreign ministers* on 8-9 May 1998 was an important innovation, resulting in a complex set of meetings (see Table 4.2 in Chapter 4) and documents:

- On 8 May G7 finance ministers had an afternoon working session, followed by a working dinner with IMF Managing Director Michel Camdessus and World Bank President James Wolfensohn. This was followed on 9 May by another session, at the end of which a document, entitled *Conclusions of G7 Finance Ministers*, was released. It deals with the world economy in general; the strengthening of the global financial system; supervision of global financial institutions; financial crime; the Financial Action Task Force; tax competition; customs procedures; and aging. This document is the basis of the G7 finance ministers' report to the G7 leaders for their Birmingham meeting, entitled *Strengthening the Architecture of the Global Financial System*.[36]

- Two other G7 finance-related documents were distributed at the 8-9 May conference in London: *Financial Stability: Supervision of Global Financial Institutions; A Report by G7 Finance Ministers*, dated May 1998; and *Promoting Financial Stability: Recent Initiatives of the Basle Committee on Banking Supervision; Submission for the G-7 Heads of Government at the 1998 Birmingham Summit*, dated Basle, March 1998.[37]

- Later in the morning of 9 May, after the release of the *Conclusions of G7 Finance Ministers*, there was a brief meeting of the G8 finance ministers. The eight ministers decided to publish eight separate *national employability action plans*.[38]

•   Concurrently with the 8 May meetings of the G7 finance ministers, the G8 foreign ministers met for a working session in the afternoon, followed by a working dinner. In the morning of 9 May the G8 foreign ministers had another working session, at the end of which they issued a document, *Conclusions of G8 Foreign Ministers.*[39] In it, the ministers addressed the following global issues: the environment, nuclear safety, UN matters, nonproliferation/arms control/disarmament, antipersonnel land mines, democracy and human rights, terrorism, infectious diseases, and crime related to intellectual property. They also discussed a whole laundry list of regional issues: Bosnia and Herzegovina, Croatia, Kosovo, Albania, Cyprus, the Middle East peace process, Iran, Iraq, Algeria, Afghanistan, Cambodia, Myanmar, the Korean peninsula, the African Great Lakes region, Nigeria, Angola, and Somalia.

•   The G8 foreign ministers also launched on 9 May a *G8 Action Programme on Forests.*[40]

•   In late morning, 9 May, the G8 foreign ministers and G8 finance ministers had a plenary meeting, followed by a working lunch with the IMF Managing Director, the World Bank President, and Renato Ruggiero, the Director-General of the WTO to discuss the Asian financial crisis and its implications.

•   The short document, *Conclusions of the Joint Meeting of G8 Foreign and Finance Ministers*, was released mid-morning, 9 May.[41] It deals with two main issues: development, and electronic commerce.

Other Official-Level Documentation

Sherpas never release public information on their invariably confidential meetings. There are, however, some writings that throw an interesting light on the summit preparatory process; for example, former French sherpa Jacques Attali's memoirs entitled *Verbatim*, and the following two short writings: François Camé's "Comment les sherpas avaient ficelé le sommet" and Estelle Ardouin's *Sherpas et sommets des 7*. Pierre Favier and Michel Martin-Roland, in *La décennie Mitterrand*, present an account of the sherpa process that differs from that of Attali's memoirs.[42]

De Guttry observes that "work groups, study groups and task forces ... prepare background documents to facilitate discussion among the Seven ... , they also present specific reports to the G-7 leaders or their personal representatives ... ".[43] One version of the report of the work group on technology, growth and employment, established by the 1982 Versailles Summit, has appeared as a British government publication.[44] The Financial Action Task Force, set up by the 1989 Summit of the Arch to co-ordinate efforts to fight drug-related money laundering, has since become a broader-than-G7 entity and has been publishing annual reports.[45] The three working groups of the Group of 22 (G22) issued in October 1998 the following reports concerning the international financial architecture: on enhancing transparency and accountability; on strengthening financial systems; and on managing international financial crises. The reports were submitted to the IMF Managing Director and the President of the World Bank, to be forwarded to the finance ministers and central bank directors who were meeting in the context of the 1998 annual meetings of the World Bank and the IMF.[46]

The existence of otherwise not publicly available reports of task forces and working groups may be inferred through references in summit documents. For example, studies prepared by the International Nuclear Fuel Cycle Evaluation Group, established by the 1977 London Summit, are acknowledged in the *Declaration* of the 1980 Venice Summit. The same Venice *Declaration* also supports the recommendations of the International Energy Technology Group which was initiated at the 1979 Tokyo Summit. The 1985 Bonn Summit's communiqué, *The Bonn Economic Declaration*, refers to its creation of an expert group on aid to Sub-Saharan Africa which was to report to the G7 foreign ministers by September of that year.[47] The Chemical Action Task Force, set up by the 1990 Houston Summit, was asked by that summit to report within a year; the appropriate report was duly welcomed and endorsed by the 1991 London Summit.[48]

The Halifax Summit charged the Counterterrorism Experts' Group (also known as Terrorism Experts' Group) to report to a ministerial-level meeting on counterterrorism measures and instructed that the appropriate meetings be held prior to the 1996 summit. The two ministerial-level meetings that have taken place so far were held in 1995 and 1996; the latter meeting endorsed twenty-five counterterrorism measures and asked the Experts' Group to follow up on those measures.[49] Subsequently, the experts held their meeting on 14-15 April 1997, in Washington, DC. The G8 foreign ministers at Halifax also established a Senior Experts' Group on Transnational Organized Crime (now known as the "Lyon Group");[50] the 1996 Lyon Summit's *Chairman's Statement* endorsed the forty recommendations developed by this group.[51] The 1998 Birmingham G8 Summit communiqué refers to the Nuclear Safety Working Group

86   *The G7/G8 System*

(established in 1992) as well as to experts on the prevention and treatment of AIDS and on export controls to prevent proliferation of weapons of mass destruction.[52]

This chapter is a survey of the types, characteristics, subject matter, production and dissemination of the documents, not only of the summits but also of other parts of the G7/G8 system; and a discussion of the evolution and importance of the documentation. A systematic assessment of the documentation will be found in Chapter 9.

Notes

1   Philippe Moreau Defarges, "The French Viewpoint on the Future of the G-7", in *The Future of the G-7 Summits*, p. 184 (*The International Spectator* 29, No. 2; April/June 1994, Special Issue).
2   William E. Whyman, "We Can't Go On Meeting Like This: Revitalizing the G-7 Process", *The Washington Quarterly* 18, No. 3 (Summer 1995), pp. 153-54.
3   Other sources of the texts of the final communiqués include the US Department of State *Bulletin* (now defunct but continued by the *US Department of State Dispatch* and by *Foreign Policy Bulletin: The Documentary Record of United States Foreign Policy*), *La politique étrangère de la France* (issued by the Documentation française for the Ministère des relations extérieures of France), and other official publications of the summit countries. For a collected set of summit documents see *The Seven-Power Summit: Documents from the Summits of Industrialized Countries, 1975-1989* (Millwood, NY: Kraus International Publications, 1989) and its *Supplement: Documents from the 1990 Summit* (Millwood, NY: Kraus International Publications, 1991), both compiled and edited by Peter I. Hajnal. For a more recent collection of summit communiqués and declarations see *The Twenty G-7 Summits* (Rome: Adnkronos Libri in Collaboration with Istituto Affari Internazionali, 1994). The University of Toronto G8 Information Centre, an internet web site devoted to the G7/G8 and including, along with summit-related writings and other studies, a comprehensive set of G7/G8 documents, may be accessed at www.g7.utoronto.ca/.
4   Andrea De Guttry, "The Institutional Configuration of the G-7 in the New International Scenario", in *The Future of the G-7 Summits*, pp. 70-71.
5   Michael R. Hodges, "More Efficiency, Less Dignity: British Perspectives on the Future Role and Working of the G-7", in *The Future of the G-7 Summits*, p. 150.

6   Defarges, "The French Viewpoint on the Future of the G-7", p. 179; Whyman, "We Can't Go On Meeting Like This: Revitalizing the G-7 Process", p. 142.

7   Hisashi Owada, "A Japanese Perspective on the Role and Future of the G-7", in *The Future of the G-7 Summits*, p. 111.

8   The OECD ministerial communiqué for 1997 was issued as Organisation for Economic Co-operation and Development, *OECD Press Release* (Paris: OECD, 27 May 1997; SG/COM/NEWS(97)45). The 1998 communiqué appeared as SG/COM/NEWS(98)51 (Paris: OECD, 28 April 1998). The texts of OECD ministerial communiqués can also be found in each issue of the *Annual Report of the OECD* (Paris: Organisation for Economic Co-operation and Development).

9   "Draft Halifax Summit Communiqué, Dated May 27, 1995, Released June 6 by Canadian Member of Parliament Nelson Riis", *Preview of the G-7 Summit, Halifax, Canada, June 15-17, Daily Report for Executives*, No. 114, Special Issue: (Washington, DC: Bureau of National Affairs, June 14, 1995): pp. S-12–S-16. See also URL: www.library.utoronto.ca/www/g7/95com.htm.

10   See, for example, "Summit Part of Larger Process", *The Financial Post*, 22 June 1988. URL: www.library.utoronto.ca/www/g7/fp/ED880622.htm. The texts of the 1997 Denver and 1998 Birmingham draft communiqués can be accessed, respectively, at URLs www.library.utoronto.ca/www/g7/denver/comden.htm and www.library.utoronto.ca/www/g7/birmingham/comdraft.htm.

11   John J. Kirton, "Introduction", in *The Seven-Power Summit: Documents from the Summits of Industrialized Countries, 1975-1989*, p. xxxii. Comp. and ed. Peter I. Hajnal (Millwood, NY: Kraus International Publications, 1989).

12   Guido Garavoglia, and Pier Carlo Padoan, "The G-7 Agenda: Old and New Issues", in *The Future of the G-7 Summits*, p. 51.

13   Kirton, "Introduction", in *The Seven-Power Summit: Documents from the Summits of Industrialized Countries, 1975-1989*, p. xxxiii.

14   Robert D. Putnam, "Western Summitry in the 1990s: American Perspectives", in *The Future of the G-7 Summits*, p. 91.

15   [Halifax Summit], *Chairman's Statement*, June 17, 1995. In United States, Department of State, Bureau of Public Affairs, *US Department of State Dispatch* 6, Supplement 4 (July 1995), pp. 10-13. See also URL: www.library.utoronto.ca/www/g7/95chair.htm.

16   Lyon Summit, 1996, *Chairman's Statement*, para. 3. University of Toronto G8 Information Centre at URL: www.library.utoronto.ca/www/g7/96poli3.htm.

17   Birmingham Summit, 1998, *G7 Chairman's Statement.* Birmingham, 15
        May 1998. URL:
        www.library.utoronto.ca/www/g7/birmingham/chair.htm.

18   Birmingham Summit, 1998, *Response By the Presidency on Behalf of the
        G8 to the Jubilee 2000 Petition.* URL:
        http://birmingham.g8summit.gov.uk/docs/jub2000.shtml and
        www.library.utoronto.ca/www/g7/birmingham/2000.htm.

19   *G7 Leaders' Statement on the World Economy,* 30 October 1998. URL:
        www.number-10.gov.uk/public/news/uktoday/uktoday_right.asp?id=248
        and www.library.utoronto.ca/www/g7/g7_103098.html.

20   Hodges, "More Efficiency, Less Dignity: British Perspectives on the Future
        Role and Working of the G-7", p. 155.

21   United States, White House, *Press Conference of the President,* 22 June
        1997. URL: www.whitehouse.gov/WH/New/Eight/19970623-18209.html
        and www.library.utoronto.ca/www/g7/denver/clint22.htm; Great Britain,
        Prime Minister' s Office, *Press Conference Given by the Prime Minister,
        Mr Tony Blair, In Birmingham, on Sunday, 17 May 1998.* Available at
        URL: www.library.utoronto.ca/www/g7/birmingham/blaira.html and
        www.library.utoronto.ca/www/g7/birmingham/blairb.html.

22   The text of President Gorbachev's letter to President Mitterrand is
        reproduced in *The Seven-Power Summit: Documents from the Summits of
        Industrialized Countries, 1975-1989,* pp. 429-36. Bayne and Putnam note
        that the letter "was identified by the British Foreign Secretary, Geoffrey
        Howe, as a cry for help": Nicholas Bayne and Robert D. Putnam,
        "Introduction: The G-7 Summit Comes of Age" in *The Halifax G-7 Summit:
        Issues on the Table,* eds. Sylvia Ostry and Gilbert R. Wynham (Halifax:
        Centre for Foreign Policy Studies, Dalhousie University, 1995), p. 7. Maull
        reports that, in addition to Gorbachev's letter, there was another one from
        German Chancellor Kohl, on economic and political co-operation with
        Moscow: Hanns W. Maull, "Germany at the Summit", in *The Future of the
        G-7 Summits,* 128.

23   Disclosed at a UK press briefing, given by Gus O'Donnell (the Prime
        Minister's Chief Press Secretary), Francis Cornish (Press Secretary to the
        Secretary of State for Foreign and Commonwealth Affairs) and Dick
        Saunders (Press Secretary to the Chancellor of the Exchequer), 15 July
        1991.

24   Hodges, "More Efficiency, Less Dignity: British Perspectives on the Future
        Role and Working of the G-7", pp. 142-43.

25   International Monetary Fund, *IMF Survey,* Vol. 1-, 1972- (Washington, DC:
        IMF). The University of Toronto G8 Information Centre has published an
        almost comprehensive set of G7/G8 finance ministers' statements on the
        internet, at URL:
        www.library.utoronto.ca/www/g7/finance/finance_ministers.htm.

26 *Statement of G7 Finance Ministers and Central Bank Governors*, 3 October 1998. URL: www.ustreas.gov/press/releases/pr2740.htm and www.library.utoronto.ca/www/g7/finance/fm100398.htm; *Declaration of G7 Finance Ministers and Central Bank Governors*, 30 October 1998. URL: www.hm-treasury.gov.uk/pub/html/docs/g7dec.html and www.library.utoronto.ca/www/g7/finance/fm103098.htm.

27 30th Quadrilateral Trade Ministers Meeting, *Chair's Statement*, Toronto, 30 April-2 May 1997. URL: http//www.library.utoronto.ca/www/g7/quad30.htm.

28 Environment Leaders' Summit of the Eight, Miami, Florida, 5-6 May 1997, *Chair's Summary*. URL: http//www.library.utoronto.ca/www/g7/environment/envsum97.htm; *1997 Declaration of the Environment Leaders of the Eight on Children's Environmental Health*. URL: http//www.library.utoronto.ca/www/g7/environment/envchi97.htm; G8 Environment Ministers Meeting, Leeds Castle, Kent, England, *Communiqué*. URL: http://birmingham.g8summit.gov.uk/prebham/leedscastle.communique.shtml and www.library.utoronto.ca/www/g7/environment/98leeds.htm.

29 G8 Conference on Growth, Employability and Inclusion, London on 21-22 February 1998, *Chairman's Conclusions*. URL: http://birmingham.g8summit.gov.uk/prebham/finance.0298.shtml and http//www.library.utoronto.ca/www/g7/adhoc_feb2198.htm; Conference on Partnership for Economic Transition in Ukraine, Winnipeg, Canada, 27 October 1994, *Chairman's Summary*. URL: http//www.library.utoronto.ca/www/g7/94ukrai.htm.

30 *Ottawa Ministerial [P8] Declaration on Countering Terrorism*, Ottawa, Canada, 12 December 1995. URL: http//www.library.utoronto.ca/www/g7/terror96.htm; Ministerial Conference on Terrorism, *Agreement on 25 Measures*, Paris, 30 July 1996. URL: www.library.utoronto.ca/www/g7/terror25.htm; France, Présidence, *Communiqué de la Présidence de la République au nom du G7/P8*, Paris, 28 décembre 1996. URL: www.library.utoronto.ca/www/g7/perup8_f.htm; Senior Experts on Transnational Organized Crime, *P8 Senior Experts Group Recommendations*, Paris, 12 April 1996. URL: http//www.library.utoronto.ca/www/g7/40pts.htm; US, Department of Justice, *Statement by Attorney General Janet Reno on the Meeting of Justice and Interior Ministers of the Eight*, Washington, DC, 10 December 1997. URL: www.usdoj.gov/opa/pr/1997/December97/518cr.html.

31   European Union, Information Society Project Office. URL:
        www.ispo.cec.be.

32   A good source of information on the G7/G8 pilot project "A Global
        Marketplace for SMEs" is the EU web site
        www.ispo.cec.be/ecommerce/g7init.html#3.

33   "Tokyo Economic Declaration", May 6, 1986, para. 11, in *The Seven-Power
        Summit: Documents from the Summits of Industrialized Countries, 1975-
        1989*, pp. 314-15.

34   Tokyo Summit, 1993, *G-7 Chairman's Statement on Support for Russian
        Reform*, in United States, Department of State, Bureau of Public Affairs, *US
        Department of State Dispatch* 4, Supplement 2 (May 1993), pp. 16-18;
        Conference on Partnership for Economic Transition in Ukraine, Winnipeg,
        Canada, 27 October 1994, *Chairman's Summary*. URL:
        http//www.library.utoronto.ca/www/g7/94ukrai.htm.

35   *G8 Foreign Ministers Communiqué on Indian and Pakistani Nuclear Tests*.
        London, 12 June 1998. URL: www.fco.gov.uk/news/newstext.asp?1131
        and www.library.utoronto.ca/www/g7/foreign/fm980612.htm.

36   *Conclusions of G7 Finance Ministers*, London, 8 May 1998. URL:
        http://birmingham.g8summit.gov.uk/forfin/finance.shtml and
        www.library.utoronto.ca/www/g7/finance/fm980509.htm; *Strengthening the
        Architecture of the Global Financial System: Report of G7 Finance
        Ministers to G7 Heads of State or Government for Their Meeting in
        Birmingham, May 1998*. URL:
        http://birmingham.g8summit.gov.uk/docs/finmin.fri.shtml and
        www.library.utoronto.ca/www/g7/birmingham/g7heads.htm.

37   *Financial Stability: Supervision of Global Financial Institutions; A Report
        by G7 Finance Ministers*, London, May 1998 (unpublished); *Promoting
        Financial Stability: Recent Initiatives of the Basle Committee on Banking
        Supervision; Submission for the G-7 Heads of Government at the 1998
        Birmingham Summit*, Basle, March 1998 (unpublished).

38   See Great Britain, Treasury, *G8 Employability Action Plans Published*
        (Press Release 74/1988), 9 May 1998. URL:
        www.hm-treasury.gov.uk/pub/html/press98/p74_98.html. For the text of
        the eight action plans, see
        www.library.utoronto.ca/www/g7/employment/actionplans.

39   *Conclusions of G8 Foreign Ministers*, London, 9 May 1998. URL:
        http://birmingham.g8summit.gov.uk/forfin/foreign.shtml and
        www.library.utoronto.ca/www/g7/foreign/fm980509.htm.

40   *G8 Action Programme on Forests*, London, 9 May 1998. URL:
        http://birmingham.g8summit.gov.uk/forfin/forests.shtml and
        www.library.utoronto.ca/www/g7/foreign/forests.html.

41   *Conclusions of the Joint Meeting of G8 Foreign and Finance Ministers*, London, 9 May 1998. URL: http://birmingham.g8summit.gov.uk/forfin/joint.shtml and www.library.utoronto.ca/www/g7/finance/fj980509.htm.

42   Jacques Attali, *Verbatim* (Paris: Fayard, 1993-1995); François Camé, "Comment les sherpas avaient ficelé le sommet", *Libération*, 17 juillet 1989: 8-15; Estelle Ardouin, *Sherpas et sommets des 7* (Lyon: Institut d'Etudes Politiques, 1996). [Computer file]. URL: http://iep.univ-lyon2.fr/ETU/sherpa.html; Pierre Favier and Michel Martin-Roland, *La décennie Mitterrand* (Paris: Seuil, 1990-91. 3 vols.)

43   De Guttry, "The Institutional Configuration of the G-7 in the New International Scenario", p. 69.

44   Great Britain, Parliament, House of Commons, Session 1982/1983, *Technology, Growth and Employment: Report of the Working Group Set Up by the Economic Summit Meeting of 1982*, by the Science and Technology Secretariat, Cabinet Office (Cmnd. 8818; London: HMSO, 1983).

45   See, for example, *International Efforts to Combat Money Laundering*, ed. William C. Gilmore (Cambridge International Documents Series, Vol. 4; Cambridge: Grotius Publications in association with the Commonwealth Secretariat, 1992).

46   G22, *Summary of Reports on the International Financial Architecture* (Washington, DC, October 1998). URL: www.imf.org/external/np/g22/summry.pdf; *[Report of] the Working Group on Transparency and Accountability*. URL: www.imf.org/external/np/g22/index.htm#trans; *[Report of] the Working Group on Strengthening Financial Systems*. URL: www.imf.org/external/np/g22/index.htm#strength; and *[Report of the Working Group on International Financial Crises*. URL: www.imf.org/external/np/g22/index.htm#crises.

47   Venice Summit, 1980, *Declaration* (23 June 1980), paras. 14-15; Bonn Summit, 1985, *The Bonn Economic Declaration: Towards Sustained Growth and Higher Employment* (4 May 1985), para. 9, in *The Seven-Power Summit: Documents from the Summits of Industrialized Countries, 1975-1989*, pp. 84, 292. Also available, respectively, at URLs www.library.utoronto.ca/www/g7/80ecodec.htm and www.library.utoronto.ca/www/g7/85ecodec.htm.

48   Houston Summit, 1990, *Houston Economic Declaration* (July 11, 1990), para. 79, in *The Seven-Power Summit: Documents from the Summits of Industrialized Countries; Supplement: Documents from the 1990 Summit*, p. 27; London Summit, 1991, *Economic Declaration: Building World Partnership*, 17 July 1991, para. 61 (b), in *The Twenty G-7 Summits*, p. 228. Also available, respectively, at

www.library.utoronto.ca/www/g7/90ecodec.htm and
www.library.utoronto.ca/www/g7/91ecodec.htm.

49   Halifax Summit, 1995, *Chairman's Statement*, 17 June 1995, para. 9. In
United States, Department of State, Bureau of Public Affairs, *US
Department of State Dispatch* 6, Supplement 4 (July 1995), p. 11. See also
URL: www.library.utoronto.ca/www/g7/95chair.htm.

50   Halifax Summit, 1995, *Chairman's Statement*, 17 June 1995, para. 10. In
United States, Department of State, Bureau of Public Affairs, *US
Department of State Dispatch* 6, Supplement 4 (July 1995), p. 11. See also
URL: www.library.utoronto.ca/www/g7/95chair.htm.

51   Lyon Summit, 1996, *Chairman's Statement*, 29 June 1996.   URL:
www.library.utoronto.ca/www/g7/96poli.htm. See also Ministerial
Conference on Terrorism, Paris, 30 July 1996, *Agreement on 25 Measures*.
URL: www.library.utoronto.ca/www/g7/terror25.htm.

52   Birmingham Summit, 1998, *G8 Birmingham Summit Communiqué*,
paragraphs 7, 10, 24. URL:
www.library.utoronto.ca/www/g7/birmingham/finalcom.htm.

9 Assessing G7/G8 Documentation

A number of observers have commented on the content of summit documents and the extent to which those documents reflect or fail to reflect actual deliberations of the G7/G8. Cesare Merlini remarks that "distinction will have to be made in the final declarations at the end of the summits between qualifying and routine positions, between matters that have actually been discussed at the summit and matters that have been assigned to the structure .... [Conversely, w]hile it is essential that the heads of state and government exchange views and concerns, these do not necessarily all have to be listed in communiqués and declarations". G. John Ikenberry laments the "bland official communiqués that paper over dysfunctions in the global economic system, or vague joint commitments to growth and prosperity that substitute for actual accord".[1]

Guido Garavoglia and Pier Carlo Padoan recall the early years of the summit when "[f]inal documents were rather short and reflected rather accurately the issues dealt with by the heads of state and government, although the tendency to increase the length and number of subjects was already evident". Later, "[t]he increase in the number of subjects discussed has gradually led to a lengthening and a diversification of the final documents .... . These documents reflect a nominal agenda, which in many cases does not correspond to the matters actually discussed by the heads of state and government".[2]

An example of this lack of correspondence is the almost one-third of the space taken up by the topic of the environment in the communiqué of the 1989 Paris Summit of the Arch, contrasted with the relatively short time the leaders actually spent discussing that subject during their working dinner (according to a background briefing by a senior official). Despite genuine efforts by the leaders to correct that kind of imbalance between released documents and actual discussions, and some real successes in this respect in more recent summits, a certain imbalance remains. For example–again, according to a background briefing by a senior official–Russian brutality in the war in Chechnya was brought up in Halifax in 1995, with several G7 leaders expressing unhappiness if not protest to Russian President Boris

93

Yeltsin, but the Halifax *Chairman's Statement* of the P8 is silent on Chechnya, although remarks by the host leader prior to the release of the *Chairman's Statement* express "concern at the continuing conflict and the resulting loss of life and civilian casualties ... [and the participants'] strong belief that the situation in Chechnya should **not** be resolved by military means".[3] Dissatisfaction with the French decision to resume nuclear testing in the South Pacific was also voiced by several delegations in Halifax, but, keeping with the G7 tradition of not openly criticising summit colleagues, this sentiment did not find its way into the public documentation of the Summit.

C. Fred Bergsten, a prominent critic of the G7, decries this hesitancy, stating that "[t]he 'nonaggression pact' now pervades the behavior of the G7. The members have decided not to criticize each other, especially in public, where it can sometimes be more effective, because they have lost confidence in their ability to influence events and because they fear being criticized themselves".[4]

Several analysts have called for various changes in summit documentation. Hisashi Owada advocates the necessity of "a more structured approach to many vital issues through the summit process, while avoiding a bureaucratic straitjacket involving spending much time on preparing a document which basically lacks substance". Hanns W. Maull criticises the "ever longer, broader and more non-committal communiqués, which tried to hide substantive policy disagreements by focusing on elements of consensus and mutual recognition of different national approaches". He mentions the German desire to see shorter communiqués and separate chairman's summaries of political topics. Philippe Moreau Defarges concurs: the French view is that "declarations should be shorter, focusing on a few key points... . [If they] are shorter, they will be read more carefully and become more binding". John J. Kirton, similarly, points to Canada's "strong preference for a short, straightforward, comprehensible communiqué—one that reflect[s] what the leaders actually cared about, talked about and meant, and one that [is] easily understood not just by the officials ... but by the media and public at large".[5]

Michael R. Hodges laments the inflationary increase in the length of the communiqué from 1,100 words at Rambouillet to 7,000 words at Munich[*] and cites John Major's reform proposals that include the desirability

---

[*]   The Munich communiqué was actually 3,560 words in length. Houston in 1990 produced a declaration of some 6,000 words.

of "concise final communiqués that reflect the issues actually discussed and the priorities established". Quoting a British official, he adds that "instead of producing prenegotiated texts and thematic papers, the sherpa meetings should concentrate on discussing lead papers introduced by a chairman". The British preference, expressed before the 1994 Naples Summit, was for a shorter final declaration that "should integrate political and economic issues".[6]

Garavoglia and Padoan, writing in early 1994, also suggest that

> [o]nly one final document should be issued at the end of the summit and it should integrate economic and political aspects as much as possible. Furthermore, it should reflect the matters actually discussed by the leaders. This means that it would be much shorter than current communiqués, facilitating immediate public understanding of the matters discussed ... . If the non-decisional nature of the summit is to be underlined, this could be done by a less demanding "summary by the chairman" illustrating the main points on which the heads of state and government reached agreement.[7]

Real events, however, can quickly overtake even the best-considered proposals from outside the G7. One of the major new developments at the Naples Summit that took place only a few months after the above-cited proposal was Russia's formal participation in the political discussions. This resulted in an immediate change in the pattern of summit documentation, described in detail in Chapter 8: the communiqués of the 1994, 1995 and 1996 summits were issued at the end of the G7 part of the summit, on the second day, so that it was no longer the "final" document. The "chairman's statement" came to express the conclusions of the P8 which followed.

The new configuration of the 1997 Denver "Summit of the Eight" changed the nature and scope of the communiqué. Now a document of the Eight, the *Communiqué* was released at the conclusion of the summit, on 22 June.[8] The following additional documents were released in Denver:

- Financial and other economic issues, still in the purview of the G7, were represented in a separate statement by the seven heads, entitled *Confronting Global Economic and Financial Challenges* and released on 21 June, the second day of the summit.[9] This statement dealt with promoting economic growth, strengthening the stability of the global financial system, and building an integrated global economy. Significantly, the statement also discussed Ukraine at the level of the Seven, rather than the Eight.

- Also at the G7 level, the seven finance ministers submitted a *Final Report to the G-7 Heads of State and Government on Promoting Financial Stability.* The release date of this document is 21 June. In addition, this document had a separately issued two-page *Executive Summary*, a summit innovation.[10]
- A G8 heads' *Statement on Bosnia and Herzegovina*, dated 22 June.[11]
- A G8 heads' *Statement on Cambodia*, also dated 22 June.[12]
- A G8 *Foreign Ministers' Progress Report*, dated 21 June.[13]

The innovations in summit format, agenda and participation introduced in 1998 in Birmingham have been discussed in previous chapters. The pattern of documentation reflects those major changes. The documents issued at Birmingham were, as expected, fewer in number compared to documentation of earlier recent summits. The G8 Summit itself released the following:

- The *Communiqué* issued by the G8 on 17 May, at the conclusion of the summit, addresses concerns and sets out tasks related to the three major agenda items.[14]   The G8 heads welcome the   European Economic and Monetary Union; comment at length on the financial crisis in Asia, recognising the impact of the crisis on the poorest and most vulnerable sectors of society, and pointing to the role of the international financial institutions in protecting these groups; reaffirm their commitment to trade and investment liberalisation; pledge their support for developing countries in building democracy and good governance; and agree to negotiate replenishment of the International Development Association (IDA) and to provide adequate resources for the Enhanced Structural Adjustment Facility of the International Monetary Fund (IMF) and for the African Development Fund. On debt relief, the G8 endorses the Heavily Indebted Poor Countries (HIPC) initiative, declaring six countries already eligible and two more to qualify soon. The communiqué also includes support for the campaign to "Roll Back Malaria" by 2010 launched by the World Health Organization (WHO). On energy, the Eight commit themselves to encourage the development of energy markets and to work for establishing appropriate legislative and regulatory frameworks. They reaffirm their support for enhancing the safety of nuclear power plants. On climate change, they reiterate their endorsement of the Kyoto Protocol to reduce greenhouse gas emissions. On the second agenda item, "Growth, employability and inclusion", the leaders endorse earlier work by G8 ministers, notably the eight individual national action plans to advance these aims, and state their willingness to share their principles and experiences with other members of the International Labour Organisation (ILO), the Organisation for Economic Co-operation and Development (OECD) and the international financial institutions. The third item, drugs and international crime, comprises drug trade, trafficking in weapons, smuggling of human beings, money laundering, and the abuse of new technologies by criminals; the leaders agree to wide-ranging action, including negotiating a United Nations (UN) convention against transnational organised crime; supporting a ten-point action plan on high-tech crime; and instituting joint law enforcement. Finally, the communiqué deals with the issues of nonproliferation of weapons of mass destruction and the Millennium Bug.

- There were *political statements on regional issues*, released on 15 May. The first deals with the political crisis in Indonesia; violence in Kosovo; Bosnia/Herzegovina; the Middle East peace process; and the Indian nuclear explosions of 11 and 13 May which the leaders condemn without agreeing on collective sanctions. A separate statement on Northern Ireland, issued on 16 May, supports the Good Friday agreement to end sectarian violence; and yet another statement, also of 16 May, deals with drugs and international crime. The last-mentioned document is a shorter version of the relevant provisions (paragraphs 18-23) of the communiqué.[15]

Apart from the G8 summit as a whole, host leader Tony Blair issued on 16 May a *Response By the Presidency on Behalf of the G8 to the Jubilee 2000 Petition*.[16] In that document Mr Blair, on behalf of the G8 leaders, addressed the concerns of more than 50,000 demonstrators at the summit site as well as a number of organisations behind the demonstration that urged complete debt forgiveness for all poor countries by the year 2000.

The leaders at Birmingham released, at the G7 level, a *G7 Chairman's Statement*, commenting on the world economy and on the strengthening of the global financial system.[17] On the latter issue, the G7 leaders supported the eight-page report submitted to them by the G7 finance ministers entitled *Strengthening the Architecture of the Global Financial System.*[18] In this document, the ministers identified five areas needing action: enhanced transparency; helping countries prepare for integration into the global economy and for free global capital flows; strengthening national financial systems; ensuring that the private sector takes responsibility for its lending decisions; and further enhancing the role of and co-operation among the IMF, the Bank for International Settlements (BIS), the World Bank, and other international financial institutions.

The Birmingham G8 Summit issued fewer documents than its recent predecessors, even when one considers the leaders' documents still released at the G7 heads' level. This reduction in volume, however, was more than offset by the proliferating output of the joint meeting of G7/G8 finance and foreign ministers in London on 8-9 May 1998. This shifting of the workload and documentation from the leaders to their ministers is a welcome new development because it allows the leaders to concentrate on issues worthy of their time and attention. It is, moreover, a reflection of greater transparency in the work of the G7/G8. By having more documents available, the academic community, the media and the wider public will be better informed and in a better position to judge the work of the G7/G8, thereby increasing the legitimacy of this very important institution.

The documentation of the G7/G8 system, in all its variety and dynamism, is an essential source of information not only about that institution but also on a whole gamut of vital issues. It is a potentially rich mine of political, economic and historical data, although it calls for a fair amount of interpretation to get beyond its jargon-laden language and somewhat repetitive nature. One must, of course, look beyond the primary G7/G8 documentation to complementary sources, notably archives, and writings about the G7/G8 and related issues–the subject of Chapter 10.

Notes

1   Cesare Merlini, "The G-7 and the Need for Reform", in *The Future of the G-7 Summits*, p. 19 (*The International Spectator* 29, No. 2; April/June 1994, Special Issue); G. John Ikenberry, "Salvaging the G-7", *Foreign Affairs* 72, No. 2 (Spring 1993), p. 132.

2   Guido Garavoglia, and Pier Carlo Padoan, "The G-7 Agenda: Old and New Issues", in *The Future of the G-7 Summits*, pp. 53-55.

3   Halifax Summit, 1995, "Remarks by Prime Minister Jean Chrétien", June 17, 1995, para. 4. URL:

www.library.utoronto.ca./www/g7/95chr.htm.

4   C. Fred Bergsten, "Grade 'F' for the G7", *The International Economy: The Magazine of International Economic Policy* 10, No. 6 (November/December 1996), p. 19.

5   Hisashi Owada, "A Japanese Perspective on the Role and Future of the G-7", in *The Future of the G-7 Summits*, p. 110; Hanns W. Maull, "Germany at the Summit", in *The Future of the G-7 Summits*, pp. 121, 136; Philippe Moreau Defarges, "The French Viewpoint on the Future of the G-7", in *The Future of the G-7 Summits*, p. 184; John J. Kirton, "Exercising Concerted Leadership: Canada's Approach to Summit Reform", in *The Future of the G-7 Summits*, p. 163.

6   Michael R. Hodges, "More Efficiency, Less Dignity: British Perspectives on the Future Role and Working of the G-7", in *The Future of the G-7 Summits*, pp. 144, 146, 151, 154.

7   Garavoglia and Padoan, "The G-7 Agenda: Old and New Issues", p. 63.

8   Denver Summit of the Eight, 1997, *Communiqué*, 22 June 1997. URL: www.library.utoronto.ca/www/g7/denver/g8final.htm.

9   Denver Summit of the Eight, 1997, *Confronting Global Economic and Financial Challenges: Denver Summit Statement by Seven,* 21 June 1997. URL: www.library.utoronto.ca/www/g7/denver/confront.htm.

10   Denver Summit of the Eight, 1997, *Final Report to the G-7 Heads of State and Government on Promoting Financial Stability*, 21 June 1997. URL: www.library.utoronto.ca/www/g7/denver/finanrpt.htm; Denver Summit of the Eight, 1997, *Final Report to the G-7 Heads of State and Government on Promoting Financial Stability: Executive Summary*, 21 June 1997. URL: www.library.utoronto.ca/www/g7/denver/exec.htm.

11   Denver Summit of the Eight, 1997, *Statement on Bosnia and Herzegovina*, 22 June 1997. URL: www.library.utoronto.ca/www/g7/denver/bosnia.htm.

12   Denver Summit of the Eight, 1997, *Statement on Cambodia*, 22 June 1997. URL: www.library.utoronto.ca/www/g7/denver/camb.htm.

13   Denver Summit of the Eight, 1997, *Foreign Ministers' Progress Report*, 21 June 1997. URL: www.library.utoronto.ca/www/g7/denver/formin.htm.

14   Birmingham Summit, 1998, *G8 Birmingham Summit Communiqué*, 17 May 1998. URL: http://birmingham.g8summit.gov.uk/docs/final.shtml and www.library.utoronto.ca/www/g7/birmingham/finalcom.htm.

15   Birmingham Summit, 1998, *[Political Statement on Regional Issues:] Indonesia, FRY/Kosovo, Bosnia and Herzegovina, Middle East Peace Process, Indian Nuclear Tests*, 15 May 1998. URL: http://birmingham.g8summit.gov.uk/docs/regional.shtml and www.library.utoronto.ca/www/g7/birmingham/regional.htm; Birmingham Summit, 1998, *Northern Ireland*, 16 May 1998. URL: http://birmingham.g8summit.gov.uk/docs/nireland.shtml and

www.library.utoronto.ca/www/g7/birmingham/ireland.htm; Birmingham Summit, 1998, *Drugs and International Crime*, 16 May 1998. URL: http://birmingham.g8summit.gov.uk/docs/crime.shtml and www.library.utoronto.ca/www/g7/birmingham/drugs.htm.

16   Birmingham Summit, 1998, *Response By the Presidency on Behalf of the G8 to the Jubilee 2000 Petition*. 16 May 1998. URL: http://birmingham.g8summit.gov.uk/docs/jub2000.shtml and www.library.utoronto.ca/www/g7/birmingham/2000.htm.

17   *G7 Chairman's Statement*, Birmingham, 15 May 1998. URL: www.library.utoronto.ca/www/g7/birmingham/chair.htm.

18   *Strengthening the Architecture of the Global Financial System: Report of G7 Finance Ministers to G7 Heads of State or Government for Their Meeting in Birmingham, May 1998*. URL: http://birmingham.g8summit.gov.uk/docs/finmin.fri.shtml and www.library.utoronto.ca/www/g7/birmingham/g7heads.htm.

10 Other Sources of Information about the G7/G8

Archives

Presidential, prime ministerial, as well as foreign, finance and other ministry archives, and even personal papers of participants, are a significant source of further G7/G8 information. These archives will yield the best and most reliable record of G7/G8 meetings, especially if note-takers at the meetings were accurate and comprehensive in their work. The Ford Presidential Library in Ann Arbor, Michigan includes archival material related to the 1975 Rambouillet Summit and the 1976 San Juan Summit.[1] The US National Archives and Records Administration lists extensive holdings from the Carter administration concerning the 1977, 1978, 1979 and 1980 summits.[2] As and when these and other archives in summit countries are opened, their holdings will, no doubt, be explored by researchers seeking access to first-hand accounts by participants of summits and G7/G8 ministerial meetings.

Writings about the G7/G8

There is a large and growing corpus of writings about various aspects of the G7/G8: scholarly analyses; compilations of texts of documents, often accompanied by additional material of reference value; government publications, including parliamentary reviews in summit countries; memoirs and other writings by prominent former summit participants (including what may be the first work of fiction about the summit); reference works of various types; media accounts including reportage and analysis in newspapers, journals, radio and television; and, increasingly, internet resources, with some web sites devoted to the G7/G8 either on an *ad hoc* or permanent basis (Chapter 11 discusses internet resources in general and the University of Toronto's G8 Information Centre in particular.) The Appendix at the end of this chapter presents some examples of writings in each category. The bibliography is a comprehensive list of monographs, articles in periodicals, and governmental and international organisation publications.

Items covered deal entirely or partly with the G7/G8 or with G7/G8-related issues.

On the subject of news media accounts, quality of reportage is a question worthy of comment. It is clear that there are some knowledgeable reporters, especially with prominent media–such as the *Financial Times* of London–who follow economic and other G7/G8-related issues the year round and are well able to interpret and analyse fast-breaking news at the summits. Others are often sent to the summit site by their news organisations simply because they are posted nearby and thus available at lower cost; their results can be quite uneven. Still others are interested mostly in photo opportunities or in "lifestyle" reporting: What dress did Mrs Blair wear? What were Helmut Kohl's food preferences? How did Boris Yeltsin handle his drinks?

Although the documents released by the G7/G8 system are the primary source material for studying that institution, especially when examined together with the transcripts of appropriate press conferences and briefings, one must look beyond those sources to complementary information. National archives, academic and journalistic writings about the G7/G8, and memoirs and other works by summit participants complete the picture.

Appendix:
Examples of Writings About the G7/G8

The following are a few examples of the growing body of literature on the G7/G8 and related issues:

Scholarly Analyses:

- Bergsten, C. Fred, and C. Randall Henning. *Global Economic Leadership and the Group of Seven*. Washington, DC: Institute for International Economics, 1996.
- De Ménil, Georges. "De Rambouillet à Versailles: un bilan des sommets économiques" (From Rambouillet to Versailles: An Assessment of the Economic Summits). *Politique étrangère* 2 (June 1982): 403-17.
- Funabashi, Yoichi. *Samittokurashi* (Summitocracy). Tokyo: Asahi Shinbunsha, 1991.

- Herz, Bernhard, and Joachim Starbatty. "Zur Frage Internationaler Dominanzbeziehungen: Eine Analyse der Machtverteilung auf Weltwirtschaftsgipfeln". (On the Question of International Relations among Dominant Powers: An Analysis of the Distribution of Power at the World Economic Summits). *Kyklos* 44 (1991), Fasc. 1:35-55.
- Kirton, John J. "Contemporary Concert Diplomacy: The Seven-Power Summit and the Management of International Order". Paper prepared for the annual meeting of the International Studies Association and the British International Studies Association, London, March 29-April 1, 1989. Unpublished in print. [Computer file] URL: www.library.utoronto.ca/www/g7/kirtitl.htm.
- Kokotsis, Eleonore. *National Compliance with G7 Environment and Development Commitments, 1988-1995*. PhD dissertation. Toronto: University of Toronto, 1998. Unpublished.
- Ostry, Sylvia. *Summitry: The Medium and the Message*. Bissell Paper No. 3. Toronto: University of Toronto, Centre for International Studies, 1988.
- Putnam, Robert D., and Nicholas Bayne. *Hanging Together: Cooperation and Conflict in the Seven-Power Summits*. Rev. ed. Cambridge, Mass.: Harvard University Press, 1987.
- Von Furstenberg, George M., and Joseph P. Daniels. *Economic Summit Declarations, 1975-1989: Examining the Written Record of International Cooperation*. Princeton Studies in International Finance, No. 72. Princeton, N. J.: International Finance Section, Dept. of Economics, Princeton University, 1992.
- *World Economic Summits: The Role of Representative Groups In the Governance of the World Economy*. WIDER Study Group Series, No. 4. Helsinki: World Institute for Development Economics Research, United Nations University, 1989.

Compilations of Texts (often with additional comment or reference material):

- Japan. Ministry of Foreign Affairs. *G-7 Official Documents, 1975-1992*. Tokyo: MFA, 1993. 2 3½" diskettes.
- Hajnal, Peter I., comp. and ed. *The Seven-Power Summit: Documents from the Summits of Industrialized Countries, 1975-1989*. With an introduction by John J. Kirton. Millwood, NY: Kraus International Publications, 1989.

- *The Twenty G-7 Summits*. On the Occasion of the Twentieth Summit, Naples, July 8-10, 1994. Rome: Adnkronos Libri in Collaboration with Istituto Affari Internazionali, 1994.

Official Publications by G8 Countries:

- Canada. Department of Foreign Affairs and International Trade. *Canada and the G-7 Summits*. Ottawa: DFAIT, 1995.
- Canada. Department of Foreign Affairs and International Trade. *Birmingham G-8 Summit and Official Visits in Europe by Prime Minister Jean Chrétien, May 13-23, 1998: Background Information*. Ottawa: DFAIT, 1998.
- Canada. Parliament. House of Commons. Standing Committee on Foreign Affairs and International Trade. *From Bretton Woods to Halifax and beyond: Towards a 21st Summit for the 21st Century Challenge: Report of the House of Commons Standing Committee on Foreign Affairs and International Trade on the Issues of International Financial Institutions Reforms for the Agenda of the June 1995 G-7 Halifax Summit*. Minutes of Proceedings and Evidence of the Standing Committee on Foreign Affairs and International Trade, Respecting, Pursuant to Standing Order 108 (2), an Examination of the Agenda for the G-7 Summit, in Halifax and in Particular, Reform of the International Financial Institutions, Including the Fourth Report to the House. Thirty-fifth Parliament, First Session, Issue No 25, May 9, 1995. Ottawa: Queen's Printer, 1995.
- Great Britain. Foreign and Commonwealth Office. *G8 Birmingham Summit, May 1998*. Background Brief. London: FCO, 1998.
- Great Britain. Parliament. House of Commons. Session 1992/1993. [Prime Minister John Major's statement on the 1993 Tokyo Summit]. In *Parliamentary Debates*, 6th Series, Vol. 228, cols. 669-71. London: House of Commons, 12 July 1993.
- Spero, Joan. "Mount Halifax: In Sight of the Summit". *US Department of State Dispatch* 6, No. 26 (June 26, 1995): 520-21.
- United States. Congress. Senate. Committee on Foreign Relations. *Economic Summit, Latin Debt, and the Baker Plan: Hearing before the Committee on Foreign Relations, United States Senate, Ninety-ninth Congress, Second Session, May 20, 1986*. S. Hrg. 99-889. Washington, D. C.: US Government Printing Office, 1986.

Memoirs and Other Writings by Prominent Former Summit Participants:

- Attali, Jacques. *Verbatim*. Paris: Fayard, 1993-1995. [Tome 1: Chronique des années 1981-1986; Tome 2: Chronique des années 1986-1988; Tome 3: Chronique des années 1988-1991.]
- Giscard d'Estaing, Valéry. "A Communiqué for Williamsburg". *The Economist* 287, No. 7290 (May 21, 1983): 15-18.
- Heath, Edward. "The Heath Memorandum". *The Times* (London), July 20, 1981: 10.
- Hurd, Douglas. *The Shape of Ice*. London: Little, Brown, 1998. [Fiction]
- Schmidt, Helmut. *Menschen und Mächte* (Men and Powers). Berlin: Siedler, 1987-1990. 2 vols.
- Thatcher, Margaret. *The Downing Street Years*. London: Harper-Collins, 1993.

Reference Works:

- Hajnal, Peter I. "G7 Bibliography". *Canadian Foreign Policy = La Politique étrangère du Canada* 3, No. 1 (Spring 1995): 125-133.
- United States. Department of State. Bureau of Public Affairs. "Fact Sheet: Economic Summits, 1988-95". *US Department of State Dispatch* (Vol. 6, Supplement No. 4; July 1995): 15-19.

Media Accounts:

- "Bill Clinton's Golden Moment". *The Economist* 343, No. 8022 (June 21, 1997): 16-17.
- "Economic Summit". *The Wall Street Journal*, July 9, 1990: R1-R40. The Wall Street Journal Reports. New York.
- Magombe, V. P., and Enyoyam Afele. "Fruitless Gathering: Africa under the Table at the Recent G-7 Summit". *West Africa*, No. 3856 (5-11 August 1991): 1283.
- Stephens, Philip. "Major Calls for Overhaul of G7 Summits". *Financial Times* (London), September 10, 1992: 1. (Summary of John Major's unpublished letter of August 1992 to other G7 heads of state or government.)
- Sutherland, Peter. "Le Directeur général du GATT réclame une refonte du G7". (The Director General of GATT calls for

remodelling of the G7). *Le Monde*, 3 février, 1994: 18. (Summary of speech at the World Economic Forum, Davos, Switzerland, on replacing the G7 with a broader institution.)

Internet Resources (see Chapter 11 for detailed discussion):

- The University of Toronto's permanent web site, the "G8 Information Centre" (URL: www.g7.utoronto.ca).
- The Université de Lyon's web server launched before the 1996 Lyon Summit (URL: sunG7.univ-lyon2.fr/g7lyon.html). No longer active.
- The French government's 1996 Lyon Summit site (URL: www.G7lyon.gouv.fr). No longer active.
- An IBM World Wide web site, "G7 Live", devoted to the 1995 G7 ministerial conference on the Global Information Society (URL: www.ibm.com/Sponsor/g7live/). No longer active.
- The web site of the G7 Support Implementation Group in Moscow (URL: www.g7sig.org/).
- The US White House site for the Denver Summit of the Eight (URL: www.whitehouse.gov/WH/New/Eight/).
- The Denver/Birmingham summit site of the Canadian Department of Foreign Affairs and International Trade (URL: www.dfait-maeci.gc.ca/english/foreignp/policy.htm#3).
- The UK government's official site for the Birmingham G8 Summit (URL: birmingham.g8summit.gov.uk/).
- The site of the People's Summit, Birmingham, 15-17 May 1998 ("The Other Economic Summit"). URL: www.gn.apc.org/peoplessummit98/.

Notes

1   See URL: www.lbjlib.utexas.edu/ford/, especially under "Foreign Economic Policy".
2   US, National Archives and Records Administration, NARA Archival Information Locator (NAIL) URL: www.nara.gov/nara/nail.html.

11 G7/G8 Information: Internet Resources

SIAN MEIKLE

The absence of a formal secretariat for the G7/G8 has had a marked effect on the availability of G7/G8 information on the internet, as it has for G7/G8 printed documentation. Web documentation about the G7/G8 is for the most part diffuse; it is sometimes only temporarily available, and it is usually found in specialised pockets on web sites whose primary purpose is only tangentially related to the G7/G8. The web sites for government ministries, international organisations, media organisations, and a few academic sites are the primary sources of internet information, and this chapter will examine each of these resources in turn.

Government Sites

Government sites have been providing G7/G8 information on the web, roughly speaking, since 1995. Each year the amount of information available online and the speed with which it is posted improve.

The most visible sources of government information concerning the G7/G8 process are each year's host country's summit web sites. These sites are, increasingly, a comprehensive and fast distribution mechanism for G7/G8 documents as they are released at the summit. A primary function of these sites is media communication, so they may also provide some transcripts of the host country's summit press conferences, although so far these have not been complete. Usually host country background briefs on summit issues are also published online.

Some participating countries also mount summit sites; Canada has done so each year since the 1995 Halifax summit; Japan, the United States, and Britain have sometimes done so. These can provide additional information, such as the given country's background briefs and press conferences. However, these sites vary in their permanence and comprehensiveness. The Canadian sites are all still available and provide French and English versions of the documents mounted. Of the several summit sites that the United States mounted in 1997 (when it hosted the summit in Denver) only one now remains. Japan's 1997 site has also been removed.

Government ministries closely concerned with the G7/G8 process in G7/G8 countries (most usually, the finance and foreign ministries) are a primary source of G7/G8 information in their area of interest, and furthermore, frequently provide translations of G7/G8 documents into their own language. The current chair country's ministries may be quite fast to make G7/G8 statements available on the web as they are released, although this has varied somewhat from year to year. Certain ministries seem particularly geared towards publishing information on the internet. In particular, the US Department of the Treasury's web site (www.ustreas.gov) has been a fast and reliable source of finance ministers' statements for several years, and the UK Foreign and Commonwealth Office (www.fco.gov.uk) has become particularly reliable for a variety of G7/G8 statements. At the time of writing (1998), the United Kingdom is the host country, and this may have affected the speed and reliability of their information service. The Canadian Department of Foreign Affairs and International Trade at www.dfait.gov.ca is another reliable and stable, although perhaps somewhat slower source of G7/G8 documentation, and it is distinguished by its provision of French versions of G7/G8 documents. The Japanese Ministry of Foreign Affairs site at www2.nttca.com:8010/infomofa/ (English) or www.mofa.go.jp/mofaj/ (Japanese) provides G7/G8 documents in Japanese and English since 1996, together with relevant Japanese press conference transcripts. The France Diplomatie site, maintained by the French Ministère des Affaires Etrangères at www.france.diplomatie.fr, is an excellent source of G7/G8 statements since 1990, translated into French; they have also mounted many of their press conferences relating to G7/G8 matters.

It is worth noting that, quite understandably, none of these sites hosts a complete set of G7/G8 documents, as that is not their mandate. And again because the primary focus of these sites is not the G7/G8, locating relevant documents within them can take some persistence. Moreover (and this is true whenever searching for G7/G8 information on the internet) all the variants on the names of the fora (G7, G-7, G8, G-8, Group of Seven, Group of Eight) must be tried to ensure good search results at these sites.

The United States Information Agency (USIA) Public Diplomacy Calendar on the web at www.usia.gov/products/calendar/calendar.htm is another government site that can be helpful in tracking the G7/G8 ministerial meeting schedule through the year. While sherpa meetings are not usually listed, and other meetings are not listed comprehensively, it is one of the few sites that publicises any G7/G8 ministerial meetings ahead of schedule. It does not, however, provide links to statements issued by the meetings; rather, it is useful as a notice of upcoming events.

A fuller list of government web sites that have G7/G8 related material is given at www.library.utoronto.ca/g7/g7_rel.htm, in the G8 Information Centre web site.

International Organisations

Some G7/G8 material can be found on the web sites of international organisations that share common interests. For example, the International Monetary Fund (IMF) site at www.imf.org can be a good source of G7 Finance Ministers' statements. Furthermore, the IMF fairly often makes reference to the G7/G8 in its own statements and press conferences, which are published on its web site. Similarly, the World Bank Group site at www.worldbank.org, and the World Trade Organization (WTO) site at www.wto.org, contain some relevant materials.

The Organisation for Economic Co-operation and Development (OECD) site at www.oecd.org is also of particular interest. OECD meetings at the ministerial level occur each year just before the G7/G8 summit. They are publicised a year in advance on the OECD site, and their statements are published quickly after the meeting. These statements closely forecast the financial portions of the G7/G8 summit statements.

The European Union has a number of sites; in particular the Information Society Project Office (ISPO) site at www.ispo.cec.be is a good resource for information on G8-initiated projects such as MARIS (the Maritime Information Society), the Global Inventory Project, and the Global Marketplace for SMEs (small- and medium-sized enterprises) project.

A list of international organisation web sites containing G7/G8-related materials is maintained by the G8 Information Centre web site at www.library.utoronto.ca/g7/internat.htm.

Other G7/G8-Related Web Sites

Each year, G7/G8-related sites appear on the web around the time of the annual summit; generally, they are concerned mainly with the summit at hand. Some remain after the event as a record of past summits, while others are simply removed.

Several sites provide alternative views on the G7/G8 process. The Other Economic Summit (TOES) runs concurrently with the G8 Summit each year as a challenge to the summit process. The 1998 TOES summit covered "a broad range of the new economics agenda, focused around the theme of sustainable consumption"[1]. TOES web sites have been mounted annually since 1995; the 1996 and 1997 sites remain online, although the content varies with the resources available to the people who mount these sites. The Overseas Development Council (ODC) also provides some commentary about G7/G8 issues in its web site at www.odc.org.

Each year, more G7/G8 information is made available through media web sites at summit time. Local newspapers in the summit host city, the major newswires, and news organisations either create specific summit sites, or feature the summit prominently in their regular sites. However, these sites are intended for current affairs interest only, and are therefore most likely to disappear quickly after the summit. They are almost certainly not updated after the summit.

A list of other G7/G8–related sites, which necessarily varies from year to year, is maintained at www.library.utoronto.ca/g7/g7_other.htm, in the G8 Information Centre web site.

Academic Sites

For the past several years, universities in the host cities of the G7/G8 summit, and other academic groups elsewhere, have been mounting G7/G8 information sites as a learning tool for their students. For example, in 1995, during the Halifax G7 Summit, Dalhousie University in Halifax hosted a G7 site, which has since been removed. In 1996, the Institut d'Etudes Politiques de l'Université de Lyon hosted a similar site, at http://sung7.univ-lyon2.fr/sommet-lyon.html, which is still available, although no longer actively developed.

The University of Toronto founded its G7 Information Centre in 1995, when Canada was the host country for the G7 Summit. In 1998, the site was renamed the G8 Information Centre. Because this site is unique in being the only permanent, comprehensive collection of G7/G8 material thus far on the internet, its contents and the use made of it will receive close attention.

University of Toronto G8 Information Centre

History, Purpose and Philosophy

The G8 Information Centre web site (www.g7.utoronto.ca) was founded in 1995, as a permanent, focused, and comprehensive record of G7/G8 activities and documents, from the founding of the G7 forum in 1975 onwards. Its intended audiences are interested scholars, government officials, media and the business community worldwide. The site was initiated collaboratively between the G8 Research Group at the University of Toronto, and the University of Toronto Libraries. It is maintained by the Web Development Group at the University of Toronto Libraries, in close cooperation with the G8 Research Group. Peter Hajnal, as both a Government Information Specialist at the Libraries and a longtime active participant in the G8 Research Group, was a natural bridge between the two groups, and played a pivotal role in bringing the web site into existence. It was immediately apparent to all the collaborators that the large collection of summit-related materials that had been assembled by the Research Group was an excellent basis for a web site for several reasons:

- As pointed out earlier, the absence of a secretariat for the G7/G8 means that there is no formal or central record-keeping mechanism in place for the group's work. Therefore, the virtually complete collection of G7/G8 documents collected by the G8 Research Group was an important resource, and the role of warehousing and publishing the documentation collectively was not filled by any other body, on the internet or elsewhere.
- The audience for such material is thinly distributed all over the world, making the web a cheap and effective dissemination tool.
- The Libraries, with a strong interest in electronic information delivery, could supply the technical expertise and resources necessary to help the Research Group bring their work to a much wider audience. The G8 Information Centre was seen as an excellent pilot project for amassing large and specialised online collections, and the continued work of the G8 Research Group was an assurance that the web site would remain current. Furthermore, copyright was not a large

problem in launching this site (as it could be in many areas) because G7/G8 documents are free of copyright, and the Research Group itself held or had the connections to request copyright clearance for many related scholarly materials.

With all the attractions of the endeavour, several challenges were also immediately apparent.

Foremost was the difficulty in tracking G7/G8 activities. As we have seen, the G7/G8 is an informal and evolving group, with many contributing ministerial and other meetings throughout the year, and an annually rotating host country. Furthermore the participants from each country vary with their political fortunes, and finally, the various meetings are (sometimes deliberately) not always well publicised.

A second challenge was to design the web site to meet the widely disparate needs of its users. It had to function variously as an introduction to the G7/G8 for first-time visitors; an efficient and very up-to-date distribution point for new documents, especially at summit time; and an advanced research tool for G7/G8 scholars.

A third major challenge, especially at the time that the site was founded, was to deal with the very large amount of printed material that had to be digitised.

Contents

The material contained in the web site falls into several broad categories.

G7/G8 Summits A fundamental part of the site is the record of each annual summit meeting, its participants, all primary summit documents, and a selection of related materials such as press conference transcripts and draft versions of summit documents.

The work of obtaining these primary documents has been greatly simplified since 1995, when the first host country summit web site was established. These sites contain material relevant to the current summit, and usually focus on the host country's role in the summit. They now also include links to media coverage (indeed, provision of material about the summit and its participants to the media is one of the primary roles of the host country summit sites), but no such site has yet included scholarly materials or analyses of the summit process. These sites are not conceived as comprehensive or permanent sources of G7/G8 information. Therefore, they simplify the task of the G8 Information Centre without eroding its *raison d'être*.

G7/G8 Ministerial Meetings   The G8 Information Centre maintains a record of all known ministerial meetings that occur through the year in support of the summit process, with the resultant documentation.

Obtaining material for this portion of the site involves careful research. Ministerial meetings are not always well publicised, and neither are documents always issued from them.   In particular sherpa meetings (see Chapter 4 for an explanation of sherpa meetings) do not issue documents, and government officials much prefer that they are not publicised until after they have taken place, or indeed, until after the ensuing summit. While finance and foreign ministers' meetings may be announced ahead of time, most foreign ministers' and some finance ministers' meetings, again, do not issue statements.   Conversely, and with increasing frequency recently (presumably as it becomes easier to teleconference) statements are sometimes issued without any meeting. Furthermore, the regular G7/G8 ministerial meetings evolve and metamorphose over the years.   Some ministerial meetings, such as the Terrorism meetings, 1995–, have developed recently in response to the changing international climate. Others start as a G7 initiative, and evolve into something much broader, such as the Global Information Society, 1995–.   For such groups, the site includes all known information for the directly relevant time period, and links to further information at other sites where available. There are also a number of specialised working groups related to the G8, such as the Senior Experts' Group on Transnational Organized Crime ("Lyon Group").   Keeping track of these groups so they can be noted on the web site has involved careful research by the G8 Research Group.   And finally, the G8 Information Centre has chosen to include copies of the statements issued by the annual OECD Council Meetings at the ministerial level, because of their relevance to the G7/G8 process as outlined earlier.

The main sources used to track these various meetings for the web site are news releases on the web sites of relevant government ministries of G8 countries; Canadian and other G8 or EU government contacts; and the diplomacy calendars maintained online by various government and international bodies.

Scholarly publications and papers   A collection of roughly fifty scholarly papers is available on the site. This full-text collection includes Peter Hajnal's comprehensive *G7/G8 Bibliography* and the refereed journal of the G8 Research Group, *G7 Governance.*

Here, ironically because of the generosity of our own scholars, the challenge lies in maintaining a scholarly balance.   The site strives to offer as broad a critical perspective on the G7/G8 process as possible; however, it is easiest to obtain permission to mount these copyrighted materials from scholars affiliated with the G8 Research Group.

Research and teaching materials These materials include the G8 Research Group's annual country and issue analyses prepared for each summit; the proceedings of the group's annual conference, held just prior to the summit since 1996; the syllabi of relevant courses taught at the University of Toronto; and the prospectus of the Research Group.

G7/G8 News News materials at the site include the full text of *Financial Post* newspaper articles about the G7/G8; and during each summit, the G8 Research Group's daily *G8 Bulletin*, and links to other media sites' coverage of the summit.

Links to other G7/G8 related sites The G8 Information Centre provides lists of government sites, international organisation sites, and other sites of relevance to the G7/G8. As described, this list fluctuates from year to year, and expands each year at summit time.

Indexing and Searching of the Site

The site holds more than 2900 files, of which the large majority is text, rather than graphics. Altogether these files use roughly 50 megabytes of storage. The ability to search the site, then, is an important short cut to finding specific information, particularly for users who are not familiar with the site's organisation.

The site has been indexed for keyword searching; the search feature retrieves all page(s) containing all the chosen keywords. The user is offered the options of searching the site by keyword, country, year or subject. The year, country, and subject features allow the user to select from a list of any G7/G8 summit years, countries, or subjects, respectively. All pages containing the chosen term are then retrieved. Subject terms have been chosen from those in use in G7/G8 documents. It would be preferable to apply descriptive subject terms to the pages of the site, and to base the search retrieval on these terms, rather than providing searching based on simple keyword matches. This strategy would provide far more precise recall for search terms. However, pragmatism in the face of limited resources has meant that this cataloguing and the addition of the required cataloguing metatags to the site's documents have not yet been feasible.

Issues of Site Maintenance

The G8 Information Centre, like many other web sites, was built with limited staff resources; nevertheless, it is intended to serve as an enduring and comprehensive record of G7/G8 activity.   This combination of circumstances has dictated a number of decisions regarding construction and contents of the site.

Collection policy   In building any subject guide on the web, the site maintainer must choose whether to provide links to documents already mounted elsewhere, or to obtain and mount copies of these documents locally.   Wherever possible (that is, where copyright could be obtained or was not an issue) the G8 Information Centre has chosen to obtain or create local electronic copies.   While this may seem like a labour-intensive duplication of effort, it is ultimately the only way to ensure the continued availability of the material.   Thus far, the site has observed two exceptions: it has not sought to mirror other G7/G8 sites, such as government summit sites, because of the large duplication in content between these sites and the G8 Information Centre. Secondly, press articles on the summit process have not been mounted, with the exception of the site's collection of G7/G8-related articles from the *Financial Post*.   This decision has been driven by a combination of limited resources (most such articles appear at summit time, when all available resources are needed to keep up with the primary documentation) and the difficulty in obtaining copyright permission from the producers to mount such material.   Unfortunately, as discussed earlier, media articles on the G7/G8 almost always disappear shortly after each summit, because they are intended as a current information service only.   The ability to archive such articles at the G8 Information Centre site, particularly once they had been discarded from their originating sites, would seem to benefit all concerned.   For the researcher, the archives would provide a useful insight into past summits. For the media outlets, the archives would provide a useful, if modest, ongoing international exposure to their work.

Document formats   A second major decision in building such a site is the choice of format in which to mount the documents.   The documents can be fully prepared as web documents (that is, marked up in hypertext markup language, or HTML).   In this case, they can be indexed and made searchable, and they are accessible to any user with any web browser.   On the other hand, good HTML markup can be a relatively labour intensive, and therefore expensive, procedure.   At the inception of the site, in 1995, the only other viable option was to create graphical images (essentially digital photocopies) of pages. These had the drawbacks of being large, slow to retrieve, not searchable, and inaccessible altogether to some users, depending on their web browsers. The advent of Adobe Acrobat (PDF) as a widely accepted file format has made a far more attractive alternative, although again, some labour and expense remain in creating searchable and broadly accessible Acrobat documents. As a third option, web page editing software has advanced to the point where it is possible to quickly create at least marginally acceptable HTML from a variety of file formats.

The driving factors, then, for the G8 Information Centre in choosing file formats have been the size of the expected audience for the document under consideration; its size and native format; and its centrality to the G7/G8 process. Primary documents from summits and ministerial meetings are virtually always produced in HTML. However, other, less central documents have been handled differently. For example, the 1998 Employment Action Plans of the member countries, which arrived on paper, and were as much as 100 pages long, were scanned and mounted as image-based, non-indexed Acrobat files.

Acquiring the documents   A third issue has been how to obtain the source documents. The G8 Research Group has been present at each summit since 1988, and a web site representative has been present at each summit since the founding of the web site in 1995. The development of host country web sites in recent years might make this seem unnecessary. However, only by sending staff to each summit can the Group ensure that it obtains a full set of documents. Secondary documents such as press conference transcripts have sometimes been truncated when posted on the official summit sites, by, for example, omitting the questions taken at the end of the conference. For the ministerial documentation, the site relies for the most part on related web sites and government contacts, as discussed earlier, although occasionally, staff members are able to go to these meetings. While quality and availability of G7/G8 documents vary between ministry sites, they have proved increasingly reliable sources.

Users of the G8 Information Centre

Because it is the only comprehensive publicly available collection of G7/G8 materials, an analysis of the use of the G8 Information Centre is helpful to understanding the uses of G7/G8 documentation in general. Several sources of data are available for analysis. The web site use logs show how often each page on the site is requested. The site also receives questions via email from its users, and these questions cast a great deal of light on the users' interests. It should be noted that at this library-based web site, user privacy is a central concern. While aggregate statistics are collected to help in developing the site, data that could identify individual users or track individual usage of the site, such as email addresses and IP addresses of users' machines, are explicitly discarded.

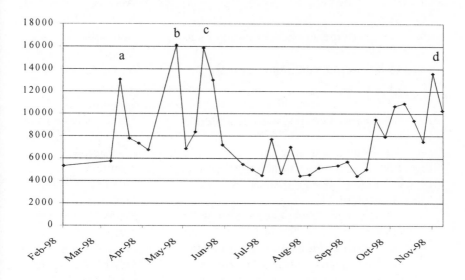

^a reason for spike unclear
^b Meeting of the OECD Council at Ministerial level
^c G8 Summit, Birmingham
^d Joint G7 leaders and G7 finance ministers' statements

Figure 11.1   Total Pages Requested from the G8 Information Centre, by Week

Most predictably, the site use varies seasonally with G7/G8 activity (see Figure 11.1). It peaks sharply each year at summit time; sizable increases in use also occur with the release of ministerial documents through the year. For example, the unusual joint statement by G7 leaders on the state of the world economy, which together with a statement by the G7 finance ministers, was released on 30 October, 1998, caused a flurry of site activity. Also, predictably, given the diffuse and specialised audience for the site, overall site usage is modest when compared to other local sites.

Table 11.1 Most Popular Thirty Pages at G8 Information Centre

	Page Title	Page Category
1.	Search by Keyword	Search
2.	G8 Centre Homepage	Homepage
3.	Search by Subject	Search
4.	What is the G7?	About G7/G8
5.	Search by Country	Search
6.	1998 Birmingham Summit Main Page	Summits
7.	What's New?	Search
8.	1998 Birmingham Summit Final Communiqué	Summits
9.	1996 Lyon Summit Delegations	Summits
10.	G8 Research Group Analytical Studies	G8 Research Group
11.	Search by Year	Search
12.	The Road to Birmingham	Ministerials
13.	List of Summits, chronological order	Summits
14.	G8-Related Government Sites	Other G7/G8 sites
15.	G8 Bulletin Homepage	News
16.	G8 Ministerial and Other Meetings	Ministerials
17.	G8 Financial Post Record	News
18.	G8 Scholarly Publications and Papers	Scholarly materials
19.	G8-Related International Organizations	Other G7/G8 sites
20.	G8 Research Group Annual Conference	G8 Research Group
21.	1998 Summit Report of G7 Finance	Summits
22.	G8 Research at the University of Toronto	G8 Research Group
23.	*G7 Governance* Journal	Scholarly materials
24.	G8 Information Centre Homepage, French	Translation
25.	About the G8 Research Group	G8 Research Group
26.	1996 Lyon Summit Main Page	Summits
27.	G7/8 Bibliography Main Page (P. Hajnal)	Scholarly materials
28.	G8 Path: Ministerial and Other Meetings	Ministerials
29.	G8-Related Nongovernmental Sites	Other G7/G8 sites
30.	40 Points: Recommendations by Senior Experts on Transnational Organized Crime, April 1996	Ministerials

To analyse the use of the site more closely, the site's pages were assigned to nine broad subject categories, reflecting its expected uses: summits, ministerial meetings, news, scholarly materials, introductory materials, other G7/G8 sites, G8 Research Group materials site searching, and translations. The top thirty most requested pages in 1998, shown in Table 11.1, show pages from all these categories, with a preponderance of primary document pages (summit and ministerial meetings pages).

Looking a little deeper, Figure 11.2 shows what proportion of requests came from each subject category, amongst the top 250 pages. Figure 11.3 shows the number of pages, as a percentage, of each subject category in the top 250 pages. Comparing the relative size of each subject group in these two figures gives an idea of how heavily each group of pages is used, in relation to its size. This sheds light on the relative value of each subject group to the user community.

It is immediately striking that the search function is a very popular choice of navigation for the users of this large and complex site. This suggests that it would be justifiable to invest in refining the search tools. It is also no small solace to the site's maintainer that the number of favourable comments and absence of negative comments received from users suggest that the search function is chosen by preference rather than necessity!

The page containing introductory material about the G7/G8 (What is the G7/G8?) is very popular. As people increasingly turn to the web as a tool for basic fact finding, the G8 Information Centre has an important role to play in providing introductory material about the G7/G8 process.

G8 primary documentation (summit and ministerial documents), when grouped together, form the most heavily used content pages, illustrating the site's usefulness as a central clearinghouse of all G7/G8 information. Of course, the current year's summit pages are the most heavily used, but interestingly, certain older documents are also frequently sought. For example, and perhaps puzzlingly, the list of delegates to the 1996 summit was the ninth most popular page on the site in 1998. Other important documents, such as the April 1996 Senior Experts Group on Transnational Crime Report to the G7 Heads (the "40 Points" document), are also heavily used. And referring once again to Figure 11.1, it is notable that use peaks almost as heavily for the release of ministerial documents as it does for the far more heavily publicised annual summit. This underlines the site's appeal as a source of G7/G8 documentation at times when no other single-purpose site is available.

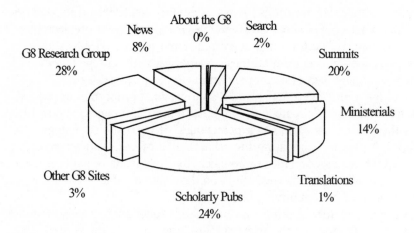

Figure 11.2 Top 250 Pages: Subject Category by Proportion of Total, 1998

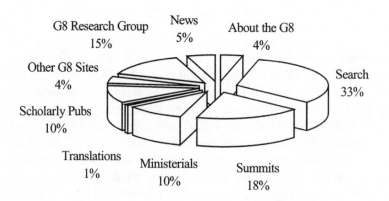

Figure 11.3 Top 250 Pages: Subject Category by Proportion of Use, 1998

A great deal of effort is invested in making scholarly and research materials available on the site, and their usefulness is underscored by their substantial proportion of use. The G8 Research Group's evaluations of country objectives and issues at each summit are particularly popular; there is a demonstrated desire for analysis of the G7/G8 process as it happens. *G7 Governance*, the refereed journal of the G8 Research Group, is also steadily popular; its main page is twenty-fifth on the list of most requested documents.

Brief news bulletins about the summit process are also well received; both the Research Group's *G8 Bulletin*, produced at the summit site, and the *Financial Post* G7/G8 articles are steadily used.

User questions cast another light on the use of the documentation: they call attention to materials that are difficult to find, issues that are hard to understand, and documents that are eagerly awaited. Questions are tracked by broad category of user, country of user, and broad category of question asked. A record of all questions asked (with identifiers removed) is also kept.

Users' affiliations (government, media, business, non-governmental organisation, or academic) cannot always be determined. As Figure 11.4 illustrates, the business community is the largest identifiable user group sending email questions, followed closely by academic users, ranging from public school students to professors. Interestingly, users from government organisations also ask a significant proportion of the questions. In the short gap between the release of G7/G8 ministerial documents and their availability on the web site, there is a noticeable spike in email to the site, of users from government organisations and international organisations seeking the new document.

Figure 11.5 displays a breakdown of email questions by broad subject category. As is usual for a web site, a significant proportion (18%) of the email questions received is not relevant to the subject matter of the site. A further 18% of users are seeking basic information about the purpose, history and membership of the G7/G8. Overall, the largest group of questions (23%) relates to current and upcoming G7/G8 activities, again demonstrating the user community's need for a central warehouse for G7/G8 information. A much smaller group of users (5%) sends fairly involved research questions, usually relating to compliance or to the economies of member countries. It is interesting to contrast this relatively low figure to the substantial use of the site's scholarly pages (Figures 11.2 and 11.3). The research community is fairly self-reliant in its information seeking, but still demonstrates an interest in the scholarly materials available on the site.

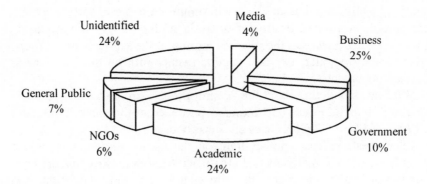

Figure 11.4 Summary of Email Questions by User Category, 1998

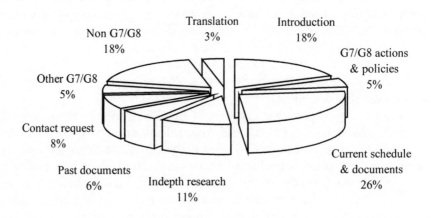

Figure 11.5 Summary of Email Questions by Subject Category, 1998

Finally, Table 11.2 tabulates the number of questions received by country of sender. While more than half of all email correspondents come from Canada and the United States, questions have been received from thirty-four countries worldwide, including seventeen countries from outside the European Union.

Table 11.2   Summary of Email Questions Received by Country, 1998

Country	Count	Country	Count
USA	59	Thailand	2
Unknown*	29	Bulgaria	1
Canada	23	Finland	1
United Kingdom	9	Ireland	1
Belgium	6	Italy	1
Germany	4	Japan	1
Switzerland	4	Jordan	1
Brazil	3	Norway	1
France	3	Pakistan	1
Netherlands	3	Peru	1
Australia	2	Russia	1
Austria	2	South Africa	1
Chile	2	South Korea	1
India	2	Spain	1
Mexico	2	Sweden	1
Nigeria	2	Taiwan	1
Singapore	2	Trinidad	1

*All these email addresses were in the .com domain, and therefore very likely American or Canadian.

In summary, the use made of the G8 Information Centre demonstrates a modest but worldwide appetite for many types of information about the G7/G8. All types of G7/G8 documentation at the G8 Information Centre are well used, from the primary documentation to the news articles reporting the process, to analysis and review of the process and scholarly work on the subject. In particular, there is a need for quick centralised access to the primary documents. As more people use the internet as a basic research tool, there is also a growing need for introductory material online about this complex forum. While a formal G7/G8 secretariat does not exist, (and such a secretariat might seem antithetical to the nature of the group), a number of web sites are important in making G7/G8 documentation available.   Currently, the University of Toronto G8 Information Centre is the only third-party clearinghouse for G7/G8 information, and as such it plays a vital role in providing a source of G8 documentation, and ensuring its ongoing availability.

Note

1 New Economics Foundation. NEF - TOES 98: The Economic Summit. Hp 1998. Web Document. Available: http://sosig.ac.uk/NewEconomics/sc.htm, 22 November, 1998.

12 Conclusion

The G7/G8 system, now twenty-four years old, is a remarkable international forum and institution which has evolved in response to and in anticipation of economic, political, and other global developments. It has increased its institutional breadth by establishing regular and *ad hoc* ministerial meetings in an ever-greater variety of portfolios as well as through working groups and expert groups. It has widened its scope beyond economics by taking on more and more issues of global importance. Although many observers, with some justification, consider the G7/G8 unrepresentative, it has, by integrating Russia and by associating several other countries with some activities, started to become somewhat more representative or at any rate less unrepresentative. Those who lament the bureaucratisation of the institution may take a modicum of consolation from recent efforts to return the summits to the early ideal (if not reality) of relative simplicity and informality, especially with the 1998 Birmingham Summit which its British host organised as a leaders-only summit.

Critics have characterised the G7/G8 as uneven in delivering on its commitments. Although this is so, it is nonetheless true that the G7/G8 has been able to secure a significant degree of compliance from its members on a number of issues. Moreover, the regular annual meetings–combined with the group's relative informality and relative lack of bureaucracy–have allowed the G7/G8 leaders to get to know one another very well and to understand one another's domestic political and economic constraints; this is not merely a political intangible but a practical aid to policy co-ordination.

Questions about the effectiveness of the G7/G8 in changing the behaviour of non-member states and multilateral institutions are more problematic, as is the institution's ability to improve broader, global conditions. Yet, the G7/G8 remains a crucial actor on the world scene, relevant beyond the borders of its member states.

The documentation of the G7/G8 system, in all its variety and dynamism, is the primary source of information about that institution and, beyond the G7/G8, a very important source on vital issues. It is a potentially rich mine of political, economic and historical data, although it calls for a fair amount of interpretation to get beyond its jargon and somewhat repetitive nature. For many years, proliferating documentation has been a serious concern. The 1998 Birmingham G8 Summit issued fewer documents than its recent predecessors, even when one also considers the leaders' documents still released at the G7 heads' level. This reduction in volume, however, was more than offset by the proliferating output of the joint meeting of G7/G8 finance and foreign ministers in London on 8-9 May 1998. This downward shift of the workload and documentation from the leaders to their ministers is a welcome new development because it allows the leaders to concentrate on issues worthy of their time and attention. It is, moreover, a reflection of greater transparency in the work of the G7/G8. By having more G7/G8 documents available, the academic community, the media and the public will be better informed and in a better position to judge the work of the G7/G8, thereby increasing the legitimacy of this very important institution.

The major primary documentation, however, is insufficient by itself. The many press conferences and briefings that are held throughout the summits provide each summit country the opportunity to present its own initiatives and positions to the news media in a manner that shows each in the best possible light internationally as well as back home. Media personnel, excluded from the actual meetings of leaders and ministers, must rely on briefings and press conferences. Even though they tend to be self-serving, news conferences allow journalists to ask probing questions of officials and other spokesmen of the summit countries and the EU, and answers to such questions can reveal additional information or insight.

Looking beyond the documents and news conference transcripts, one must also be aware of complementary sources of information, notably national archives of heads of state or government and ministerial archives, as well as writings about the G7/G8 and related issues, especially the writings of participants. And, in this technological age, the internet is not merely another medium of information about this topic; it is the easiest and often the only way to gain access to a significant portion of the material.

How will the G7/G8 evolve? The rationale continues for both the G7 and the G8. A powerful G3 of the US, Germany and Japan has been reported to exist as well, playing an important crisis-management role; for example, in the Indonesian crisis of 1997/98. As financial and other economic issues once again take centre stage in response to the global financial turmoil of the second half of 1998–and these matters remain primarily in the purview of the G7, not the G8–will the G8 decline in importance? What are the implications of this multiple configuration of the G7/G8? Will the several configurations all be formalised in the future, or, on the contrary, will the most powerful actors in the group make the G3 even less formal, for example by using technology such as teleconferencing instead of face-to-face meetings? If so, there is need for further research into and analysis of the implications for policy-making and institution-building. The evolving role of the G7/G8 will continue to occupy the attention of the academic community, government officials and the news media.

The G7/G8 faces great challenges and opportunities to improve its composition, methods and effectiveness. In the post-Cold War world, the challenges are more diffuse and diverse than they were earlier. The G7/G8–and especially the G7 which not only survives but thrives alongside the G8–has shown considerable flexibility in response to and in anticipation of world developments. It must become even more flexible and more representative; in other words, it must transform itself significantly if it is to rise to the challenges of the future.

G7/G8 Bibliography

List of monographs, articles in periodicals (journals and magazines but generally not newspapers except for analytical articles by summit personalities or reports of reference value), and governmental and international organisation publications. Items covered deal entirely or partly with the G7/G8 or with G7/G8-related issues.

Methodological note This bibliography is based on searches of the catalogues and bibliographic databases of the Joint Library of the World Bank and the International Monetary Fund, Harvard University libraries, the University of Toronto Library, *Business Abstracts*, *PAIS International*, *ABI/Inform* and various other databases and printed indexes and bibliographies. Wherever possible, items were inspected prior to inclusion in the bibliography.

Note on internet addresses Web sites tend to appear, change or disappear, often without warning. Addresses cited in this bibliography were accurate and active at the time of writing (early December 1998).

Books, Shorter Writings, and Publications in Series

Ardouin, Estelle. *Sherpas et sommets des 7* (Sherpas and Summits of the 7). Lyon: Institut d'Etudes Politiques, 1996. [Computer file] URL: http://iep.univ-lyon2.fr/ETU/sherpa.html.

Armstrong of Ilminster, Robert Temple. *Economic Summits: A British Perspective*. Bissell Paper No. 4. Toronto: University of Toronto, Centre for International Studies, 1988. Also available as computer file. URL: www.library.utoronto.ca/www/g7/armtitl.htm.

Armstrong of Ilminster, Robert Temple. *Summits: A Sherpa's Eye View*. Montague Burton Lecture on International Relations, No. 44. Leeds, Eng.: University of Leeds, 1992.

Artis, Michael J., Zenon G. Kontolemis, and Denise R. Osbom. *Classical Business Cycles for G-7 and European Countries*. Discussion Paper Series, No. 1137. London: Centre for Economic Policy Research, 1995.

Artis, Michael J., and Sylvia Ostry. *International Economic Policy Coordination*. Chatham House Papers, Vol. 30. London and New York: Routledge & Kegan Paul, 1986.

Aschauer, David Alan. *Back of the G-7 Pack: Public Investment and Productivity Growth in the Group of Seven*. Working Paper Series, WP-89-13: Macro Economic Issues. [Chicago, Ill.]: Federal Reserve Bank of Chicago, 1989.

Ash, Ahmad, and others. *Formal and Informal Investment Barriers in the G-7 Countries*. By Ahmad Ash. Occasional Paper, No. 1, Vols. 1-2. Ottawa: Industry Canada, 1994.

Attali, Jacques. *Verbatim*. Paris: Fayard, 1993-1995. [Tome 1: Chronique des années 1981-1986; Tome 2: Chronique des années 1986-1988; Tome 3: Chronique des années 1988-1991.]

Baker, James A. *The Politics of Diplomacy: Revolution, War, and Peace, 1989-1992*. New York: G.B. Putnam's Sons, 1995.

Barnes, James N. *Promises, Promises! A Review: G-7 Economic Summit Declarations on Environment and Development*. [S.l.:] Friends of the Earth, 1994.

Barrell, Ray, and Simon Wren-Lewis. *Fundamental Equilibrium Exchange Rates for the G-7*. Centre for Economic Policy Research, Discussion Paper Series, No. 323. London: National Institute of Economic and Social Research, 1989.

Bayne, Nicholas. "History of the G7 Summit: The Importance of American Leadership". Keynote address delivered at a conference "Explaining Summit Success: Prospects for the Denver Summit of the Eight", sponsored by the University of Colorado at Denver and the Metropolitan State College of Denver in cooperation with the University of Toronto G7 Research Group, Denver, Colorado, June 19, 1997. [Computer file] URL: www.library.utoronto.ca/www/g7/annual/bayneg8.htm.

Bayne, Nicholas. *Impressions of the Denver Summit*. Toronto: University of Toronto G7 Research Group, 22 June 1997. [Computer file] URL: www.library.utoronto.ca/www/g7/evaluations/forepol.htm.

Beccarello, Massimo. *Time Series Analysis of Market Power: Evidence from G-7 Manufacturing*. Papers, No. 312. London: Queen Mary and Westfield College, University of London, Dept. of Economics, 1994.

Becher, Klaus, and others. *The Munich Summit: Analyses by the Research Institute, German Society for Foreign Affairs [Deutsche Gesellschaft für Auswärtige Politik]*. Bonn: Inter Nationes, 1992.

Bergsten, C. Fred, and C. Randall Henning. *Global Economic Leadership and the Group of Seven*. Washington, D.C.: Institute for International Economics, 1996.

Berridge, G. R. *Diplomacy: Theory and Practice*. London: Prentice Hall/Harvester Wheatsheaf, 1995.

Blommestein, Hans J., ed. *The Reality of International Economic Policy Coordination*. Contributions to Economic Analysis, No. 199. Amsterdam; New York; Oxford; Tokyo: North- Holland, 1991.

Board Directors and Corporate Governance: Trends in the G7 Countries over the Next Ten Years: Executive Report. Prepared for Russell Reynolds Associates, Price Waterhouse, Goldman Sachs International Ltd. [and] Gibson, Dunn & Crutcher [by] Oxford Analytica Limited. Oxford: Oxford Analytica, 1992.

Bortoli, Georges. *La cour des grands: les coulisses des sommets* (The Court of the Great: The Corridors of the Summits). Paris: Perrin, 1991.

Brzezinski, Zbigniew. *Power and Principle: Memoirs of the National Security Adviser, 1977-1981*. New York: Farrar Straus Giroux, 1983.

Ch`ien, Kuo-jung. *Hsi fang ch`i kuo kao feng hui i yü kuo chi ching chi cheng ts`e hsieh t`iao = The Summit and the Policy Coordination*. Shen-yang shih: Liao-ning ta hsüeh ch`u pan she, 1992. [Introduction (abstract) also in English.]

Chossudovsky, Michel. "Destroying National Currencies". Ottawa, 1997. [Computer file] URL: www.interlog.com/~cjazz/chossd.htm, pp. 30-31.

Chossudovsky, Michel. "Financial Warfare". Ottawa, 21 September 1998. [Computer file] URL: www.interlog.com/~cjazz/chossd.htm, pp. 1-8.

Chossudovsky, Michel. "The Global Financial Crisis". Ottawa, 20 January 1998. [Computer file] URL: www.interlog.com/~cjazz/chossd.htm, pp. 9-16.

Chossudovsky, Michel. "The G7 Policy Agenda Creates Global Poverty". Ottawa, 13 June 1995. [Computer file] URL: www.interlog.com/~cjazz/chossd.htm, pp. 16-23.

Chossudovsky, Michel. "The G7 'Solution' To The Global Financial Crisis: A Marshall Plan For Creditors And Speculators". [Computer file] Ottawa, 3 December 1998. URL: http://x9.dejanews.com/getdoc.xp?AN=418389663&CONTEXT= 912874705.1431568471&h.

Clausen, A. W.   "Upcoming Versailles Summit: Keeping the Global Economy Open".   Remarks before the Commercial Club, Chicago, May 21, 1982. Unpublished.

Cooper, Richard N., ed.   *Can Nations Agree?   Issues in International Economic Cooperation.*   Studies in International Economics. Washington, D. C.: Brookings Institution, 1989.

Cooper, Shelley. *Cross-Border Savings Flows and Capital Mobility in the G7 Economies.*   Discussion Paper, No. 54; Technical Series. London: Bank of England, 1991.

Daniels, Joseph P.   *The Meaning and Reliability of Economic Summit Undertakings, 1975-1989.* New York; London: Garland Publishing, 1993.

Daniels, Joseph P., and Eleonore Kokotsis.   "Summit Compliance: Are Summit Commitments Meaningful?"   Remarks delivered at a conference "Explaining Summit Success: Prospects for the Denver Summit of the Eight", sponsored by the University of Colorado at Denver and the Metropolitan State College of Denver in cooperation with the University of Toronto G7 Research Group, Denver, Colorado, June 19, 1997. [Computer file] URL: www.library.utoronto.ca/www/g7/annual/daniels.htm.

De Ménil, Georges. *Les Sommets économiques: les politiques nationales à l'heure de l'interdépendance* (Economic Summits: National Policies at the Time of Interdependence). Paris: Economica, 1983.

De Ménil, Georges, and Anthony M. Solomon. *Economic Summitry.* New York: Council on Foreign Relations, 1983.

Dimock, W. Blair. *The Benefits of Teamplay: Italy and the Seven Power Summits.* Country Study No. 5. Toronto: University of Toronto, Centre for International Studies, 1989. Also available as computer file. URL: www.library.utoronto.ca/www/g7/scholar/dimock/dimcon.htm.

DiRita, Lawrence T., and Bryan T. Johnson. *An Agenda for Leadership: The G-7 Summit in Naples.* Heritage Talking Points. Washington, D.C.: Heritage Foundation, [1994].

Dobson, Wendy. *Economic Policy Coordination: Requiem or Prologue?* Policy Analyses in International Economics, Vol. 30. Washington, D. C.: Institute for International Economics, 1991.

Dornbusch, Rüdiger. *World Economic Problems for the Summit: Co-ordination, Debt and the Exchange Rate System.* Bissell Paper No. 6. Toronto: University of Toronto, Centre for International Studies, 1988. Also available as computer file. URL: www.library.utoronto.ca/www/g7/scholar/dornbusch/dorncont.htm.

Eatwell, John. *Disguised Unemployment: The G7 Experience.* Annual Lecture. Cambridge: Centre for International Business Studies, South Bank University Business School, Trinity College, 1995. Also issued as Discussion Papers, No. 106. Geneva: United Nations Conference on Trade and Development, 1995.

The Economic Summit: A Pictorial History of the Economic Summits of Industrialized Nations, 1975-1990. Houston, Texas: Economic Summit of Industrialized Nations in Cooperation with the Houston Economic Summit Host Committee, 1990.

Ekins, Paul, ed. *The Living Economy: A New Economics in the Making.* London; New York: Routledge & Kegan Paul, 1986. [Thirty-nine essays based on The Other Economic Summit.]

Les enjeux du g7: regards croisés sur la mondialisation. Edited by Denis Samuel-Lajeunesse and Michel Foucher. Paris: Economica, 1997.

Farrow, Maureen. *The Toronto Economic Summit: Great Expectations Need To Be Tempered with Realism.* Commentary, No. 16. Toronto: C. D. Howe Institute, 1988.

Favier, Pierre, and Michel Martin-Roland. *La décennie Mitterrand*. Paris: Seuil, 1990-91. 3 vols.

The Financial System under Stress: An Architecture for the World Economy. Edited by Marc Uzan. New York: Routledge, 1996.

Fowler, Henry H., and W. Randolph Burgess. *Harmonizing Economic Policy: Summit Meetings and Collective Leadership; Report of the Atlantic Council's Working Group on Economic Policy*. Atlantic Council of the United States Policy Papers. Boulder, Co.: Westview Press, 1977.

Funabashi, Yoichi. *Managing the Dollar: From the Plaza to the Louvre*. Washington, D. C.: Institute for International Economics, 1988.

Funabashi, Yoichi. *Samitto no shiso* (Philosophy of the Summits). Tokyo: Asahi Shinbunsha, 1980.

Funabashi, Yoichi. *Samittokurashi* (Summitocracy). Tokyo: Asahi Shinbunsha, 1991.

G7: Napoli Summit '94: The Record, Key Players, Preliminaries and Expectations; Data. Roma: Agenzia ANSA, 1994.

Gerlach, Stefan, and Frank Smets. *Monetary Transmission Mechanism: Evidence from the G-7 Countries*. Discussion Paper Series, No. 1219. London: Centre for Economic Policy Research, 1995.

Gilmore, William C., ed. *International Efforts to Combat Money Laundering*. Cambridge International Documents Series, Vol. 4. Cambridge: Grotius Publications in association with the Commonwealth Secretariat, 1992.

Giscard d'Estaing, Valéry. *Le pouvoir et la vie*. (*Power and Life*). [s.l.:] Compagnie 12, 1988.

Gotlieb, Allan. *Canada and the Economic Summits: Power and Responsibility*. Bissell Paper No. 1. Toronto: University of Toronto, Centre for International Studies, 1987. Also available as computer file. URL: www.library.utoronto.ca/www/g7/scholar/gotcont.htm.

Group of Thirty. *The Summit Process and Collective Security: Future Responsibility Sharing; A Study Group Report*. Washington, D. C.: Group of Thirty, 1991.

Guth, Wilfried, moderator. *Economic Policy Coordination; Proceedings of an International Seminar Held In Hamburg* [May 5-7, 1988]. Washington, D. C.: International Monetary Fund; Hamburg: HWWA Institut für Wirtschaftsforschung, 1988.

Hagemann, Helmut. *Not Out of the Woods Yet: The Scope of the G-7 Initiative for a Pilot Program for the Conservation of the Brazilian*

Rainforests. Forschungen zu Lateinamerika, Bd. 32. Saabrücken : Verlag für Entwicklungspolitik Breitenbach, 1994.

Hainsworth, Susan. *Coming of Age: The European Community and the Economic Summit*. Country Study No. 7. Toronto: University of Toronto, Centre for International Studies, 1990. Also available as computer file. URL: www.library.utoronto.ca/www/g7/biscon.htm.

Hajnal, Peter I., comp. and ed. *The Seven-Power Summit: Documents from the Summits of Industrialized Countries, 1975-1989*. With an introduction by John J. Kirton. Millwood, N.Y.: Kraus International Publications, 1989.

Hajnal, Peter I., comp. and ed. *The Seven-Power Summit: Documents from the Summits of Industrialized Countries; Supplement: Documents from the 1990 Summit*. With an introduction by John J. Kirton. Millwood, N.Y.: Kraus International Publications, 1991.

The Halifax G-7 Summit: Issues on the Table. Edited by Sylvia Ostry and Gilbert R. Wynham. Halifax: Centre for Foreign Policy Studies, Dalhousie University, 1995.

The Halifax Initiative: First Annual G7 Report Card on Bretton Woods Reform: Report on the Commitments Made by the G7 Leaders at the Halifax Summit, June 1995. Ottawa: Canadian Coalition for Global Economic Democracy, 1996.

Heeney, Timothy. *Canadian Foreign Policy and the Seven Power Summits*. Country Study No. 1. Toronto: University of Toronto, Centre for International Studies, 1988. Also available as computer file. URL: www.library.utoronto.ca/www/g7/heentoc.htm.

Hein, John. *From Summit to Summit: Policymaking in an Interdependent World*. Conference Board Report No. 774. New York: The Conference Board, 1980.

Heiwa Anzen Hosho Kenkyujo (Tokyo, Japan). *After the Collapse: G-7 Policy toward Russia and the C.I.S.* RIPS Special Report. Tokyo: Research Institute for Peace and Security, [1994].

Hellmann, Rainer. *Weltwirtschaftsgipfel Wozu?* (Whither Economic Summits?) Baden-Baden: Nomos Verlagsgesellschaft, 1982.

Henning, C. Randall. "International Monetary Policymaking within the Countries of the Group of 5". Paper presented at the Annual Meeting of the American Political Science Association, San Francisco, August 29-September 2, 1990. Unpublished.

Henning, C. Randall. *Macroeconomic Diplomacy in the 1980s: Domestic Politics and International Conflict among the United States, Japan,*

---

and Europe. Atlantic Paper No. 65. London; New York: Croom Helm for the Atlantic Institute for International Affairs, 1987.

Henrikson, A. K. "US-Japanese Cooperation, the 'Summit Alliance' (G-7) and the New World Order". Address to the Policy Study Group, Tokyo, March 16, 1993. Unpublished.

Hibbs, Mark [Center for War, Peace, and the News Media, New York University, Department of Journalism and Mass Communication]. *The G-7 Summit on Nuclear Safety and Security: A Summit Primer*. The Global Reporting Network, Issue Brief, No. 12. Lyon: Institut d'Etudes Politiques, 1996. [Computer file] URL: www.library.utoronto.ca/www/g7/moscou-i.htm.

Hodges, Michael R., John J. Kirton, and Joseph P. Daniels, eds. *The G8: Its Role in the New Millennium*. Aldershot; Brookfield, MA; Singapore; Sydney: Ashgate, forthcoming, 1999.

Hoehmann, Hans-Hermann, and Christian Meier. *Zwischen Neapal und Halifax: Die G7, Russland und die Ukraine vor und auf dem "Gipfel der Bescheidenheit"* (Between Naples and Halifax: The G7, Russia and Ukraine before and at the "Modest Summit". Berichte des Bundesinstituts für Ostwissenschaftliche und Internationale Studien, 0435-7183; 44-1995. Köln: Bundesinstitut für Ostwissenschaftliche und Internationale Studien, 1995.

Holmes, John W., and John J. Kirton, eds. *Canada and the New Internationalism*. Toronto: Canadian Institute of International Affairs, and University of Toronto, Centre for International Studies, 1988.

Hornung, Robert. *Sharing Economic Responsibility: The United States and the Seven Power Summits*. Country Study No. 4. Toronto: University of Toronto, Centre for International Studies, 1989. Also available as computer file. URL: www.library.utoronto.ca/www/g7/scholar/hornung/horcon.htm.

Hurd, Douglas. *The Shape of Ice*. London: Little, Brown, 1998.

Ingham, Graham, ed. *Employability and Exclusion: What Governments Can Do*. Conference Volume: A Major One Day Conference Hosted by the Centre for Economic Performance and the London School of Economics on 6 May 1998. London: Centre for Economic Performance, London School of Economics and Political Science, 1998.

International Economic Cooperation. Edited and with an Introduction by Martin Feldstein. A National Bureau of Economic Research Conference Report. Chicago: University of Chicago Press, 1988.

International People's Tribunal To Judge the G-7, 1993, Tokyo, Japan. *The People vs. Global Capital: The G-7, TNCs, SAPs, and Human Rights: Report of the International People's Tribunal To Judge the G-7, Tokyo, July 1993.* Tokyo: Pacific Asia Resource Center, 1994.

International Policy Coordination and Exchange Rate Fluctuations. Edited by William H. Branson, Jacob A. Frenkel, and Morris Goldstein. A National Bureau of Economic Research Conference Report. Chicago: University of Chicago Press, 1990.

Istituto Affari Internazionali. *Economic Summits, 1975-1986: Declarations.* Isola San Giorgio, Italy: Fondazione Cini, 1987.

"Jobs, Crime and Money: Challenges for the G8 Summit in 1998: Conference at the Plaisterers' Hall, London, 13 May 1998". London: Clifford Chance; London School of Economics and Political Science; G8 Research Group, 1998. Unpublished.

Kaiser, Karl; Winston Lord; Thierry De Montbrial; and David David. *Western Security: What Has Changed? What Should Be Done?* [New York:] Council on Foreign Relations; [London: Royal Institute of International Affairs,] 1981.

Kenen, Peter B., ed. *From Halifax to Lyons: What Has Been Done about Crisis Management?* Essays in International Finance, No. 200. Princeton: Dept. of Economics, International Finance Section, Princeton University, 1996.

Kenen, Peter B., ed. *From Rambouillet to Versailles: A Symposium.* Essays in International Finance, No. 149. Princeton: Dept. of Economics, International Finance Section, Princeton University, 1982.

Kirton, John J. "Canada, the G7 and the Denver Summit of the Eight: Implications for Asia and Taiwan". Based on a paper prepared for the conference Canada-Taiwan Relations in the 1990's, Department of Diplomacy, National Chengchi University, Taipei, Taiwan, 13-16 November 1997. [Computer file] URL: www.library.utoronto.ca/www/g7/scholar/taicon.htm.

Kirton, John J. "Contemporary Concert Diplomacy: The Seven-Power Summit and the Management of International Order". Paper prepared for the annual meeting of the International Studies Association and the British International Studies Association,

London, March 29-April 1, 1989. Unpublished in print. URL: www.library.utoronto.ca/www/g7/kirtitl.htm.

Kobayashi, Tomohiko. *The Japanese Perspective on the Toronto Economic Summit and the Uruguay Round*. Bissell Paper No. 8. Toronto: University of Toronto, Centre for International Studies, 1988. Also available as computer file. URL: www.library.utoronto.ca/www/g7/scholar/kobatitl.htm.

Kokotsis, Eleonore. *National Compliance with G7 Environment and Development Commitments, 1988-1995*. Ph.D. dissertation. Toronto: University of Toronto, 1998. Unpublished.

Kokotsis, Eleonore. *Promises Kept*. New York; London: Garland Publishing, forthcoming, 1999.

Kokotsis, Eleonore, and John J. Kirton. "National Compliance with Environmental Regimes: The Case of the G7, 1988-1995". Paper prepared for the annual convention of the International Studies Association, Toronto, March 18-22, 1997. Unpublished.

Labohm, Hans H. J. *G-7 Economic Summits: A View from the Lowlands*. The Hague: Netherlands Institute of International Relations Clingendael, 1993.

Lamy, Pascal. *The Economic Summit and the European Community*. Bissell Paper No. 4. Toronto: University of Toronto, Centre for International Studies, 1988. Also available as computer file. URL: www.library.utoronto.ca/www/g7/scholar/lamtitl.htm.

Lawson, Nigel. *The View from No. 11: Memoirs of a Tory Radical*. London; New York: Bantam Press, 1992.

Lee, Kevin C. *Economic Fluctuations in a Model of Output Growth in the G7 Economies, 1960-1991*. Department of Applied Economics Working Paper, No. 9409. Cambridge, England: University of Cambridge, Dept. of Applied Economics, May 1994.

Lieberman, Sima. *The Economic and Political Roots of the New Protectionism*. Totowa, N. J.: Rowman & Littlefield, 1988.

Managing the World Economy: Fifty Years after Bretton Woods. Edited by Peter B. Kenen. Washington, D.C.: Institute for International Economics, 1994.

Martiri, Gail. *The Right Kind of Club: Britain and the Seven Power Summit*. Country Study No. 8. Toronto: University of Toronto, Centre for International Studies, 1991. Unpublished.

McMillan, Charles. *Comparing Canadian and Japanese Approaches to the Seven Power Summit*. Bissell Paper No. 2. Toronto: University of

Toronto, Centre for International Studies, 1988. Also available as computer file. URL: www.library.utoronto.ca/www/g7/mcmtitl.htm.

Merlini, Cesare, ed. *Economic Summits and Western Decision-Making.* London: Croom Helm; New York: St. Martin's Press in association with the European Institute of Public Administration, 1984.

Merlini, Cesare, ed. *I Vertici: Cooperazione e Competizione tra Paesi Occidentali* (The Summits: Cooperation and Competition Among the Western Countries). Rome: ADN Kronos, 1985.

Il Mondo a Napoli: I Preparativi, l'Accoglienza, i Fatti, le Curiosità del G7 = The World Gathers In Naples: Preparations, Welcome, Events, Curiosities of "G7". Milano: G. Mondadori, 1994.

Moving Beyond Assistance: Final Report of the IEWS Task Force on Western Assistance to Transition in the Czech and Slovak Federal Republic, Hungary and Poland. Rev. ed. By Krzysztof Ners. New York; Prague; Štiřín: Institute for EastWest Studies, European Studies Center, 1992.

Munich G-7 Summit, 6-8 July 1992 = Sommet économique de Munich = Wirtschaftsgipfel München: de la morosité constatée à la reprise souhaitée de l'économie. Compiled by Tristan Mage. Paris: T. Mage, 1992. 4 vols. (Vol. 4: table of contents.)

The 1991 Envirosummit: A Critical View of the Environmental Performance of the G7 Governments. Produced by G7 environmental groups led by Friends of the Earth International, World Wide Fund for Nature, and the Environmental Defense Fund. London: Friends of the Earth, 1991.

Ortona, Egidio. *The Problem of International Consultations: Report of the Trilateral Task Force on Consultative Procedures to the Trilateral Commission.* Egidio Ortona, J. Robert Schaetzel, and Nobuhiko Ushiba, rapporteurs. The Triangle Papers, Vol. 12. New York: Trilateral Commission, 1976.

Ostry, Sylvia. *Summitry: The Medium and the Message.* Bissell Paper No. 3. Toronto: University of Toronto, Centre for International Studies, 1988. Also available as computer file. URL: www.library.utoronto.ca/www/g7/med_tab.htm.

Owen, David; Zbigniew Brzezinski; and Saburo Okita. *Democracy Must Work: A Trilateral Agenda for the Decade; A Task Force Report of the Trilateral Commission.* The Triangle Papers, 28. New York; London: New York University Press, 1984.

Oxenstierna, Rosario F., ed. *The 1992 Group of Seven Summit and Its Impact on the Middle East.* Contemporary Strategic Issues in the Arab Gulf. London: Gulf Centre for Strategic Studies, 1993.

Pauly, Louis W. *Who Elected the Bankers? Surveillance and Control in the World Economy.* Ithaca; London: Cornell University Press, 1997.

The Political Economy of International Co-operation. Edited by Paolo Guerrieri and Pier Carlo Padoan. London; New York; Sydney: Croom Helm, 1988.

Pons, Michael. *West German Foreign Policy and the Seven Power Summits.* Country Study No. 2. Toronto: University of Toronto, Centre for International Studies, 1988. Also available as computer file. URL: www.library.utoronto.ca/www/g7/scholar/pons/poncont.htm.

Public Opinion in the "S8" Countries on Key Issues at the Start of the US Hosted Summit. [Toronto:] Angus Reid Group, June 20, 1997.

Putnam, Robert D., and C. Randall Henning. *The Bonn Summit of 1978: How Does International Economic Policy Coordination Actually Work?* Brookings Discussion Papers in International Economics, No. 53. Washington, D. C.: Brookings Institution, 1986.

Putnam, Robert D., and Nicholas Bayne. *Hanging Together: Cooperation and Conflict in the Seven-Power Summits.* Rev. ed. Cambridge, Mass.: Harvard University Press, 1987.

Putnam, Robert D., and Nicholas Bayne. *Hanging Together: The Seven-Power Summits.* Cambridge, Mass.: Harvard University Press, 1984.

Putnam, Robert D., and Nicholas Bayne. *Weltwirtschaftsgipfel im Wandel* (World Economic Summits Amid Change). Bonn: Europa Union Verlag, 1985.

Reuther, Helmut, ed. *Wirtschaftsgipfel München 1992: Eine Dokumentation, 1975-1991* (The Munich Economic Summit, 1992: Documentation, 1975-1991.) Bonn: Transcontact Verlags-gesellschaft, 1992.

Roberge, François. *French Foreign Policy and the Seven Power Summits.* Country Study No. 3. Toronto: University of Toronto, Centre for International Studies, 1988. Also available as computer file. URL: www.library.utoronto.ca/www/g7/scholar/roberge/robercon.htm.

Rollo, J. "Economic Policy Co-ordination". Speech to the Royal Institute of International Affairs, 7 October 1993. Unpublished.

Saito, Shiro. *Japan at the Summit: Its Role in the Western Alliance and in Asian Pacific Co-operation.* London; New York: Routledge for the Royal Institute of International Affairs, 1990.

Sakurada, Daizo. *Japan and the Management of the International Political Economy: Japan's Seven Power Summit Diplomacy.* Country Study No. 6. Toronto: University of Toronto, Centre for International Studies and University of Toronto/York University Joint Centre on Asia-Pacific Studies, 1989. Also available as computer file. URL: www.library.utoronto.ca/www/g7/scholar/sakurada/sakcon.htm.

Schmidt, Helmut. *Men and Powers: A Political Perspective.* New York: Random House, 1989. (Translation of Volume 1 of *Menschen und Mächte.*)

Schmidt, Helmut. *Menschen und Mächte* (Men and Powers). Berlin: Siedler, 1987-1990. 2 vols.

The Seven-Power Summits. Tokyo: TBS-Britannica, 1986.

Shafer, Byron E., ed. *Postwar Politics in the G-7: Orders and Eras in Comparative Perspective.* Madison: University of Wisconsin Press, 1996.

Shultz, George P. *Turmoil and Triumph: My Years As Secretary of State.* New York: Scribner's, 1993.

Shultz, George P., and Kenneth W. Dam. *Economic Policy Beyond the Headlines.* New York: Norton, 1977.

Solomon, Robert. *Forums for Intergovernmental Consultations about Macroeconomic Policies.* Brookings Discussion Papers in International Economics, No. 15. Washington, D. C.: Brookings Institution, 1984.

Sommet économique de Londres, 15-17 juillet 1991: un tournant décisif dans les relations Est-Ouest = London Economic Summit: A Turning Point in East-West Relations. Textes réunis et présentés par Tristan Mage. Paris: T. Mage, 1991. 8 vols., 839 p. ISBN (éd. complète) 2-87891-049-4.

Sommet économique de Lyon, 27-29 juin 1996: de la priorité absolue à la lutte contre le terrorisme à la réussite de la mondialisation au bénéfice de tous = Lyon G7 Summit, 27-29 June 1996: The Fight against Terrorism To Be Absolute Priority To Making a Success of Globalization for the Benefit of All. Textes réunis et présentés par Tristan Mage. Paris: T. Mage, 1996. 4 vols.

Sovrani Ma Interdipendenti: I Vertici dei Paesi Più Industrializzati (Sovereign But Interdependent: The Summits of the Most Industrialised Countries). Bologna: Il Mulino, 1987.

Staines, Nicholas. "The G7: Economic Outlook and Policy. Paper delivered at a conference "Explaining Summit Success: Prospects for the

Denver Summit of the Eight", sponsored by the University of Colorado at Denver and the Metropolitan State College of Denver in cooperation with the University of Toronto G7 Research Group, Denver, Colorado, June 19, 1997. [Computer file] URL: www.library.utoronto.ca/www/g7/annual/staineg8.htm.

Summit Magazine, June 20-22, 1997. [Denver:] Denver Summit of the Eight Committee, 1997.

Summit Meetings and Collective Leadership in the 1980's. Charles Robinson and William C. Turner, co-chairmen; Harald B. Malmgren, rapporteur. Atlantic Council of the United States Policy Papers. Washington, D. C.: Working Group on Political Affairs, Atlantic Council of the United States, 1980.

Summitwatch: Prospects for the 1988 Toronto Summit. 3d ed. Toronto: The Research Group, University of Toronto, Centre for International Studies, 1988. Also available as computer file. URL: www.library.utoronto.ca/www/g7/scholar/summitwatch/swatcont. htm.

Sutherland, Peter. "Global Trade: The Next Challenge". Davos, Switzerland: World Economic Forum, 28 January 1994. Unpublished.

Taniguchi, Yoichiro. *Japan and Seven-power Summitry: Toward a More Assertive Foreign Policy.* [Senior thesis.] [s.l.: s.n.,] 1986. 172 leaves. [Harvard University Archives HU 92. 86.821.]

Taylor, Rupert J., ed. *Canada in action: Canada and the G-7.* Waterloo, Ont.: R/L Taylor Publishing, 1995.

Thatcher, Margaret. *The Downing Street Years.* London: Harper-Collins, 1993.

Thygesen, Niels. *An Agenda for the London Economic Summit: Policy Convergence, Exchange Rates, and International Liquidity; With a Statement by the 1984 Quadrangular Forum.* CEPS Papers, No. 10. Brussels: Centre for European Policy Studies, 1984.

Tokyo G-7 Summit: 7-9 July 1993 = Sommet économique de Tokyo = Wirtschaftsgipfel Tokio: un sommet soumis à la crise et aux pressions = A Summit Subject to Crisis and Pressures. Compiled by Tristan Mage. Paris: T. Mage, c1993. 4 v. Volumes 1-3: news media articles in English, German, and French; Vol. 4: table of contents.

The Twenty G-7 Summits. On the Occasion of the Twentieth Summit, Naples, July 8-10, 1994. Rome: Adnkronos Libri in Collaboration with Istituto Affari Internazionali, 1994.

Vasa, Barbara. *Global Information Society: Bibliography.* University of Toronto. May 1998. [Computer file] URL: www.library.utoronto.ca/www/g7/gis_bibliography/index.htm.

Von Furstenberg, George M., and Joseph P. Daniels. *Economic Summit Declarations, 1975-1989: Examining the Written Record of International Cooperation.* Princeton Studies in International Finance, No. 72. Princeton, N. J.: International Finance Section, Dept. of Economics, Princeton University, 1992.

Watt, David. *Next Steps for Summitry: Report of the Twentieth Century Fund International Conference on Economic Summitry; Background Paper.* New York: Priority Press, 1984.

Weber, Axel A. *Testing Long-run Neutrality: Empirical Evidence for G7 Countries with Special Emphasis on Germany.* Centre for Economic Policy Research. Discussion Paper, No. 1042. Bonn: University of Bonn, 1994.

Whitehead, John C. *Towards a Stronger International Economy.* Bissell Paper No. 7. Toronto: University of Toronto, Centre for International Studies, 1988. Also available as computer file. URL: www.library.utoronto.ca/www/g7/whittitl.htm.

Why Do the G7 Bother? They Can't Control the Global Economy, So They Might As Well Stay Home. By Oxford Analytica Limited. Oxford: Oxford Analytica, 1997. URL: www.slate.com/GlobalVision/97-06-24/GlobalVision.asp.

Williams, John. *The G-7, the CIS and Nuclear Proliferation.* Bristol, Eng.: Saferworld, 1993.

Williamson, John. *Targets and Indicators: A Blueprint for the International Coordination of Economic Policy.* Policy Analyses in International Economics, No. 22. Washington, D. C.: Institute of International Economics, 1987.

Chapters in Books

Bassi, Carlo. "The G-7 Summit: A Short History". In *The Twenty G-7 Summits*, 39-53. Rome: Adnkronos Libri in collaboration with Estated Affari Internazionali, 1994.

Bayne, Nicholas, and Robert D. Putnam. "Introduction: The G-7 Summit Comes of Age". In *The Halifax G-7 Summit: Issues on the Table.* Edited by Sylvia Ostry and Gilbert R. Wynham. Halifax: Centre for

Foreign Policy Studies, Dalhousie University, 1995, 1-13. Also available as computer file. URL: www.library.utoronto.ca/www/g7/bay95con.htm.

Becker, Kurt. "Between Image and Substance: The Role of the Media". In *Economic Summits and Western Decision-Making*, 153-66. Edited by Cesare Merlini. London: Croom Helm; New York: St. Martin's Press in association with the European Institute of Public Administration, 1984.

Bergsten, C. Fred. "Managing the World Economy of the Future". In *Managing the World Economy: Fifty Years after Bretton Woods*, edited by Peter B. Kenen, 341-74. Washington, D.C.: Institute for International Economics, 1994.

Blackwill, Robert D. "Russia and the G-7". In *The Halifax G-7 Summit: Issues on the Table*. Edited by Sylvia Ostry and Gilbert R. Wynham. Halifax: Centre for Foreign Policy Studies, Dalhousie University, 1995, 85-101.

Cooper, Richard N. "Reform of Multilateral Financial Institutions". In *The Halifax G-7 Summit: Issues on the Table*. Edited by Sylvia Ostry and Gilbert R. Wynham. Halifax: Centre for Foreign Policy Studies, Dalhousie University, 1995, 15-34.

Courtis, Kenneth S. "The First New Era Summit". In *Japan's Relations with North America: The New Pacific Interface*, 111-14. Edited by Richard A. Matthew and K. Lorne Brownsey. Halifax, N.S.: Institute for Research on Public Policy; Santa Fe, N.M.: North American Institute, 1990.

Dobson, Wendy. "Economic Policy Coordination Institutionalized? The G-7 and the Future of the Bretton Woods Institutions". In Bretton Woods Commission, *Bretton Woods: Looking to the Future: Commission Report, Staff Review, Background Papers*, C143-48. Washington, D.C.: Bretton Woods Commission, 1994.

Eichengreen, Barry, and Peter B. Kenen. "Managing the World Economy under the Bretton Woods System: An Overview". In *Managing the World Economy: Fifty Years after Bretton Woods*, edited by Peter B. Kenen, 3-57. Washington, D.C.: Institute for International Economics, 1994.

Frankel, Jeffrey A. "The Obstacles to Macro-economic Policy Co-ordination in the 1990s, and an Analysis of International Nominal Targeting". In *International Trade and Global Development: Essays in Honour of Jagdish Bhagwati,* edited by Ad Koekkoek and L. B. M. Mennes, 211-36. London; New York: Routledge, 1991.

Garavoglia, Guido. "The G-7 Summits: Between Continuity and Change". In *The Twenty G-7 Summits,* 11-28. Rome: Adnkronos Libri in collaboration with Istituto Affari Internazionali, 1994.

Good, Len. "The World Bank". In *The Halifax Summit, Sustainable Development, and International Institutional Reform.* Edited by John Kirton and Sarah Richardson. Ottawa: National Round Table on the Environment and the Economy, 1995, 54-57.

Hajnal, Peter I. "The G7". In *International Information: Documents, Publications, and Electronic Information of International Governmental Organizations,* 2nd ed., 202-40. Edited by Peter I. Hajnal. Englewood, Colo.: Libraries Unlimited, 1997.

Hiss, Dieter. "Weltwirtschaftsgipfel: Betrachtungen eines Insiders" (World Economic Summits: Observations of an Insider). In *Empirische Wirtschaftsforschung: Konzeptionen, Verfahren und Ergebnisse; Festschrift für Rolf Krengel aus Anlass seines 60. Geburtstages* (Empirical Economic Research: Concepts, Means and Ends; Festschrift for Rolf Krengel on the Occasion of his Sixtieth Birthday), edited by Joachim Frohn and Reiner Staeglin, 279-89. Berlin: Duncker & Humblot, 1980.

Jervis, Robert. "From Balance To Concert: A Study of International Security Cooperation". In *Co-operation Under Anarchy,* edited by Kenneth A. Oye, 58-79. Princeton: Princeton University Press, 1985.

Kaufmann, Johan. "Summit Diplomacy: Conference Style". In *Effective Negotiation: Case Studies in Conference Diplomacy,* edited by Johan Kaufmann, 165-71. Dordrecht, Netherlands: Nijhoff; New York: United Nations Institute for Training and Research, 1989.

Kawai, Masao. "A Japanese Perspective". In *The Halifax Summit, Sustainable Development, and International Institutional Reform.* Edited by John Kirton and Sarah Richardson. Ottawa: National Round Table on the Environment and the Economy, 1995, 99-101.

Kenen, Peter B. "Summing Up and Looking Ahead". In *Managing the World Economy: Fifty Years after Bretton Woods,* edited by Peter B. Kenen, 395-405. Washington, D.C.: Institute for International Economics, 1994.

Kirton, John J. "Economic Cooperation: Summitry, Institutions, and Structural Change". Paper prepared for a conference on "Structural Change and Co-operation in the Global Economy". Center for

International Business Education and Center for Global Change and Governance, Rutgers University, New Brunswick, N.J., May 19-20, 1997. [Computer file] URL: www.library.utoronto.ca/www/g7/scholar/rutcon.htm. To appear in *Structural Change and Co-operation in the Global Economy*, edited by John Dunning and Gavin Boyd (London: Edward Elgar, forthcoming, 1999).

Kirton, John J. "The Emerging Pacific Partnership: Japan, Canada, and the United States at the G-7 Summit". In *The North Pacific Triangle: The United States, Japan, and Canada at Century's End*, edited by Michael Fry, John J. Kirton, and Mitsuru Kurosawa, 292-313. Toronto; Buffalo; London: University of Toronto Press, 1998.

Kirton, John J. "Forging a Pacific Partnership: Canadian and Japanese Approaches to the U.S. in the Seven Power Summit". In *The Triangle of Pacific States*. Tokyo: Sairyusha Press, 1995. (In Japanese.)

Kirton, John J. "Managing Global Conflict: Canada and International Summitry". In *Canada Among Nations 1987: A World of Conflict*, edited by Maureen A. Molot and Brian W. Tomlin, 22-40. Toronto: James Lorimer, 1988.

Kirton, John J. "The Seven-Power Summit as a New Security Institution". In *Building a New Global Order: Emerging Trends in International Security*, edited by David Dewitt, David Haglund, and John Kirton, 335-57. Toronto; Oxford: Oxford University Press, 1993. Also available as computer file. URL: www.library.utoronto.ca/www/g7/scholar/kircont.htm.

Kirton, John J. "The Significance of the Houston Summit". In *The Seven-Power Summit: Documents from the Summits of Industrialized Countries; Supplement: Documents from the 1990 Summit*, compiled and edited by Peter I. Hajnal, ix-xvii. Millwood, N.Y.: Kraus International Publications, 1991. Also available as computer file. URL: www.library.utoronto.ca/www/g7/kircon90.htm.

Kirton, John J. "The Significance of the Seven-Power Summit". In *The Seven-Power Summit: Documents from the Summits of Industrialized Countries, 1975-1989*, compiled and edited by Peter I. Hajnal, xxi-li. Millwood, N.Y.: Kraus International Publications, 1989. Also available as computer file. URL: www.library.utoronto.ca/www/g7/kircon89.htm.

Kudrle, Robert T., and Davis B. Bobrow. "The G7 after Hegemony: Compatibility, Cooperation and Conflict". In *World Leadership and Hegemony*, 147-67. Edited by David P. Rapkin. Boulder, Colo.; London: Lynne Rienner Publisher, 1990.

Maull, Hanns W., and Angelika Volle. "Der Gipfelprozess [The Summit Process]". In *Der Gipfel in München: Analysen aus dem Forschungsinstitut der Deutschen Gesellschaft für Auswärtige Politik* (The Summit in Munich: Analyses of the Forschungsinstitut der Deutschen Gesellschaft für Auswärtige Politik), 1-14. Bonn: Deutsche Gesellschaft für Auswärtige Politik, 1993.

Ostry, Sylvia. "Canada, Europe and the Economic Summits". In *Canada on the Threshold of the 21st Century: European Reflections upon the Future of Canada: Selected Papers at the First All-European Canadian Studies Conference, The Hague, October 24-27, 1990*, 521-28. Edited by C. H. W. Remie and J.-M. Lacroix. Amsterdam; Philadelphia: John Benjamins Pub. Co., 1991. An earlier version available as computer file. URL: www.library.utoronto.ca/www/g7/osttoc.htm.

Ostry, Sylvia, and Gilbert R. Winham. "Post-Uruguay Round Trade Policy". In *The Halifax G-7 Summit: Issues on the Table*. Edited by Sylvia Ostry and Gilbert R. Wynham. Halifax: Centre for Foreign Policy Studies, Dalhousie University, 1995, 59-84.

Schrettl, Wolfram, and Ulrich Weissenburger. "Russia: Success Story or Collapse?" In *The Halifax G-7 Summit: Issues on the Table*. Edited by Sylvia Ostry and Gilbert R. Wynham. Halifax: Centre for Foreign Policy Studies, Dalhousie University, 1995, 103-126.

Solomon, Anthony M. "International Economic Policy Coordination: Present Shortcomings, Future Opportunities". In *The Quest for National and Global Economic Stability*, edited by Wietze Eizenga, E. Frans Limburg, and Jacques J. Polak, 217-29. Dordrecht; Boston; London: Kluwer Academic Publishers, 1988.

Summers, Lawrence H. "Shared Prosperity and the New International Economic Order". In *Managing the World Economy: Fifty Years after Bretton Woods*, edited by Peter B. Kenen, 419-26. Washington, D.C.: Institute for International Economics, 1994.

Triffin, Robert. "Before and After the Bonn Summit Meeting". In *International Trade and Exchange Rates in the Late Eighties*, edited by Theo Peeters and others, 405-11. Amsterdam; New York; Oxford: North-Holland, 1985.

Volcker, Paul. "Comment [on C. Fred Bergsten's 'Managing the World Economy of the Future']". In *Managing the World Economy: Fifty Years after Bretton Woods*, edited by Peter B. Kenen, 381-85. Washington, D.C.: Institute for International Economics, 1994.

Wallace William "Political Issues at the Summits: A New Concert of Powers?" In *Economic Summits and Western Decision-Making*, edited by Cesare Merlini, 137-52. London: Croom Helm; New York: St. Martin's Press in association with the European Institute of Public Administration, 1984.

Webb, Michael C. "Canada and the International Monetary Regime". In *Canadian Foreign Policy and International Economic Regimes*, edited by A. Claire Cutler and Mark W. Zacher, 153-85. Vancouver: UBC Press, 1992.

Williamson, John, and C. Randall Henning. "Managing the Monetary System". In *Managing the World Economy: Fifty Years after Bretton Woods*, edited by Peter B. Kenen, 83-111. Washington, D.C.: Institute for International Economics, 1994.

Yoshitomi, Masaru. "Main Issues of Macroeconomic Coordination: The Peso, Dollar and Yen Problems". In *The Halifax G-7 Summit: Issues on the Table*. Edited by Sylvia Ostry and Gilbert R. Wynham. Halifax: Centre for Foreign Policy Studies, Dalhousie University, 1995, 35-58.

Articles in Periodicals

"After the Debacle". *Time* 142, No. 7 (August 16, 1993): 12-17.

"All Smiles on the Western Front". *The Economist* 287, No. 7292 (June 4, 1983): 23-24.

"America Loses its Afrophobia". *The Economist* 343, No. 8014 (April 26, 1997): 23-24.

Artis, Michael J., and Wenda Zhang. "BVAR Forecasts for the G-7". *International Journal of Forecasting* 6, No. 3 (October 1990): 349-362.

Attali, Jacques. "La meilleure façon de dire 'non', c'est de dire 'non' (The Best Way To Say No Is To Say No)". *Le Monde*, 12 July 1996, 17.

Awanohara, Susumu. "Yeltsin's Yoke: Japan Strives for G-7 Backing in Islands Dispute. *Far Eastern Economic Review* 155, No. 28 (July 16, 1992): 11.

Bacon, Louis. "Devalue the Yen: How the G7–and Even its Tokyo Contingent–Misreads Japan's Trade Imbalances. *The International Economy: The Magazine of International Economic Policy* 11, No. 6 (November/December 1997): 18-19, 55.

Baldassarri, Mario. "Il G7 di Napoli: Problemi e Prospettive dell'Economia Internazionale (Problems and Prospects of the International Economy)". *Rivista di Politica Economica* 84, No. 7 (July 1994): 125-28.

Barber, Lionel. "Europe's Summit Agenda. *Europe: Magazine of the European Union* 366 (May 1997): 20-21.

Barber, Lionel. "Three G's. *Europe: Magazine of the European Union*" 366 (May 1997): 12-14.

Barnard, Bruce. "The Euro Is Coming to Denver". *Europe: Magazine of the European Union*" 366 (May 1997): 22-23.

Barrell, R. J. "Manufacturing Export Prices for the G7". *National Institute Economic Review*, No. 128 (May 1989): 90-91.

"The Basket-Case Summit". *The Economist* 324, No. 7766 (July 4, 1992): 13-14.

Bayne, Nicholas. "Britain, the G8 and the Commonwealth: Lessons of the Birmingham Summit". *The Round Table*, No. 348 (October 1998): 445-57.

Bayne, Nicholas. "Changing Patterns at the G7 Summit". *G7 Governance*, No. 1 (May 1997). [Computer file]. URL: www.library.utoronto.ca/www/g7/governance/g7gove1.htm.

Bayne, Nicholas. "The Course of Summitry". *The World Today* 48, No. 2 (February 1992): 27-30. Also available as computer file. URL: www.library.utoronto.ca/www/g7/baytoc.htm.

Bayne, Nicholas. "The G7 Summit and the Reform of Global Institutions". *Government and Opposition* 30, No. 4 (Autumn 1995): 492-509. Also available as computer file. URL: www.library.utoronto.ca/www/g7/bayn2toc.htm.

Bayne, Nicholas. "Western Economic Summits: Can They Do Better?" *The World Today* 40, No. 1 (January 1984): 4-12.

Bayne, Nicholas. "Die Westlichen Wirtschafts-Gipfeltreffen: Rückblick und Anregungen (The Western Economic Summit Meetings: Retrospective View and Recommendations.)" *Europa-Archiv* 39, 2. Folge (25 Januar 1984): 43-52.

Bayne, Nicholas, and Heidi Ullrich. "The School and the Summit". *LSE Magazine* 10, No. 2 (Winter 1998): 14-15.

Bergsten, C. Fred. "The Decline of the G7". *The International Economy: The Magazine of International Economic Policy* 10, No. 4 (July/August 1996): 10-14.

Bergsten, C. Fred. "Grade 'F' for the G7". *The International Economy: The Magazine of International Economic Policy* 10, No. 6 (November/December 1996): 18-21, 68.

Bergsten, C. Fred. "Missed Opportunity". *The International Economy: The Magazine of International Economic Policy* 12, No. 6 (November/December 1998): 26-27.

Bergsten, C. Fred. "The Paris Summit: Lost Opportunities". *Challenge* 32, No. 5 (September/October 1989): 52-53.

Bergsten, C. Fred. "A Qualified Success: Plaza Was a Ten-strike". Then Officials Dropped the Ball. *The International Economy: The Magazine of International Economic Policy* 9, No. 5 (September/October 1995): 15-16.

Bergsten, C. Fred, and Lawrence R. Klein. "The Need for a Global Strategy". *The Economist* 287, No. 7286 (April 23, 1983): 18-20.

"Big Deal". *The Economist* 268, No. 7038 (July 22, 1978): 73-74.

"Bill Clinton's Golden Moment". *The Economist* 343, No. 8022 (June 21, 1997): 16-17.

Bird, Graham. "The Bretton Woods Institutions and the Political Economy of International Monetary Reform: Introduction". *The World Economy* 19, No. 2 (March 1996): 143-46.

Bird, Graham. "From Bretton Woods to Halifax and Beyond: The Political Economy of International Monetary Reform". *The World Economy* 19, No. 2 (March 1996): 149-72.

Blackwell, Michael P. "From G-5 to G-77: International Forums for Discussion of Economic Issues". *Finance & Development* 23, No. 4 (December 1986): 40-41.

Boehm, Peter. "There Was a Summit in Halifax: Behind the Scenes at the 21st Birthday of the G-7". *Bout de papier* 13, No. 1 (Spring 1996): 5-7.

"The Bonn Summit and the U.S. Trade Deficit". *World Financial Markets* (New York: Morgan Guaranty Trust Company), March/April 1985: 1-13.

Borrus, Amy, and others. "To Russia with Hope: Clinton Bets His Aid Will Spur the G-7 To Do More To Help Stabilize Russia". *Business Week*, No. 3315 (April 19, 1993): 46.

Brzezinski, Zbigniew. "Let's Add 4 to the G-7". *The New York Times*, June 25, 1996, A11.

"The Buck Stops Here: Would a Stronger U.S. Dollar in 1993 Wreak Havoc on the G7?" *International Economy: The Magazine of International Economic Policy* 7, No. 1 (January/February 1993): 12-19.

"Buck-passing at Williamsburg". *The Economist* 287, No. 7291 (May 28, 1983): 16-17.

"Bumbling in Bavaria". *The Economist* 324, No. 7767 (July 11, 1992): 44.

Busetto, Guido. "Vertice di Tokyo: Tutti Insieme in Ordine Sparso (Tokyo Summit: All Together, in Open Order)". *Mondo Economico*, No. 18 (May 12 1986): 36-39.

Camé, François. "Comment les sherpas avaient ficelé le sommet (How the Sherpas Had Wrapped Up the Summit)". *Libération*, 17 juillet 1989: 8-15.

"Can the G7 Ride Again?" *The Economist* 339, No. 7971 (June 22, 1996): 96.

"Canada and the 1995 G7 Halifax Summit: Developing Canada's Positions". *Canadian Foreign Policy = La Politique étrangère du Canada* 3, No. 1 (Spring 1995).

Carabini, Orazio, and Beppe Caravita. "A Williamsburg senza Rete (In Williamsburg without a Safety Net)". *Mondo Economico*, No. 38 (June 1 1983): 16-19.

Catte, Pietro; Giampaolo Galli; and Salvatore Rebecchini. "Report on the G-7: Exchange Markets Can Be Managed!" *International Economic Insights* 3 (September-October 1992): 17-21.

Chadha, Bankim, and Eswar Prasad. *Are Prices Countercyclical? Evidence from the G-7*. IMF Working Paper, No. WP/94/91. Washington, D.C.: International Monetary Fund, Research and Western Hemisphere Departments, 1994. See also Chadha and Prasad, "Are Prices Countercyclical? Evidence from the G-7", *Journal of Monetary Economics* 34, No. 2 (October 1994): 239-57.

Charpin, Jean-Michel. "Le sommet de Tokyo peut être utile (The Tokyo Summit May Be Useful)". *Economie prospective internationale: revue du Centre d'études prospectives et d'informations internationales*, No. 26 (2e trimestre 1986): 3-10.

Chauveau, Thierry, and Rahim Loufir. "L'avenir des régimes publics de retraite dans les pays du G7 (The Future of Public Pension Regimes in G7 Countries)". *Observations et diagnostics économiques: revue de l'OFCE* 52 (January 1995): 49-103.

Checchi, Daniele. "L'Esperienza dei Summit del G-7 (The Experience of the G-7 Summits.)" *Rivista di Diritto Valutario e di Economia Internazionale* 41, No. 4 (dicembre 1989): 703-22.

"Checking the G-7 Pulse". *The International Economy: The Magazine of International Economic Policy* 3, No. 5 (September/October 1989): 46-47.

Chertkow, Paul S. "Dollar Will Slip Eventually Despite G-7 Accord". *Asian Finance* 13, No. 3 (March 15, 1987): 100-101.

Chertkow, Paul S. "G-7 Rhetoric Will Not Stop Dollar Plunge: Britain Gives Priority to War on Inflation". *Asian Finance* 14, No. 5 (May 15, 1988): 84-85.

"A China Primer: Five Experts Address Five Key Questions Which Should Preoccupy the G7". *The International Economy: The Magazine of International Economic Policy* 12, No. 6 (November/December 1998): 38-42.

Ching, Frank. "G7 Leaders Should Welcome Dialogue with Poorer Nations". *Far Eastern Economic Review* 156, No. 22 (June 3, 1993): 30.

"Cinderella Gorbachev". *The Economist* 320, No. 7716 (July 20, 1991): 47-48.

Cohen, Stephen. "G-7 Con Job". *The International Economy: The Magazine of International Economic Policy* 11, No. 6 (November/December 1988): 83-86.

Colombo, Antonio. "Il Coordinamento Internazionale: da Bretton Woods alle Riunioni del G5, G7 nelli anni '80 (International Co-ordination: from Bretton Woods to the Meetings of the G5 [and] G-7 in the 80s)". *Rivista di Politica Economica* 79 (June 1989): 297-314.

"Competing Interests: A Guide to EC and G7 Competition Law". *International Financial Law Review* 10 (June 1991), Special Supplement.

"Conferences: Sticking to the Plan". *Asiaweek* 10 (June 22, 1984): 44-46.

Conthe, Manuel. "La Cumbre de Williamsburg: Valio la Pena la Ascensión? (The Williamsburg Summit: Worth the Climb?" Spain, Ministerio de Economía y Hacienda, *Información Comercial Española: Revista de Economía*, No. 601 (Setiembre 1983): 12-25.

Cook, David. "The Selling of the Summit, 1983". *Johns Hopkins Magazine* 34, No. 4 (August 1983): 33-37.

Cook, George. "Summitry Comes to U of T". *University of Toronto Alumni Magazine* 15, No. 4 (Summer 1988): 8-10.

Crawford, Malcolm. "Third World Debt Is Here to Stay". *Lloyds Bank Review*, No. 155 (January 1985): 13-31.

Crow, John W. "The New World of International Finance: Implications for Business and Labor". *North American Outlook* 5, No. 3 (June 1995): 19-28.

"La 'Cumbre' de Williamsbourg y la VI^a UNCTAD (The Williamsburg Summit and UNCTAD VI)". *FIDE [Fundación de Investigaciones para el Desarrollo] Coyuntura y Desarrollo*, No. 58 (Junio 1983): 36-43.

Currie, David. "G-7 Process: Which Way Forward?" *International Economic Insights* 4 (September/October 1993): 13-16.

Davidson, Ian. "Of Summits, and Their Uses". *Financial Times* (London), April 2, 1984: 17.

De Haan, J., and H. Garretsen. "Falende Internationale Macro-economische Beleidscöordinatie? (Failing International Macroeconomic Policy Co-ordination?)" *Internationale Spectator* 43, No. 2 (Februari 1989): 104-11.

De Ménil, Georges. "De Rambouillet à Versailles: un bilan des sommets économiques" (From Rambouillet to Versailles: An Assessment of the Economic Summits). *Politique étrangère* 2 (June 1982): 403-17.

De Ménil, Georges. "Si le sommet de Versailles n'avait pas eu lieu" (If the Versailles Summit Had Not Taken Place). *Commentaire*, No. 20 (Winter 1982/83): 571-79.

"Deathly in Venice". *The Economist* 303, No. 7502 (June 13, 1987): 69-70.

"Debtspeak for the G7". *Economist Financial Report* 13 (January 26, 1989):1.

Defarges, Philippe Moreau. "The French Viewpoint on the Future of the G-7". In "The Future of the G-7 Summits", 177-185. *The International Spectator* 29, No. 2 (April/June 1994), Special Issue. Also available as computer file. URL: www.library.utoronto.ca/www/g7/scholar/defartab.htm.

Delamaide, Darrell. "The Coming of Age of G7". *Euromoney*, No. 293 (September 1993: 70-78.

Denters, Erik. "Hoe de G-7 het Internationale Monetaire Systeem Reviseert" (How the G-7 Revised the International Monetary System). *Internationale Spectator* 42 (August 1988): 478-85.

"Denver Summit of the Eight, June 20-22, 1997". *Daily Report for Executives*, No. 118, Special Issue. Washington, D.C.: Bureau of National Affairs, June 19, 1997.

"Directorate of the Rich". *The Economist* 263, No. 6976 (May 14, 1977): 104-105.

"A Disquieting New Agenda For Trade". *The Economist* 332, No. 7872 (July 16, 1994): 55-56.

Dobson, Wendy. "Rethinking the G-7: A New World Coordination Process". *International Economic Insights* 2 (March/April 1991): 34-35.

Dobson, Wendy. "Should G-7 Cooperation Be Buried?" *International Economic Insights* 4 (May-June 1993): 35-37.

Dobson, Wendy. "Summitry and the International Monetary System: The Past as Prologue". *Canadian Foreign Policy = La Politique étrangère du Canada* 3, No. 1 (Spring 1995): 5-13.

"Don't 'Save' the Yen". *The Economist* 342, No. 8003 (February 8, 1997): 18.

Dornbusch, Rüdiger. "The Ridiculous G7". *The International Economy: The Magazine of International Economic Policy* 10, No. 5 (September/October 1996): 40-42.

"Draft Halifax Summit Communiqué, Dated May 27, 1995 Released June 6 by Canadian Member of Parliament Nelson Riis". "Preview of the G-7 Summit, Halifax, Canada, June 15-17". *Daily Report for Executives*, No. 114, Special Issue. Washington, D.C.: Bureau of National Affairs, June 14, 1995: S12-S16.

"Economic Summit". *The Wall Street Journal*, July 9, 1990: R1-R40. The Wall Street Journal Reports. New York.

"Economic Summit Issues". *World Financial Markets* (New York: Morgan Guaranty Trust Company), May 1982: 1-13.

"Emerging Africa". *The Economist* 343, No. 8021 (June 14, 1997): 13-14

Engelen, Klaus. "Benign Neglect Revisited: It's Time for the G7 To Stop Talking and Start Acting on the Worldwide Jobs Crisis". *The International Economy: The Magazine of International Economic Policy* 7, No. 6 (November/December 1993): 42-44.

Engelen, Klaus. "For Once the G7 Can Talk and Chew Gum at the Same Time". *The International Economy: The Magazine of International Economic Policy* 9, No. 5 (September/October 1995): 5.

Fase, M. M. G. "In Search for Stability: An Empirical Appraisal of the Demand for Money in the G7 and EC Countries". *De Economist* 142, No.4 (1994): 421-54.

Fayolle, Jacky, and Alexandre Mathis. "Tendances et cycles stylisés dans les pays du G7: une approche stochastique (Trends and Stylised Cycles in G7 Countries: A Stochastic Approach". *Observations et diagnostics économiques: revue de l'OFCE* 47 (October 1993): 201-33.

Fernandez, David G. "Waiter, There Are No Choices on My Menu! The Shrinking Set of Options for Reforming the International Monetary System". *North American Outlook* 5, No. 3 (June 1995): 29-42.

Finch, C. David. "G7 Corruption Project: It's Time the World Bank and IMF Address the Corruption Issue Head On". *The International Economy: The Magazine of International Economic Policy* 10, No. 6 (November/December 1996): 22-26.

Finch, C. David. "Let the G7 Deputies Run the IMF!" *The International Economy: The Magazine of International Economic Policy* 7, No. 5 (September/October 1993): 54-56.

Fiorito, Riccardo, and Tryphon Kollintzas. "Stylized Facts of Business Cycles in the G7 from a Real Business Cycles Perspective". *European Economic Review* 38, No. 2 (February 1994): 235-69. See also Centre for Economic Policy Research. Discussion Paper Series, No. 681 (July 1992).

"The First Green Summit". *The Economist* 312, No. 7611 (July 15, 1989): 13-14.

"Flushing Funny Money into the Open". *The Economist* 315, No. 7653 (May 5, 1990): 91-92.

Fotheringham, Allan. "Scaling Another Economic Summit". *Maclean's: Canada's Weekly Newsmagazine* 108, No. 26 (June 26, 1996): 60.

Foucher, Michel. "Les réunions du G7 incarnent ce que l'on appelle à tort ou à raison la globalisation (The Meetings of the G7 Embody What Is Called–Rightly or Wrongly–Globalisation)". *La lettre de l'O.e.g. [Observatoire européen de géopolitique]*, No. 3 (1er semestre 1996), [2-4].

Fréchette, Louise. "Canada and the 1995 G7 Halifax Summit". *Canadian Foreign Policy = La Politique étrangère du Canada* 3, No. 1 (Spring 1995): 1-4.

Fréchette, Louise. "The Halifax Summit: A Canadian Perspective". *North American Outlook* 5, No. 3 (June 1995): 7-13.

Friedland, Jonathan. "Direct Approach: Clinton Uses G7 Summit To Woo Japanese Consumers". *Far Eastern Economic Review* 156, No. 28 (July 15, 1993): 78.

"The Future of the G-7 Summits". *The International Spectator* 29, No. 2 (April/June 1994), Special Issue.

"G-7 Against More IMF Payout for the Poor". *Pakistan & Gulf Economist* 13 (October 8-14, 1994): 15.

G7 Bulletin. Issues 1-4, June 19-22, 1997. Editor: Lynne Driscoll. Published in cooperation with the University of Toronto and the G7 Research Group. Denver, 1997. [Computer file] URL: www.library.utoronto.ca/www/g7/g7bulletin.index.htm.

"The G7 Charade". *The Economist* 315, No. 7650 (April 14, 1990): 16.

"The G7 and the Euro-11". *The Economist* 349, No. 8089 (October 10, 1998): 17.

"G7 Consumers: Debt, Saving and Economic Growth". *AMEX Bank Review* 20 (January 25, 1993): 1-7.

"Le G7 court après le dollar (The G7 Is Running after the Dollar)". *Le nouvel économiste*, No. 679 (January 29, 1989): 40-41.

"G7 Leaders Welcome Dialogue with Poorer Nations". *Far Eastern Economic Review* 156, No. 22 (June 3, 1993): 30.

G7 Raises Level of Debt Write-off. *Africa Economic Digest* 12 (July 29-August 11, 1991): 21.

The G-7 Report: A Publication for International Trade & Investment. 1992-. Toronto: W. B. Z. Vukson.

"The G7 Summit: A Modest Proposal". *The Economist* 335, No. 7918 (June 10, 1995): 19-21.

Galimberti, Fabrizio, and Luca Paolazzi. "Recessione, debiti chi offre di più?" (Recession, debts, Who Is Offering More?) *Mondo Economico*, No. 22 (June 8, 1987): 34-36.

Garavoglia, Guido and Pier Carlo Padoan. "The G-7 Agenda: Old and New Issues". In "The Future of the G-7 Summits", 49-65. *The International Spectator* 29, No. 2 (April/June 1994), Special Issue. Also available as computer file. URL: www.library.utoronto.ca/g7/scholar/garatbl.htm.

Garavoglia, Guido, and Cesare Merlini, eds. *Il Vertice dei Sette: ruolo e prospettive del G-7 nel mutato scenario internazionale* (The Summit of the Seven: Role and Prospects of the G7 on the Changing International Scene). Lo Spettatore Internazionale. Milano: Franco Angeli, 1994. English version: *International Spectator* 29, No. 2 (April/June 1994), Special issue (*q.v.*).

Garten, Jeffrey E. "Munich Madness". *The International Economy: The Magazine of International Economic Policy* 6, No. 3 (May/June 1992): 23-26.

Garten, Jeffrey E. "The 100-day Economic Agenda". *Foreign Affairs* 72, No. 5 (Winter 1992/93): 16-31.

"Getting Away from It". *The Economist* 275, No. 7139 (June 28, 1980): 13-14.

Giscard d'Estaing, Valéry. "A Communiqué for Williamsburg". *The Economist* 287, No. 7290 (May 21, 1983): 15-18.

"Going for Gold: The G7 and Debt Relief". *The Economist* 339, No. 7971 (June 22, 1996): 95.

Gorbachev, Mikhail. "The G7 Behaves Like an Executive Committee Ruling the World". *The Globe and Mail*, July 9, 1997, A14.

Gotlieb, Sondra. "Keep on Summiting". *Saturday Night*, 110, No. 7 (September 1995): 76-79.

Goybet, Catherine. "Williamsburg, un sommet 'tranquille'" (Williamsburg, a 'Quiet' Summit). *Revue du Marché commun*, No. 268 (juin/juillet 1983): 287-89.

Graham, Bill. "The 1995 Halifax G7 Summit: A View from Parliament". *Canadian Foreign Policy = La Politique étrangère du Canada* 3, No. 1 (Spring 1995): 31-37.

Guttry, Andrea de. "The Institutional Configuration of the G-7 in the New International Scenario". In "The Future of the G-7 Summits", 67-80. *The International Spectator* 29, No. 2 (April/June 1994), Special Issue. Also available as computer file. URL: www.library.utoronto.ca/g7/scholar/guttrtab.htm.

Hajnal, Peter I. "The Documentation of the G7/G8 System". *G7 Governance*, No. 4 (June 1998). [Computer file] URL: www.library.utoronto.ca/www/g7/governance/gov4/index.html.

Hajnal, Peter I. "Documents of the Seven-Power Summit". *INSPEL: Official Organ of the IFLA Division of Special Libraries* 26, No. 2 (1992): 127-37.

Hajnal, Peter I. "G7 Bibliography". *Canadian Foreign Policy = La Politique étrangère du Canada* 3, No. 1 (Spring 1995): 125-133.

Hajnal, Peter I. "The G-7 Summit and Its Documents". *Government Information in Canada* [Electronic Journal] 1, No. 3.3 (Winter 1995). URL: www.usask.ca/library/gic/v1n3/hajnal/hajnal.html.

Hale, David D. "The F/X Maginot Line: It's Time for the G7 To Know Its Limitations". *The International Economy: The Magazine of the International Economic Policy* 7, No. 1 (January/February 1993): 25-27.

Hale, David D. "Picking Up Reagan's Tab". *Foreign Policy* 74 (Spring 1989): 145-67.

Hall, Tammy, and others. *The Halifax 21st G-7 Summit: En Route to the 21st Century*. Halifax: Centre for Foreign Policy Studies, Dalhousie University; Canadian Institute of International Affairs (Halifax Branch); *International Insights: A Dalhousie Journal of International Affairs*, 1996.

Hardouvelis, Gikas A. "The Term Structure Spread and Future Changes in Long and Short Rates in the G7 Countries: Is There a Puzzle?" *Journal of Monetary Economics* 33, No. 2 (April 1994): 255-83.

Healey, Denis. "The Power of the Weak". *The Economist* 287, No. 7286 (April 23, 1983): 17-18.

Heath, Edward. "The Heath Memorandum". *The Times* (London), July 20, 1981: 10.

Hein, John. "Uphill after the Summit". *Across the Board* 23, No. 7-8 (July/August 1986): 7-8.

Hein, John. "Why the Summit? Because It's There". *Across the Board* 20, No. 7 (July/August 1983): 5-7.

Helliwell, John F., and others. "INTERMOD 1.1: a G7 version of the IMF's MULTIMOD". *Economic Modelling* 7, No. 1 (January 1990): 3-62.

Henning, C. Randall. "G-7 Dilemma: Agreeing on Cost Sharing". *International Economic Insights* 11 (May-June 1991): 2-6.

Herz, Bernhard, and Joachim Starbatty. "Zur Frage Internationaler Dominanzbeziehungen: Eine Analyse der Machtverteilung auf Weltwirtschaftsgipfeln". (On the Question of International Relations among Dominant Powers: An Analysis of the Distribution of Power at the World Economic Summits). *Kyklos* 44 (1991), Fasc. 1:35-55.

Hirsh, Michael. "G-7 at 20". *Institutional Investor* (International ed.) 18 (November 1993): 42-48.

Hodges, Michael R. "More Efficiency, Less Dignity: British Perspectives on the Future Role and Working of the G-7". In "The Future of the G-7 Summits", 141-159. *The International Spectator* 29, No. 2 (April/June 1994), Special Issue. Also available as computer file. URL: www.library.utoronto.ca/www/g7/hodtoc.htm.

Hoehmann, Hans-Hermann, and Christian Meier. "Before and After Yeltsin's Election Victory: On the Prospects of Western Cooperation with Russia". *Aussenpolitik: German Foreign Affairs Review* 47, No. 3 (1996): 263-74.

Hoehmann, Hans-Hermann, and Christian Meier. "The Halifax G7 Summit and Western Assistance for Russia and the Ukraine". *Aussenpolitik: German Foreign Affairs Review* 47, No. 1 (1996): 53-60.

Hoehmann, Hans-Hermann, and Christian Meier. "Russia, `Summit of the Eight' and International Economic Organisations". *Aussenpolitik: German Foreign Affairs Review* 48, No. 4 (1997): 335-45.

Hoehmann, Hans-Hermann, and Christian Meier. "The World Economic Summit in Naples: A New Political Role for Russia?". *Aussenpolitik: German Foreign Affairs Review* 45, No. 4 (1994): 336-45.

Hollohan, Brian. "The Magnificent Seven: A Primer on G-7 Summits". *The Canadian Business Review* 16, No. 3 (Autumn 1989): 37-41.

"Hold Back, G7". *Economist Financial Report* 12 (December 10, 1987): 3.

Hormats, Robert D. "New Era, New Pie: The Group of 7 Needs To Expand". *The New York Times*, July 1, 1994: A25.

Hormats, Robert D. "Redefining Europe and the Atlantic Link". *Foreign Affairs* 68 (Fall 1989): 71-91.

Hormats, Robert D. "Summits Aren't for Sleeping". *The International Economy: The Magazine of International Economic Policy* 2, No. 2 (March/April 1988): 94-97.

Horňák, Petr. "K Výsledkům Schůzky Představitelů 'Sedmičky' ve Williamsburgu". (On the Results of the Williamsburg Meeting of G-7 Representatives). *Mezinárodní Vztahy* 18, No. 7 (1983): 47-52.

"How To Stabilize Exchange Rates". *The Economist* 283, No. 7241 (June 12, 1982): 71.

Hsieh, Edward, and Kon S. Lai. "Government Spending and Economic Growth: The G-7 Experience". *Applied Economics* 26, No. 5 (May 1994): 535-42.

Humphreys, Gary. "G7 Currencies". *Euromoney: The 1993 Guide to Currencies* (February 1993): 3-12.

Hunt, John, and Henry Owen. "Taking Stock of the Seven-Power Summits: Two Views". Review of *Hanging Together: The Seven-Power Summits*, by Robert D. Putnam and Nicholas Bayne. *International Affairs* 60, No. 4 (Autumn 1984): 657-61.

I., S. G. "Stern Financial Discipline–for the Poor: London Economic Summit". *Economic and Political Weekly* (Bombay) 19, No. 26 (June 30, 1984): 981.

Ikenberry, G. John. "Market Solutions for State Problems: The International and Domestic Politics of American Oil Decontrol". *International Organization* 42, No. 1 (Winter 1988): 151-77.

Ikenberry, G. John. "Salvaging the G-7". *Foreign Affairs* 72, No. 2 (Spring 1993): 132-39.

"The IMF Fights Back". *The International Economy: The Magazine of International Economic Policy* 12, No. 1 (January/February 1998): 6- 9, 59.

"In Praise of Summits". *The Economist* 291, No. 7346 (June 16, 1984): 12-13.

"In Time for Toronto, America Finds the Curve In Its J-curve". *The Economist* 307, No. 7555 (June 18, 1988): 65-66, 69.

Inoguchi, Kuniko. "The Changing Significance of the G-7 Summits". *Japan Review of International Affairs* 8, No. 1 (Winter 1994): 21-38.

Inoue, Yuko. "G-7 Commodity Basket Featuring Gold Draws Mixed Reaction in Japan". *Japan Economic Journal* (International ed.) 26 (April 30, 1988): 1-2.

"An Insider's Behind-the-Scenes Account of Session on Clinton's Trade Initiative". *The Wall Street Journal*, July 11, 1994: A3.

James, Antoinette M., and Bruce T. Elmslie. "Testing Heckscher-Ohlin-Vanek in the G-7". *Weltwirtschaftliches Archiv* 132, No. 1 (1996): 139-59.

Jayawardena, Lal. "World Economic Summits: The Role of Representative Groups In the Governance of the World Economy". *Development: Journal of the Society for International Development*, 1989, No. 4: 17-20. [Reproduces portions of WIDER Study Group Series, No. 4, *q.v.,* Entry No. 309.]

Kemme, David M. "The Houston Report: The Failure of Perestroika". *International Economic Insights* 11, No. 1 (January/February 1991): 9-13.

Kindleberger, Charles P. ...[et al.]. "Return to Tribalism? Implications for the EC and the G7". *The International Economy: The Magazine of International Economic Policy* 7, No. 5 (September/October 1993): 11-17.

Kirton, John J. "The Diplomacy of Concert: Canada, the G7 and the Halifax Summit". *Canadian Foreign Policy = La Politique étrangère du Canada* 3, No. 1 (Spring 1995): 63-80. Also available as computer file. URL: www.library.utoronto.ca/www/g7/cfp95con.htm.

Kirton, John J. "Exercising Concerted Leadership: Canada's Approach to Summit Reform". In "The Future of the G-7 Summits", 161-176. *The International Spectator* 29, No. 2 (April/June 1994), Special Issue. Also available as computer file. URL: www.library.utoronto.ca/www/g7/scholar/kirtotab.htm.

Kirton, John J. "The G-7, the Halifax Summit, and International Financial System Reform". *North American Outlook* 5, No. 3 (June 1995): 43-66. Also available as computer file. URL: www.library.utoronto.ca/www/g7/kir95con.htm.

Kirton, John J. "Le rôle du G7 dans le couple integration régionale/sécurité globale". *Etudes internationales* 28 (juin 1997): 255-70. Also in English: "The Role of the G7 in the Regional Integration-Global Security Link". *G7 Governance*, No. 2 (June 1997). [Computer file]. URL: www.library.utoronto.ca/www/g7/governance/g7gove2.htm.

Kirton, John J. and Eleonore Kokotsis. "La revitalisation du G-7: Perspectives pour le Sommet des Huit à Birmingham, en 1998". *G7 Governance*, No. 3 (May 1998). [Computer file]. URL: www.library.utoronto.ca/www/g7/governance/gov3.htm.

Kirton, John J. and Eleonore Kokotsis. "Revitalizing the G-7: Prospects for the 1998 Birmingham Summit of the Eight". *International Journal* 53, No. 1 (Winter 1997/1998): 38-56. Also available as computer file. URL: www.library.utoronto.ca/www/g7/scholar/bircon.htm.

Kitamatsu, Katsuro. "G7 Nations Lukewarm to Japan Initiatives". *Japan Economic Journal* (International ed.) 26 (October 8, 1988): 2.

Koenig, Peter. "Into the Maelstrom". *Euromoney*, June 1987: 67-79.

Koenig, Peter. "The Last Days of the G7". *Euromoney*, May 1995: 21-23.

Krämer, Jörg. "Determinants of the Expected Real Long-Term Interest Rates in the G7 Countries". *Applied Economics* 30, No. 2 (February 1998): 279-85.

Kronsten, Gregory. "After G7 Jargon, One Debt Plan Stands Out". *Africa Analysis*, No. 50 (June 24, 1988): 4.

Krugman, Paul. "Harmless Shmoozing: But Plaza Did Produce Some Gread Head-of-State Vacation Spots". *The International Economy: The Magazine of International Economic Policy* 9, No. 5 (September/October 1995): 17-19.

Krugman, Paul. "Regional Blocs: The Good, the Bad and the Ugly: a Leading Scholar Charts the G7's Next 'Inevitable Uncertainty'". *The International Economy: The Magazine of International Economic Policy* 5, No. 6 (November/December 1991): 54-56.

Kuttner, Bob. "Silent Summit: Why Are We in Williamsburg?" *New Republic* 188, No. 22 (June 6, 1983): 9-13.

Kuttner, Robert. "The Toronto Summit's Achilles' Heel". *The International Economy: The Magazine of International Economic Policy* 2, No. 3 (May/June 1988): 78-83.

Leachman, Lori L., and Bill Francis. "Long-Run Relations among the G-5 and G-7 Equity Markets: Evidence on the Plaza and Louvre Accords". *Journal of Macroeconomics* 17, No. 4 (Fall 1995): 551-77.

"Let's All Now Wring Our Hands". *The Economist* 335, No. 7912 (April 29, 1995): 80.

Lewis, Flora. "The 'G-7½' Directorate". *Foreign Policy*, No. 85 (Winter 1991-92): 25-40.

"Lies at Versailles". *The Economist* 283, No. 7241 (June 12, 1982): 14, 16. ["Alternative communiqué".]

"A Lift in Tokyo". *The Economist* 299, No. 7443 (April 26, 1986): 14-15.

Lipsey, R. G. "Agendas for the 1988 and Future Summits". *Canadian Public Policy* 15 (February 1989): S86-S91.

"London Summit". *Pakistan & Gulf Economist* 3 (June 16, 1984): 5-6.

"Londres: le sommet américain (London: The American Summit". *Le nouvel économiste*, No. 443 (11 juin 1984): 40-41.

Losoncz, Miklós. "A Vezető Tőkés Országok Gazdasági Stratégiája a Williamsburg-i Csúcstalálkozó Tükrében". (Economic Strategy of the Leading Capitalist Countries As Reflected by the Williamsburg Summit). *Külgazdaság* 27, No. 8 (1983): 34-44.

"Lots To Do". *The Economist* 320, No. 7715 (July 13, 1991): 13-14.

"Lyon or Mouse?" *The Economist* 340, No. 7973 (July 6, 1996): 64.

MacDonald, Ronald. "Exchange Rate Survey Data: A Disaggregated G-7 Perspective". *Manchester School of Economic and Social Studies*, No. 60, Supplement (June 1992): 47-62.

MacFarlane, S. Neil. "Russia and the G7". *Canadian Foreign Policy = La Politique étrangère du Canada* 3, No. 1 (Spring 1995): 81-89.

Magombe, V. P., and Enyoyam Afele. "Fruitless Gathering: Africa under the Table at the Recent G-7 Summit". *West Africa*, No. 3856 (5-11 August 1991): 1283.

Malmgren, Harald B. "It's Time for a G7 Task Force". *The International Economy: The Magazine of International Economic Policy* 6, No. 1 (January/February 1992): 26, 28-29, 57-59.

Mardirosyan, Ara. "Sommet: échec de la concertation économique des Sept à Londres". (The Summit: Failure of the Economic Concert in London). *Jeune Afrique Economie* 41 (7 juin 1984): 15-17.

Maull, Hanns W. "Germany at the Summit". In "The Future of the G-7 Summits", 112-139. *The International Spectator* 29, No. 2 (April/June 1994), Special Issue. Also available as computer file. URL: www.library.utoronto.ca/www/g7/scholar/maultab.htm.

McNamar, Richard T. "Changing Priorities: New Issues for the Economic Summit". *Speaking of Japan* 10, No. 106 (October 1989): 7-13.

McNamar, Richard T. "New Issues for the Economic Summit: The Environment and Growth". *Vital Speeches of the Day* 56, No. 2 (November 1, 1989): 60-64.

"Mercantilists in Houston". *The Economist* 316, No. 7662 (July 7, 1990): 14-15.

"Merchants of Venice". *The Economist* 275, No. 7135 (May 31, 1980): 9-11.

"Merge the IMF and the World Bank: It's Time To Prepare for the 21st Century". *The International Economy: The Magazine of International Economic Policy* 12, No. 1 (January/February 1998): 14-16.

Merlini, Cesare. "The G-7 and the Need for Reform". In "The Future of the G-7 Summits", 5-25. *The International Spectator* 29, No. 2 (April/June 1994), Special Issue. Also available as computer file. URL: www.library.utoronto.ca/www/g7/scholar/merltitl.htm.

Mikhailov, Viktor. "Nuclear Issues at th Moscow Summit". *International Affairs* 42, No. 2 (1996): 38-47.

Milani, Hamid. "Exchange Rate Behaviour under Flexible Exchange Rate: Some Empirical Evidence from G-7". *Foreign Trade Review: Quarterly Journal of the Indian Institute of Foreign Trade* 28 (July-December 1993): 166-71.

"Mountain Climbing May Not Be the Best Exercise for Nakasone". *The Economist* 299, No. 7445 (May 10, 1986): 33-34.

"Mr Schmidt's Summits". *The Economist* 268, No. 7037 (July 15, 1978): 13-14.

Mulford, David, and David M. Smick. "The G7 Strikes Back! A Mulford Interview". *The International Economy: The Magazine of International Economic Policy* 5, No. 4 (July/August 1991): 15-23.

Mulford, David. "Mulford Memorandum: America Has Blown It with the G7". *The International Economy: The Magazine of International Economic Policy* 12, No. 1 (January/February 1998): 10-13,60.

Mwanza, Allast M. "G7 Ignores Africa's Debt Plight". *Africa Analysis*, No. 127 (July 26, 1991): 15.

"Objective for the 1980s". *The Banker* 133, No. 688 (June 1983): 5.

Odom, William E. "How To Create a True World Order". *Orbis* 39, No. 2 (Spring 1995): 155-72.

"OPEC Gets Up Energy for the Summit". *The Economist* 271, No. 7086 (June 23, 1979): 85-86.

Owada, Hisashi. "A Japanese Perspective on the Role and Future of the G-7". In "The Future of the G-7 Summits", 95-112. *The International Spectator* 29, No. 2 (April/June 1994), Special Issue. Also available as computer file. URL: www.library.utoronto.ca/www/g7/scholar/owadtab.htm.

Owen, Henry. "Defending the G7: Why Fred Bergsten Should See the Glass as Half Full". *The International Economy: The Magazine of International Economic Policy* 11, No. 1 (January/February 1997): 30-33.

Owen, Henry. "High Time for Europe to Act in Concert". *Financial Times* (London), May 16, 1984: 17.

Owen, Henry. "Summitry Revisited". *The Atlantic Monthly* 231, No. 3 (March 1973): 6-10.

Owen, Henry. "A U.S. Perspective on Reform of the International Monetary System". *North American Outlook* 5, No. 3 (June 1995): 14-18.

Owen, Henry. "The World Economy: The Dollar and the Summit". *Foreign Affairs* 63, No. 2 (Winter 1984/85): 344-59.

Parboni, Riccardo. "Reflections on Williamsburg". *New Left Review*, No. 141 (September/October 1983): 72-78.

"The Path Down from the Summit Is Paved with Good Intentions". *The Economist* 280, No. 7195 (July 25, 1981): 61-62.

Pelkmans, Jacques. "Economische Topconferenties (Economic Summits)". *Internationale Spectator* 38, No. 2 (Februari 1984): 69-77.

"People Who Live in Glass Houses ...". *The Economist* 320, No. 7716 (July 20, 1991): 47-48.

"Per Ardua ad Ottawa". *The Economist* 280, No. 7194 (July 18, 1981): 12-13.

Perpiñá, Román. "Reflexiones ante las Cumbres Económicos y la de Williamsburgo". (Reflections before the Economic Summits and the

Summit of Williamsburg). *Moneda y Crédito: Revista de Economía*, 167 (Diciembre 1983): 7-20.

"Playing to the Balconies". *The Economist* 328, No. 7819 (July 10, 1993): 57-58.

"Preview of the G-7 Summit, Halifax, Canada, June 15-17" *Daily Report for Executives*, No. 114, Special Issue. Washington, D.C.: Bureau of National Affairs, June 14, 1995.

Primakov, Yevgeni and Grigori Yavlinski. "A Gorbachev-Yeltsin Deal for the G7". *The International Economy: The Magazine of International Economic Policy* 5, No. 3 (May/June 1991), 12, 14-15.

Putnam, Robert D. "Diplomacy and Domestic Politics: The Logic of Two-Level Games". *International Organization* 42, No. 3 (Summer 1988): 427-60.

Putnam, Robert D. "Summit Sense". *Foreign Policy* 55 (Summer 1984): 73-91.

Putnam, Robert D. "Western Summitry in the 1990s: American Perspectives". In "The Future of the G-7 Summits", 81-93. *The International Spectator* 29, No. 2 (April/June 1994), Special Issue. Also available as computer file. URL: www.library.utoronto.ca/www/g7/scholar/putnmtab.htm.

Putnam, Robert D. "Der Zweite Bonner Weltwirtschaftsgipfel (The Second Bonn World Economic Summit)". *Europa-Archiv* 40, 8. Folge (25 April 1985)): 233-42.

"Pygmies of G7: Interest Groups Tower over `Leaders' at Tokyo Summit". *Far Eastern Economic Review* 156, No. 29 (July 22, 1993): 5.

"The Rambouillet Declaration". *The Atlantic Community Quarterly* 13, No. 4 (Winter 1975-76): 506-12.

Ramirez de la O, Rogelio. "Reform of International Financial Institutions: A Mexican View". *North American Outlook* 5, No. 3 (June 1995): 67-74.

"Reform of the International Monetary System: Views from North America". *North American Outlook* 5, No. 3 (June 1995).

"The Regan [US Treasury Secretary Donald Regan] Initiative" *Institutional Investor* (International ed.), February 1983: 79-83.

Riaz, M. H. "London Summit: Flickering Ray of Hope for Third World". *Pakistan & Gulf Economist* 3 (June 23, 1984): 18-20.

Richter, Rudolf. "The Louvre Accord from the Viewpoint of the New Institutional Economics". *Journal of Institutional and Theoretical Economics* 145, No. 4 (December 1989): 704-19.

Rosenberg, Michael R. "Is G-7 Coordinated Intervention Responsible for Greater Stability of Exchange Rates?" *Journal of Asian Economics* 4, No. 2 (Fall 1993): 397-405.

"A Route Map for the Seven Summiteers". *The Economist* 307, No. 7555 (June 18, 1988): 17-19. ["Alternative communiqué" drafted by ten experts.]

Rowley, Anthony. "G-7 Reshapes Bretton Woods". *The Banker* 144, No. 824 (October 1994): 37-42.

Rowley, Anthony. "Greenlight in Paris: G-7 Leaders Launch Initiative on Environment". *Far Eastern Economic Review* 145, No. 30 (July 27, 1989): 58-59.

"Rulers' Rusty Rules". *The Banker* 146, No. 850 (December 1996): 18.

"Running the World: The Mulford Gang of Five, Plus Poehl". *The International Economy: The Magazine of International Economic Policy* 3, No. 5 (September/October 1989): 44-45, 48.

Sachs, Jeffrey. "Global Capitalism: Making It Work". *The Economist* 348, No. 8085 (September 12, 1998): 23-25.

Sachs, Jeffrey. "Russian Sachs Appeal: The G7 Has One Last Chance". *The International Economy: The Magazine of International Economic Policy* 7, No. 1 (January/February 1993): 50-53.

Samuel-Lajeunesse, Denis. "A propos du G7: 'beaucoup de bruit pour rien'? (About the G7: Much Ado about Nothing)?" *La lettre de l'O.e.g. [Observatoire européen de géopolitique]*, No. 3 (1er semestre 1996), [1].

Samuelson, Robert J. "Doing Something by Doing Nothing". *National Journal* 15, No. 21 (May 21, 1983): 1070.

Sassoon, Enrico. "Ricominciare de Venezia". (Starting Over from Venice). *Mondo Economico*, No. 24 (June 22, 1987): 22-23.

"The Saudis Help Those Who Sort of Help Themselves". *The Economist* 272, No. 7088 (July 7, 1979): 87-88.

Schaetzel, J. Robert, and Harald B. Malmgren. "Talking Heads". *Foreign Policy* 39 (Summer 1980): 130-42.

Schmidt, Helmut. "The Inevitable Need for American Leadership". *The Economist* 286, No. 7278 (February 26, 1983): 19-24, 27-30.

Schmidt, Helmut. "The Trade War Threat: Failure of the Bonn Economic Summit Puts Even More Pressure on the American Economy". *The Washington Post Magazine*, June 16, 1985: 11, 13, 35-36.

Sen, Sudhir. "Economic Summits: Empty Ritual". *Economic and Political Weekly* (Bombay) 18, No. 27 (July 2, 1983): 1169-70.

Séréni, Jean-Pierre. "Sommet de Bonn: le grand marchandage". (The Bonn Summit: The Big Haggle). *Le nouvel économiste*, No. 488 (3 mai 1985): 58-63.

Shelley, Toby. "Plenty of Nothing". *West Africa*, No. 3754 (31 July-6 August 1989): 1240-42.

Shida, Tomio. "Has G-7 Intervention Reached Its Limit?" *Japan Economic Journal* (International ed.) 28:1-2 October 21, 1989.

Silvestri, Stefano. "Between Globalism and Regionalism: The Role and Composition of the G-7". In "The Future of the G-7 Summits", 27-48. *The International Spectator* 29, No. 2 (April/June 1994), Special Issue. Also available as computer file. URL: www.library.utoronto.ca/www/g7/scholar/silvestri.htm.

Simandjuntak, Djisman S. "Expanding the Focus of the G-7". *Japan Review of International Affairs* 8, No. 1 (Winter 1994): 39-64.

Smith, Murray. "International Financial Institutions and the World Trade Organization: Making the Linkages Work". *Canadian Foreign Policy = La Politique étrangère du Canada* 3, No. 1 (Spring 1995): 23-30.

Smith, Steven K., and Douglas A. Wertman. "Summing Up before the Economic Summit". *Public Opinion* 11 (March/April 1989): 41-45.

Smouts, Marie-Claude. "Les Sommets des pays industrialisés" (The Summits of Industrialised Countries). *Revue de droit international* (1980): 668-85.

Smyser, W. R. "Goodbye, G-7". *The Washington Quarterly* 16, No. 1 (Winter 1993): 15-28.

Smyslov, Dmitrii V. "External Assistance: The Magic of Numbers and Reality". *Russian and East European Finance and Trade* 31, No. 2 (March/April 1995): 6-26.

Solomon, Hyman. "Summit Reflections". *International Perspectives* 17, No. 4 (July/August 1988): 8-10.

"Special Report: The Denver Economic Summit". *Newsweek* 129, No. 25 (June 23, 1997): 12-31.

"The Spirit of Rambouillet". *The Economist* 257, No. 6900 (November 22, 1975): 77-78.

Stark, Jürgen. "The G7 at Work". *The International Economy: The Magazine of International Economic Policy* 9, No. 5 (September/October 1995): 52-54.

Stephens, Gina. "The G-7 Summit: Lyon, France". *Centre News* (Centre for Russian & East European Studies, University of Toronto), September 1996: 3-5.

Stephens, Philip. "Major Calls for Overhaul of G7 Summits". *Financial Times* (London), September 10, 1992: 1. (Summary of John Major's unpublished letter of August 1992 to other G-7 heads of state or government.)

Summers, Lawrence H. "In Defense of the G7". *The International Economy: The Magazine of International Economic Policy* 10, No. 4 (July/August 1996): 8-9, 57-59.

"Summit in Slump". *The Economist* 257, No. 6899 (November 15, 1975): 81-84.

"Summit Is As Summit Does". *The Economist* 260, No. 6931 (July 3, 1976): 91-92.

"A Summit or a Cliff?" *The Economist* 283, No. 7239 (May 29, 1982): 13-14.

"A Summit Package". *The Economist* 295, No. 7391 (April 27, 1985): 15-16.

"The Summit Process in Review". *Japan Review of International Affairs* 8, No. 1 (Winter 1994): 3-64.

"The Summit Round". *The Economist* 291, No. 7345 (June 9, 1984): 12.

"The Summit: Well, the Weather Was Fine". *The Economist* 307, No. 7556 (June 25, 1988): 66, 68.

"Summitspeak". *The Economist* 299, No. 7445 (May 10, 1986): 12-13.

Sutherland, Peter. "Le Directeur général du GATT réclame une refonte du G7". (The Director General of GATT calls for remodelling of the G7). *Le Monde*, 3 février, 1994: 18. (Summary of speech at the World Economic Forum, Davos, Switzerland, on replacing the G-7 with a broader institution.)

Suzuki, Motoshi. "Economic Interdependence, Relative Gains, and International Cooperation: The Case of Monetary Policy Coordination". *International Studies Quarterly* 38, No. 3 (September 1994): 475-98.

Takase, Junichi. "The Second Politicisation of G7 Summits". [In Japanese] *Gaiko Jiho = Revue Diplomatique*, June 1993: 81-93.

Taylor, James H. "Preparing for the Halifax Summit: Reflections on Past Summits". *Canadian Foreign Policy = La Politique étrangère du Canada* 3, No. 1 (Spring 1995): 31-46.

Taylor, John B. "International Coordination in the Design of Macroeconomic Policy Rules". *European Economic Review* 28, No. 1/2 (June/July 1985): 53-81. [*See also Comments* by Giampaolo Galli (83-87) and William Nordhaus (89-92).]

"A Test of Confidence at the Summit". *Business Week*, No. 2846 (June 11, 1984): 40-41.

Theulet, Xavier. "Dette: les belles promesses du G7 (Debt: The Fine Promises of the G7)". *Jeune Afrique Economie*, No. 222 (July 15, 1996): 8-10.

Thiel, Elke. "Atlantischer Wirtschaftskonflikt vor und nach Versailles". (Atlantic Economic Conflict Before and After Versailles). *Aussenpolitik* 33, No. 4 (1982): 371-84.

Thiel, Elke. "Wirtschaftsgipfel von Rambouillet bis Venedig". (Economic Summits from Rambouillet to Venice). *Aussenpolitik* 32, No. 1 (1981): 3-14.

"This Year's Summit". *The Economist* 335, No. 7918 (June 10, 1995): 13-14.

Tietmeyer, Hans. "Probleme und Perspektiven der Weltwirtschaft vor Williamsburg". (Problems and Perspectives of the World Economy before Williamsburg). *Europa-Archiv* 38, 10. Folge (25 Mai 1983): 295-304.

"Toeing the G-7 Line". *Economic and Political Weekly* (Bombay) 24, No. 7 (February 18, 1989): 343-44.

"Tokyo Summit: Er ... Exchange Rates and Budgets?" *The Economist* 299, No. 7444 (May 3, 1986): 78, 82.

"Towards Harmony, and Williamsburg". *The Economist* 287, No. 7286 (April 23, 1983): 23-24.

"Transparent Hype". *The Economist* 349, No. 8093 (November 7, 1998): 80.

"Triple Detente". *The Economist* 316, No. 7663 (July 14, 1990): 27-29.

"Tutte le promesse dei sette grandi". (All the Promises of the Great Seven). *Mondo Economico*, No. 24 (June 22, 1987): 24-25.

Ugochukwu, Onyema. "London Summit: Consensus among Believers". *West Africa*, No. 3487 (18 June 1984): 1257-58.

Ullmann, Owen, and others. "Summit of the Damned: The Not-so-magnificent G-7 Leaders Are Limping into Tokyo". *Business Week*, No. 3327 (July 12, 1993): 44-45.

Ullrich, Heidi, and Alan Donnelly. "The Group of Eight and the European Union: The Evolving Partnership". *G7 Governance*, No. 5 (November 1998). [Computer file]. URL: http://www.library.utoronto.ca/www/g7/governance/gov5/.

"Un-magnificent G7". *Economist Financial Report* 13 (February 9, 1989): 1.

Vastel, Michel.   "Trudeau on Summitry".   *International Perspectives*, November/December 1982: 10-12.

Vogel, Heinrich.   "The London Summit and the Soviet Union". *Aussenpolitik: German Foreign Affairs Review* 42, No. 4 (1991): 315-25.

Von Furstenberg, George M. "Accountability and a Metric for Credibility and Compliance". *Journal of Institutional and Theoretical Economics = Zeitschrift für die Gesamte Staatswissenschaft* 151, No. 2 (June 1995): 304-25.

Von Furstenberg, George M., and Joseph P. Daniels. "Can You Trust G-7 Promises?"   *International Economic Insights* 3, No. 5 (September/October 1992): 24-27. Also available as computer file. URL: www.library.utoronto.ca/www/g7/furst_dan.htm.

Von Furstenberg, George M., and Joseph P. Daniels. "Policy Undertakings by the Seven 'Summit' Countries: Ascertaining the Degree of Compliance". *Carnegie-Rochester Conference Series on Public Policy* 35 (Autumn 1991): 267-308.

Wallis, W. Allen. "A Sherpa's View of Economic Summits". *The American Enterprise*, July/August 1990: 63-69.

Watanabe, Akio. "The G-7 Summits and the Formation of a New World Political Order". *Japan Review of International Affairs* 8, No. 1 (Winter 1994): 3-20.

Waverman, Leonard, and Tom Wilson, eds. "Macroeconomic Co-ordination and the Summit". *Canadian Public Policy* 15 (February 1989), Special Supplement.

Webb, Michael C. "International Economic Structures, Government Interests, and International Coordination of Macroeconomic Adjustment Policies". *International Organization* 45, No. 3 (Summer 1991): 308-42.

Westlake, Melvyn. "Cold Hearts and Cherry Blossom". *South: The Third World Magazine*, No. 69 (July 1986): 93-94.

Westlake, Melvyn. "London Summit: The Bits and Peaces Strategy". *South: The Third World Magazine*, No. 45 (July 1984): 36.

"Where Have All the Leaders Gone?" *Time*, July 12, 1993: 14-19.

Whyman, William E. "We Can't Go On Meeting Like This: Revitalizing the G-7 Process". *The Washington Quarterly* 18, No. 3 (Summer 1995): 139-65.

"Williamsburg: les dossiers des présidents". (Williamsburg: the Presidents' Files). *Le nouvel économiste*, No. 390 (30 mai 1983): 52-56.

Williamson, John. "Reform of the International Financial Institutions". *Canadian Foreign Policy = La Politique étrangère du Canada* 3, No. 1 (Spring 1995): 15-22.

Wojnilower, Albert. "How Gorbachev Is Threatening G-7 Coordination". *The International Economy: The Magazine of International Economic Policy* 2, No. 2 (March/April 1988): 32-33.

Wolfe, Robert. "Should Canada Stay in the Group of Seven?" *Canadian Foreign Policy = La Politique étrangère du Canada* 3, No. 1 (Spring 1995): 47-62.

"Woof, Thank You, Lac St-Jean". *The Economist* 307, No. 7556 (June 25, 1988): 44-45.

"World Economic Summit: Straws To Clutch". *The Economist* 275, No. 7139 (June 28, 1980): 82-83.

Yamamoto, Yoshinobu. "The Role of the G-7 Summit in the New International System". *Japan Review of International Affairs* 7, No. 2 (Spring 1993): 161-76.

"Yeltsin Gets Aid Package from G-7 in Tokyo". *The Current Digest of the Post-Soviet Press* 45, No. 27 (August 4, 1993): 14-17.

"Yeltsin Hosts G-7 for Nuclear Security Summit". *The Current Digest of the Post-Soviet Press* 48, No. 16 (May 15 1996): 1-6.

"Yeltsin in Munich: G-7 Backs Aid to Russia". *The Current Digest of the Post-Soviet Press* 44, No. 27 (August 5 1992): 1-5.

Zhao Zonglu. "G-7 Summit More Positive on Aid". *Beijing Review* 39, No. 30 (July 22, 1996): 10.

Government Publications

Canada. Department of External Affairs. *The Houston Economic Summit, Houston, Texas, July 9-11, 1990.* [Ottawa], 1990.

Canada. Department of External Affairs. *The Munich Economic Summit, July 6-8, 1992: Background Information.* [Ottawa], 1992.

Canada. Department of External Affairs. *The Summit of the Arch, Paris, July 14-16, 1989.* [Ottawa], 1989.

Canada. Department of External Affairs. *Toronto Economic Summit, June 19-21, 1988*. [Ottawa], 1988.

Canada. Department of External Affairs. *Venice Economic Summit, June 8-10, 1987*. [Ottawa], 1987.

Canada. Department of External Affairs and International Trade. *The London Economic Summit, July 15-17, 1991: Background Information*. Ottawa: DEAIT, 1991.

Canada. Department of External Affairs and International Trade. *The Tokyo Economic Summit, July 7-9, 1993: Background Information*. Ottawa: DFAIT, 1993.

Canada. Department of Foreign Affairs and International Trade. *Canada and the G-7 Summits*. Ottawa: DFAIT, 1995.

Canada. Department of Foreign Affairs and International Trade. *The Denver Summit, June 20-22, 1997: Background Information*. Ottawa: DFAIT, 1997.

Canada. Department of Foreign Affairs and International Trade. *The Halifax Summit, June 15-17, 1995: Background Information*. Ottawa: DFAIT, 1995.

Canada. Department of Foreign Affairs and International Trade. *The Lyon Summit, June 27-29, 1996: Background Information*. Ottawa: DFAIT, 1996.

Canada. Department of Foreign Affairs and International Trade. *The Naples Economic Summit, July 8-10, 1994: Background Information*. Ottawa: DFAIT, 1994.

Canada. Department of Foreign Affairs and International Trade. *1995, Canada's Year As G7 Chair: The Halifax Summit Legacy*. Ottawa: DFAIT, 1996. See also the Department's Web site at www.dfait-maeci.gc.ca/english/g7summit/hfax2.htm.

Canada. Environment Canada. *G-7 Environment Ministers' Meeting, Hamilton, Canada, April 30 and May 1, 1995*. [Computer file] Ottawa: Environment Canada, 1995. URL: www.doe.ca/issues/g7/e-g7.html.

Canada. Parliament. House of Commons. Standing Committee on Foreign Affairs and International Trade. *From Bretton Woods to Halifax and beyond: Towards a 21st Summit for the 21st Century Challenge: Report of the House of Commons Standing Committee on Foreign Affairs and International Trade on the Issues of International Financial Institutions Reforms for the Agenda of the June 1995 G-7 Halifax Summit*. Minutes of Proceedings and Evidence of the

Standing Committee on Foreign Affairs and International Trade, Respecting, Pursuant to Standing Order 108 (2), an Examination of the Agenda for the G-7 Summit, in Halifax and in Particular, Reform of the International Financial Institutions, Including the Fourth Report to the House. Thirty-fifth Parliament, First Session, Issue No 25, May 9, 1995. Ottawa: Queen's Printer, 1995.

Canada. Parliament. House of Commons. Standing Committee on Foreign Affairs and International Trade. *Minutes of Proceedings and Evidence of the Standing Committee on Foreign Affairs and International Trade, Respecting, Pursuant to Standing Order 108 (2), a Round Table Discussion of the Agenda for the G-7 Summit in Halifax.* Thirty-fifth Parliament, First Session, Issue Nos. 16, February 21-22, 1995; 18, March 14, 1995; 21, March 28, 1995; 22, March 30, 1995; 23, April 4, 1995. Ottawa: Queen's Printer, 1995. Minutes of Meeting No. 40, May 2, 1995 (URL: www.library.utoronto.ca/www/g7/min40.htm); *Evidence,* Meeting No. 40, May 2, 1995 [unpublished].

Cappe, Mel. "From Hamilton to Halifax". In *The Halifax Summit, Sustainable Development, and International Institutional Reform.* Edited by John Kirton and Sarah Richardson. Ottawa: National Round Table on the Environment and the Economy, 1995, 38-41.

Crenna, C. D. *Working Towards an Environmental Information Statement: Summary Paper / International Forum on Environmental Information for the Twenty-first Century, Montreal, 1991.* Ottawa: Environmental Information Forum Secretariat, State of the Environment Reporting, Environment Canada, 1991.

Dam, Kenneth W. "Looking toward Williamsburg: U.S. Economic Policy". United States, Department of State, *Department of State Bulletin* 83, No. 2075 (June 1983): 21-24.

Dolzer, Rudolph. "A German Perspective". In *The Halifax Summit, Sustainable Development, and International Institutional Reform.* Edited by John Kirton and Sarah Richardson. Ottawa: National Round Table on the Environment and the Economy, 1995, 95-98.

Eglin, Richard. "The World Trade Organization". In *The Halifax Summit, Sustainable Development, and International Institutional Reform.* Edited by John Kirton and Sarah Richardson. Ottawa: National Round Table on the Environment and the Economy, 1995, 70-72.

Esty, Dan. "A Global Environment Organization: The Fourth Bretton Woods Pillar?" In *The Halifax Summit, Sustainable Development, and International Institutional Reform*. Edited by John Kirton and Sarah Richardson. Ottawa: National Round Table on the Environment and the Economy, 1995, 75-79.

Evans, Charles L., and Fernando Santos. *Monetary Policy Shocks and Productivity Measures in the G-7 Countries*. Federal Reserve Bank of Chicago. Working Paper Series, Macro Economic Issues, No. WP-93-12. Chicago: Federal Reserve Bank of Chicago, November 1993.

Gandhi, Ved. "The International Monetary Fund". In *The Halifax Summit, Sustainable Development, and International Institutional Reform*. Edited by John Kirton and Sarah Richardson. Ottawa: National Round Table on the Environment and the Economy, 1995, 45-53.

Godbout, Todd M., and Constance Sorrentino. *International Labor Comparisons among the G-7 Countries: A Chartbook*. Report, No. 890. Washington, D.C.: U.S. Dept. of Labor, Bureau of Labor Statistics, 1995.

Gotlieb, Allan. "The Western Economic Summit". Canada. Department of External Affairs. *Statements and Speeches*, No. 81/13. Ottawa, 1981.

Great Britain. Foreign & Commonwealth Office. *The G7 process*. Background Brief. London, 1996.

Great Britain. Foreign & Commonwealth Office. *Western Assistance to the Former Soviet Union*. Background Brief. London: Foreign & Commonwealth Office, 1992.

Great Britain. Parliament. House of Commons. Session 1982/1983. *Technology, Growth and Employment: Report of the Working Group Set Up by the Economic Summit Meeting of 1982*. By the Science and Technology Secretariat, Cabinet Office. Cmnd. 8818. London: HMSO, 1983.

Great Britain. Parliament. House of Commons. Session 1983/1984. *Report of the Technology, Growth and Employment Working Group to the London Economic Summit 1984*. By the Science and Technology Secretariat, Cabinet Office. Cmnd. 9269. London: HMSO, 1984.

Great Britain. Parliament. House of Commons. Session 1992/1993. [Prime Minister John Major's statement on the 1993 Tokyo Summit]. In *Parliamentary Debates*, 6th Series, Vol. 228, cols. 669-71. London: House of Commons, 12 July 1993.

Hale, David. "An American Perspective". In *The Halifax Summit, Sustainable Development, and International Institutional Reform*.

Edited by John Kirton and Sarah Richardson. Ottawa: National Round Table on the Environment and the Economy, 1995, 89-94.

Hashmi, I. "Energy Consumption among the G-7 Countries". *Canadian Economic Observer* 8 (Ottawa: Statistics Canada; Catalogue No. 11-010; May 1995): 3.1-3.9.

Hopkinson, Nicholas. *The Evolving World Debt Problem.* Wilton Park Papers, No. 17. London: Her Majesty's Stationery Office, 1991. [Based on Wilton Park Conference 336, 2-6 May 1989.]

International Forum on Environmental Information for the Twenty-first Century, Montreal, 1991. *Proceedings, Environmental Information Forum.* Ottawa: Environmental Information Forum Secretariat, State of the Environment Reporting, Environment Canada, 1992.

Japan. Ministry of Foreign Affairs. *G-7 Official Documents, 1975-1992.* Tokyo: MFA, 1993. 2 3½" diskettes.

Johnson, Pierre Marc, and John J. Kirton. "Sustainable Development and Canada at the G7 Summit". In *The Halifax Summit, Sustainable Development, and International Institutional Reform: Preliminary Discussion Paper and Background Material.* Montreal: Task Force on Foreign Policy and Sustainability, The National Round Table on the Environment and the Economy, 1995, Tab 1, 14 p. [Workshop on the Halifax Summit, Sustainable Development, and International Institutional Reform, Montreal, February 27, 1995.]

Johnson, Pierre Marc, and John J. Kirton. "Sustainable Development and Canada at the G7 Summit". In *The Halifax Summit, Sustainable Development, and International Institutional Reform.* Edited by John Kirton and Sarah Richardson. Ottawa: National Round Table on the Environment and the Economy, 1995, 19-29.

Kirton, John J. "Sustainable Development at the Houston Summit". Paper prepared for the Foreign Policy Committee, National Roundtable on Environment and the Economy, Ottawa, September 6, 1990. Unpublished in print. [Computer file]URL: www.library.utoronto.ca/www/g7/scholar/sdh.htm.

Kirton, John J., and Sarah Richardson, eds. *The Halifax Summit, Sustainable Development, and International Institutional Reform.* Ottawa: National Round Table on the Environment and the Economy, 1995. Also available as computer file. URL: www.library.utoronto.ca/www/g7/rt95con.htm.

Kokotsis, Eleonore. "Keeping Sustainable Development Commitments: The Recent G7 Record". In *The Halifax Summit, Sustainable*

Development, and International Institutional Reform: Preliminary Discussion Paper and Background Material. Montreal: Task Force on Foreign Policy and Sustainability, The National Round Table on the Environment and the Economy, 1995, Tab 2, 28 p. [Workshop on the Halifax Summit, Sustainable Development, and International Institutional Reform, Montreal, February 27, 1995.] Also published in *The Halifax Summit, Sustainable Development, and International Institutional Reform*, edited by John Kirton and Sarah Richardson (Ottawa: National Round Table on the Environment and the Economy, 1995), 117-133. Also available as computer file. URL: www.library.utoronto.ca/www/g7/kitcon95.htm.

MacNeill, Jim. "UN Agencies and the OECD". In *The Halifax Summit, Sustainable Development, and International Institutional Reform*. Edited by John Kirton and Sarah Richardson. Ottawa: National Round Table on the Environment and the Economy, 1995, 81-85.

Page, Robert. "International Trade and the Environment: The WTO and the New Beginning". In *The Halifax Summit, Sustainable Development, and International Institutional Reform*. Edited by John Kirton and Sarah Richardson. Ottawa: National Round Table on the Environment and the Economy, 1995, 61-69.

Previous Summits. Paris: Secrétariat général du Sommet des pays industrialisés; Service d'information et de diffusion du Premier ministre, 1989.

Richardson, Sarah, and John Kirton. "Conclusion". In *The Halifax Summit, Sustainable Development, and International Institutional Reform*. Edited by John Kirton and Sarah Richardson. Ottawa: National Round Table on the Environment and the Economy, 1995, 102-111.

Richardson, Sarah, and John Kirton. "Introduction". In *The Halifax Summit, Sustainable Development, and International Institutional Reform*. Edited by John Kirton and Sarah Richardson. Ottawa: National Round Table on the Environment and the Economy, 1995, 1-5.

Ricketts, Nicholas, and David Rose. *Inflation, Learning and Monetary Policy Regimes in the G-7 Economies*. Working Paper, No. 95-6. Ottawa: Bank of Canada, 1995.

Smith, Gordon. "Canada and the Halifax Summit". In *The Halifax Summit, Sustainable Development, and International Institutional Reform*. Edited by John Kirton and Sarah Richardson. Ottawa: National Round Table on the Environment and the Economy, 1995, 33-37.

Spain. Ministerio de Economía y Hacienda. "Algunas Reflexiones sobre tres conferencias económicas internacionales en el 83: desde Paris a Belgrado, pasando por Williamsburg". (Some reflections on three international economic conferences in '83: from Paris to Belgrade, via Williamsburg). Por Ramón Tamames. *Información Comercial Española: Revista de Economía,* No. 601 (September 1983): 5-11.

Spero, Joan. "Mount Halifax: In Sight of the Summit". *US Department of State Dispatch* 6, No. 26 (June 26, 1995): 520-21.

Stone, Nat. *Public Opinion Background: The G7, Globalization and Trade.* Ottawa: Department of Foreign Affairs and International Trade, 1996.

Strong, Maurice F. "Post-Rio Sustainable Development and the Summit". In *The Halifax Summit, Sustainable Development, and International Institutional Reform.* Edited by John Kirton and Sarah Richardson. Ottawa: National Round Table on the Environment and the Economy, 1995, 9-18.

Ulan, Michael, William G. Dewald, and James B. Bullard. "U.S. Official Forecasts of G-7 Economies, 1976-90". *Review (Federal Reserve Bank of St. Louis)* 77, No. 2 (March/April 1995): 39-47.

United States. Congress. House. Committee on Banking, Finance, and Urban Affairs. Subcommittee on International Finance, Trade, and Monetary Policy. *Venice Economic Summit: Hearing before the Subcommittee on International Finance, Trade, and Monetary Policy of the Committee on Banking, Finance, and Urban Affairs, House of Representatives, One Hundredth Congress, First Session, June 4, 1987.* Washington, D. C.: U.S. Government Printing Office, 1987.

United States. Congress. House. Committee on Foreign Affairs. *Economic Summit: Joint Hearing before the Committee on Foreign Affairs and the Joint Economic Committee, Congress of the United States, Ninety-ninth Congress, First Session, April 30, 1985.* Washington, D. C.: U.S. Government Printing Office, 1985.

United States. Congress. House. Committee on Foreign Affairs. Subcommittee on Europe and the Middle East. *Prospects for the London Economic Summit: Joint Hearings before the Subcommittees on Europe and the Middle East, and on International Economic Policy and Trade of the Committee on Foreign Affairs, House of Representatives, and the Subcommittee on Economic Goals and Intergovernmental Policy of the Joint Economic Committee,*

Congress of the United States, Ninety-eighth Congress, Second Session, May 14 and 20, 1984. Washington, D. C.: U.S. Government Printing Office, 1984.

United States. Congress. House. Committee on Foreign Affairs. Subcommittee on Europe and the Middle East, and on International Economic Policy and Trade. *The Venice Economic Summit: Hearing before the Subcommittees on Europe and the Middle East, and on International Economic Policy and Trade of the Committee on Foreign Affairs, House of Representatives, One Hundredth Congress, First Session, June 3, 1987.* Washington, D. C.: U.S. Government Printing Office, 1988.

United States. Congress. House. Committee on International Relations. Subcommittee on International Economic Policy and Trade. *The Bonn Summit: Its Aftermath and New International Economic Initiatives: Hearing before the Subcommittees on International Economic Policy and Trade, and International Development of the Committee on International Relations, House of Representatives, Ninety-fifth Congress, Second Session, September 20 and 21, 1978.* Washington, D. C.: U.S. Government Printing Office, 1978.

United States. Congress. Joint Economic Committee. *Issues at the Summit: Hearings before the Joint Economic Committee, Congress of the United States, Ninety-fifth Congress, First Session, April 20, 21 and 22, 1977.* Washington, D. C.: U.S. Government Printing Office, 1978.

United States. Congress. Joint Economic Committee. *Issues at the Summit: Report of the Joint Economic Committee, Congress of the United States, Together with Additional and Supplementary Views.* Washington, D. C.: U.S. Government Printing Office, 1977.

United States. Congress. Joint Economic Committee. *The London Economic Summit: Hearing before the Joint Economic Committee, Congress of the United States, One Hundred Second Congress, First Session, July 9, 1991.* S. Hrg. 102-185. Washington, D. C.: U.S. Government Printing Office, 1991.

United States. Congress. Joint Economic Committee. *The Ottawa Summit and U.S. International Economic Policy: Hearings before the Joint Economic Committee, Congress of the United States, Ninety-seventh Congress, First Session, July 14 and 16, 1981.* Washington, D. C.: U.S. Government Printing Office, 1982.

United States. Congress. Joint Economic Committee. *The Paris Economic Summit: Hearing before the Joint Economic Committee, Congress of the United States, One Hundred First Congress, First Session, July 6, 1989.* S. Hrg. 101-510. Washington, D. C.: U.S. Government Printing Office, 1990. [Includes testimonies by Robert Hormats, C. Fred Bergsten and Jeffrey Sachs.]

United States. Congress. Joint Economic Committee. *Review of the Houston Economic Summit: Hearing before the Joint Economic Committee, Congress of the United States, One Hundred First Congress, Second Session, July 25, 1990.* Washington, D. C.: U.S. Government Printing Office, 1991.

United States. Congress. Joint Economic Committee. *Review of the Paris Economic Summit: Hearing before the Joint Economic Committee, Congress of the United States, One Hundred First Congress, First Session, July 19, 1989.* S. Hrg. 101-506. Washington, D. C.: U.S. Government Printing Office, 1990.

United States. Congress. Joint Economic Committee. *Venice Economic Summit: Hearing before the Joint Economic Committee, Congress of the United States, One Hundredth Congress, First Session, April 28, 1987.* S. Hrg. 100-274. Washington, D. C.: U.S. Government Printing Office, 1987. [Includes statements by Stephen Marris, Jeffrey Sach and Ralph Bryant.]

United States. Congress. Joint Economic Committee. *Versailles Summit and the World Economy: High Interest Rates and Protectionism; Hearings before the Joint Economic Committee, Congress of the United States, Ninety-seventh Congress, Second Session, May 25, 26 and 27, 1982.* Washington, D. C.: U.S. Government Printing Office, 1982.

United States. Congress. Joint Economic Committee. *Williamsburg Economic Summit: Hearing before the Joint Economic Committee, Congress of the United States, Ninety-eighth Congress, First Session, May 24, 1983.* Washington, D. C.: U.S. Government Printing Office, 1983.

United States. Congress. Senate. Committee on Foreign Relations. *Economic Summit, Latin Debt, and the Baker Plan: Hearing before the Committee on Foreign Relations, United States Senate, Ninety-ninth Congress, Second Session, May 20, 1986.* S. Hrg. 99-889. Washington, D. C.: U.S. Government Printing Office, 1986.

United States. Congress. Senate. Committee on Foreign Relations. Subcommittee on International Economic Policy, Trade, Oceans, and Environment. *Paris Economic Summit and the International Environmental Agenda: Hearing before the Subcommittee on International Economic Policy, Trade, Oceans, and Environment of the Committee on Foreign Relations, United States Senate, One Hundred First Congress, First Session, August 3, 1989*. S. Hrg. 101-420. Washington, D. C.: U.S. Government Printing Office, 1990.

United States. Department of State. *Bonn Economic Summit*. Gist. Washington, D. C.: Bureau of Public Affairs, Dept. of State, 1985.

United States. Department of State. "G-7 Chairmen's Statement on Support for Russian Reform: Text of the Chairmen's Statement of the G-7 Joint Ministerial Meeting and the Following Meeting with Russian Ministers, Tokyo, Japan, April 15, 1993". *US Department of State Dispatch; Supplement* (Vol. 4, Suppl. 2; May 1993): 16-18. Washington, D.C.: U.S. G.P.O., 1993.

United States. Department of State. "Global Environmental Initiatives: The Environment and G7". *US Department of State Dispatch* 6, No. 4 (July 1995). Washington, D.C.: U.S. G.P.O., 1995.

United States. Department of State. "Group of Seven (G-7) 1992 Economic Summit, Munich, Germany, July 6-8, 1992". *US Department of State Dispatch; Supplement* (Vol. 3, Suppl. 5; 1992). Washington, D.C.: U.S. G.P.O., 1992.

United States. Department of State. "Group of Seven (G-7) 1993 Economic Summit, Tokyo, Japan, July 7-9, 1993". *U.S. Department of State Dispatch; Supplement* (Vol. 4, Suppl. 3; August 1993). Washington, D. C.: Bureau of Public Affairs, Dept. of State.

United States. Department of State. "Group of Seven (G-7) 1994 Economic Summit and G-7 Plus One Political Meeting, Naples, Italy, July 8-10, 1994". *U.S. Department of State Dispatch; Supplement* (Vol. 5, Suppl. 6; 1994). Washington, D.C.: U.S. G.P.O., 1994.

United States. Department of State. "Group of Seven (G-7) 1995 Economic Summit, Halifax, Nova Scotia, June 15-17, 1995". *U.S. Department of State Dispatch; Supplement* (Vol. 6, Suppl. 4; 1995). Washington, D.C.: Department of State, 1995.

United States. Department of State. "Group of Seven (G-7) 1996 Economic Summit, Lyon, France, June 26-30, 1996". *U.S. Department of State Dispatch; Supplement* (Vol. 7, Suppl. 2; 1996). Washington, D.C.: Department of State, 1996.

United States. Department of State. *London Economic Summit.* Gist. Washington, D. C.: Bureau of Public Affairs, Dept. of State, 1984.

United States. Department of State. *Tokyo Economic Summit.* Gist. Washington, D. C.: Bureau of Public Affairs, Dept. of State, 1986.

United States. Department of State. Bureau of Public Affairs. *Economic Summits, 1981-89.* Public Information Series. Washington, D. C.: Dept. of State, 1990.

United States. Department of State. Bureau of Public Affairs. "Fact Sheet: Economic Summits, 1988-95". *US Department of State Dispatch* (Vol. 6, Supplement No. 4; July 1995): 15-19.

United States. Department of the Treasury. *Survey of G-7 Laws and Regulations on Foreign Direct Investment: General Summary.* Washington, D.C.: Dept. of the Treasury, [1988].

Wallis, W. Allen. "Looking Toward London: Ten Years of Economic Summitry". Current Policy, No. 579. Washington, D. C.: Bureau of Public Affairs, Department of State, 1984.

Wallis, W. Allen. *The Tokyo Economic Summit.* Current Policy, No. 818. Washington, D. C.: Bureau of Public Affairs, Department of State, 1986.

Wallis, W. Allen. "The Tokyo Economic Summit". United States, Department of State, *Department of State Bulletin* 86, No. 2112 (July 1986): 64-68.

Wallis, W. Allen. *U.S.-Japan Economic Relations: The Tokyo Summit and Beyond.* Current Policy, No. 826. Washington, D. C.: Bureau of Public Affairs, Department of State, 1986.

Whitehead, John C. "Toward a Stronger International Economy". United States, Department of State, *Department of State Bulletin* 88, No. 2136 (July 1988): 39-43.

International Organisation Publications

Bartolini, Leonardo, Assaf Razin, and Steve Symansky. *Fiscal Restructuring in the Group of Seven Major Industrial Countries in the 1990s: Macroeconomic Effects.* IMF Working Paper, No. WP/95/35. Washington, D.C.: International Monetary Fund, Research Dept., 1995.

Bomhoff, Eduard J. *Stability of Velocity in the G-7 Countries: A Kalman Filter Approach.* International Monetary Fund Seminar Series, No. 1990-5:1. Washington, D.C.: International Monetary Fund, 1990.

Brittan, Samuel. "How To Make Sense of the Tokyo Summit Indicators". In *Interdependence and Co-operation in Tomorrow's World: A Symposium Marking the Twenty-fifth Anniversary of the OECD*, 95-101. Paris: Organisation for Economic Co-operation and Development, 1987.

Castells, Manuel, and Yuko Aoyama. "Paths towards the Informational Society: Employment Structure in G-7 Countries, 1920-90". *International Labour Review* 133, No 1 (1994): 5-33.

"Combating Unemployment and Exclusion: The Essence of an ILO Approach". *International Labour Review* 135, No 2 (1996): 227-30.

Executive summary of the ILO contribution to the G7 Employment Conference at Lille, France, 1-2 April 1996: *Combating Unemployment and Exclusion: Issues and Policy Options.*

De Larosière, Jacques. "De Larosière UNCTAD Speech: World Economy at Threshold of Recovery; Marked Pickup Anticipated in Second Half". *IMF Survey* 12, No. 11 (June 13, 1983): 161-66.

Eatwell, John. *Disguised Unemployment: The G7 Experience.* Discussion Papers, No. 106. Geneva: United Nations Conference on Trade and Development, 1995. Also issued as Annual Lecture. Cambridge: Centre for International Business Studies, South Bank University Business School, Trinity College, 1995.

European Commission. *G7 Ministerial Conference on the Global Information Society: Ministerial Conference Summary.* Luxembourg: Office for Official Publications of the European Communities, 1995.

"G-7 Leaders Urge Strong IMF-Supported Policies in States of Former U.S.S.R". *IMF Survey* 21, No. 15 (July 20, 1992): 225-26.

"G-7 Ministerial Communiqué...: Economic Policy Coordination Is Essential for Stable Growth". *IMF Survey* 20, No. 20 (November 4, 1991): 324-25.

"G-7 Ministers Finalize Debt Agreement with Soviet Union and Republics". *IMF Survey* 20, No. 22 (December 2, 1991): 363-64.

"G-7 Offers Proposals To Strengthen Bretton Woods Institutions". *IMF Survey* 24, No. 13 (July 3, 1995): 201-5.

"G-7 Statement". *IMF Survey* 20, No. 3 (February 4, 1991): 41.

G22. *Summary of Reports on the International Financial Architecture* (Washington, DC, October 1998). [Computer File] URL: www.imf.org/external/np/g22/summry.pdf.

Golub, Stephen S. *Comparative Advantage, Exchange Rates, and G-7 Sectoral Trade Balances*. IMF Working Paper, No. WP/94/5. Washington, D.C.: International Monetary Fund, Research Dept., 1994.

Grilli, Vittorio, and Nouriel Roubini. *Liquidity and Exchange Rates: Puzzling Evidence from the G-7 Countries*. International Monetary Fund Seminar Series, No. 1993-46. Washington, D.C.: IMF, 1993. Also in New York University, Leonard N. Stern School of Business, Department of Economics, Working Paper Series, No. EC-95-17 (New York: NYU, 1995).

Grosser, Gunter. "The Empirical Evidence for the Effects of Policy Coordination among the Major Industrial Countries since the Rambouillet Summit Meeting of 1975". Paper Prepared for the Conference on National Economic Policies and Their Impact on the World Economy, organized by the International Monetary Fund and the HWWA-Institut für Wirtschaftsforschung, Hamburg, May 5-7, 1988. Washington, D.C.: International Monetary Fund; Hamburg: HWWA-Institut für Wirtschaftsforschung, 1988.

Heller, Peter S. *Aging, Savings and Pensions in the Group of Seven Countries, 1980-2025*. IMF Working Paper, No. WP/89/13. Washington, D.C.: International Monetary Fund, 1989.

Horne, Jocelyn P, and Paul R. Masson. "Scope and Limits of International Economic Cooperation and Policy Coordination". International Monetary Fund. *Staff Papers* 35, No. 2 (June 1988): 259-96.

International Monetary Fund. *Macroeconomic Policies in an Interdependent World*. Edited by Ralph C. Bryant *et al*. Washington, D. C.: IMF; Centre for Economic Policy Research; Brookings Institution, 1989.

James, Harold. *International Monetary Cooperation since Bretton Woods*. Washington, D.C.: International Monetary Fund; New York; Oxford: Oxford University Press, 1996.

Kaslow, Amy. "Getting Tough in Munich". *Europe: Magazine of the European Community*" 318 (July/August 1992): 18-20.

Kopinski, Thaddeus C. "Focus on Global Economic Issues Underscores Shift in Paris Summit". United Nations, Department of Public Information, *Development Business: The Business Edition of Development Forum*, No. 276 (16 August 1989): 1, 20.

Lane, Timothy D., and Stephen S. Poloz. *Currency Substitution and Cross-border Monetary Aggregation: Evidence from the G-7.* IMF Working Paper, WP/92/81. Washington, D.C.: International Monetary Fund, Research Dept., 1992.

"Much Is At Stake for G-7 in Today's Globalized World". *IMF Survey* 25, No. 14 (July 15, 1996): 229, 235-37.

O'Callaghan, G., and others. *Recent Fiscal Developments in the European Countries of the G-7.* Papers on Policy Analysis and Assessment, No. PPAA/94/13. Washington, D.C.: International Monetary Fund, 1994.

Poloz, Stephen S. *Tests of the Twin Deficits Hypothesis for the G-7 Countries.* International Monetary Fund Seminar Series, No. 1992-10. Washington, D.C.: IMF, 1992.

Rosen, Gerald R. "G-7 Backs Technical Aid to U.S.S.R". *IMF Survey* 20, No. 15 (July 29, 1991): 225, 233.

Schuchat, Frank. "Denver: Home of the 1997 Summit of the Eight". *Europe: Magazine of the European Union*" 366 (May 1997): 15-16.

Stein, Jerome L. *The Fundamental Determinants of the Real Exchange Rate of the U.S. Dollar Relative to Other G-7 Currencies.* IMF Working Paper, WP/95/81. Washington, D.C.: International Monetary Fund, Research Dept., 1995.

"Summit Adopts Debt Relief Plan To Help Poorest Countries, Reinforces G-7 Policy Coordination, Stresses Structural Reforms". *IMF Survey* 17, No. 13 (June 27, 1988): 209, 219-23.

"Valéry Giscard d'Estaing [interviewed by Robert J. Guttman]". *Europe: Magazine of the European Union*" 366 (May 1997): 17-19.

"Venice Summit Strengthens Policy Coordination, Backs More Stable Exchange Rates, Enhanced SAF". *IMF Survey* 16, No. 11 (June 15, 1987): 177, 188-89.

"Williamsburg Meeting: Summit Stresses Need to Achieve Stable Recovery". *IMF Survey* 12, No. 11 (June 13, 1983): 161, 172-73.

Wood, Barry D. "Behind the Scenes at the Economic Summit: The (Almost) Invisible Players". *Europe: Magazine of the European Community* 318 (July/August 1992): 21-23.

Wood, Barry D. "The London Economic Summit". *Europe: Magazine of the European Community* 308 (July/August 1991): 12-15.

Wood, Barry D. "Looking Toward Tokyo". *Europe: Magazine of the European Community*" 327 (June 1993): 8-11.

World Bank. *G-7 Backgrounder*. Washington, D.C.: World Bank, 1996. Also available at URL: www.library.utoronto.ca/www/g7/96wb.htm.

World Economic Summits: The Role of Representative Groups In the Governance of the World Economy. WIDER Study Group Series, No. 4. Helsinki: World Institute for Development Economics Research, United Nations University, 1989.

World Trade Organization. *Reshaping the World Trading System: A History of the Uruguay Round*. By John Croome. Geneva: WTO, 1995.

Internet Resources

Canada. Dept. of Foreign Affairs and International Trade. *[G7/G8 Summit Information]*. Ottawa, 1995-. [Computer File] URL: www.dfait-maeci.gc.ca/english/g7summit/table-e.htm and www.dfait-maeci.gc.ca/english/foreignp/policy.htm#3.

European Union. Information Society Project Office. *ISPO*. Brussels; Luxembourg: ECSC-EC-EAEC, 1995-. [Computer File] URL: www.ispo.cec.be/.

G7 Governance. No. 1-, 1997-. G8 Research Group. Toronto. [Computer file] URL: www.library.utoronto.ca/www/g7/governance/index.htm.

G7 Support Implementation Group, Moscow, Russia. [Computer File] URL: www.g7sig.org/.

G8 Bulletin. Vol. 1-, June 1997-. Toronto. [Computer File] URL: www.library.utoronto.ca/www/g7/g7bulletin/index.htm.

Great Britain. Foreign & Commonwealth Office. *Birmingham G8 Summit Web Site*. London, 1998. [Computer file] URL: http://birmingham.g8summit.gov.uk.

Lyon–Sommet du G7 (Lyon–G7 Summit). Lyon: Institut d'Etudes Politiques, Université de Lyon, 1996-. [Computer File] URL: http://sunG7.univ-lyon2.fr/g7lyon.html.

United States. Dept. of State. *Birmingham Summit of the Eight*. Washington, DC, 1998. [Computer File] URL: www.state.gov/www/issues/economic/summit/98_g8_summit.html.

United States. Dept. of State. *Denver Summit of the Eight*. Washington, DC, 1997. [Computer File] URL: www.state.gov/www/issues/economic/summit/g8.html.

United States. Dept. of State. *Halifax Summit*. Washington, DC, 1995.
[Computer File] URL:
www.state.gov/www/issues/economic/summit/halifaxsummit.html.
United States. Dept. of State. *Lyon Summit*. Washington, DC, 1996.
[Computer File] URL:
www.state.gov/www/issues/economic/summit/lyonsummit.html.
United States. White House. *Denver Summit of the Eight*. Washington, DC,
1997. [Computer file] URL:
www.whitehouse.gov/WH/New/Eight/.
University of Toronto G8 Information Centre. Toronto: University of
Toronto Library and University of Toronto G7 Research Group,
1995-. [Computer File] URL: www.g7.utoronto.ca/.

Index

Ad hoc ministerial meetings, 20, 35-
    36, 39-40
  documents 82
Afele, Enyoyam 105
Afghanistan 57, 68, 76, 84
Africa 62, 68, 70, 77, 83-84 *See
    also* South Africa, Southern
    Africa
  Sub-Saharan 36
    Expert Group on Aid to 36,
    85
African Development Bank 50
African Development Fund 63, 96
Aging 62, 83
Agricultural policies 58
AIDS 57-58, 61, 63, 76, 79, 86 *See
    also* UNAIDS
  Expert Group on the Prevention
    and Treatment of 37
  International Ethics Committee
    on 37, 42
Aircraft hijacking 57, 76
Albania 62, 84
Algeria 84
Americas 77 *See also* Central
America, Latin America, North
America
Angola 84
Annan, Kofi 48
Anti-terrorism *See* Terrorism
Arab-Israeli Conflict 79 *See also*
    Israel, Lebanon, Middle East,
    Palestinians
Archives 98, 101-102
Ardouin, Estelle 84
Argentina 41-42

Arms control 13, 15, 57-59, 61-63,
    70, 76-77, 84, 97 *See also*
    Chemical weapons, Biological
    weapons, MTCR,
Nonproliferation, Nuclear
weapons, Weapons of mass
destruction
Asia-Pacific 77
Asian financial crisis (1997/98) 32,
    38, 50, 52, 62, 64, 75, 84, 96
Asian Development Bank 50, 62
Atlantic alliance 2, 7, 21
Attali, Jacques 84, 105
Australia 28, 30, 42

Balance of payments 20, 57, 68
Baltic states 77, 81
Banking and securities regulations
    46, 51
Basle Committee 46, 83
Bayne, Nicholas 3, 19, 47, 58, 60,
    62, 67-68, 103
Belgium 25, 28
Bergsten, C. Fred 20, 30, 32, 94,
    102
Berridge, R. G. 3
Biodiversity 70
Biological weapons 58
Birmingham Summit (1998) 1-3, 7-
    8, 14-15, 19, 25-27, 39, 43, 67-
    70, 74, 78, 96, 106, 125
  agenda 25, 39, 62-64, 96
  documents 39, 49-50, 62-64, 75-
    76, 79-80, 83, 85, 96-98, 126
BIS (Bank for International
    Settlements) 49, 98

Blair, Tony 14, 27, 50-51, 63, 80, 97
Bonn Summit (1978) 14, 20, 35, 57, 101
  documents 76
Bonn Summit (1985) 14, 58, 67-68
  documents 76, 85
Borges, Jorge Luis 73
Bosnia 61, 64, 77-79, 84, 96-97
Brady Plan 58
Brazil 28-30, 42
  financial rescue 52
  Pilot Program on Tropical Forests 37
Bretton Woods institutions 4, 6, 37, 61 *See also* IMF, World Bank
  reform 46, 50-51
Brzezinski, Zbigniew 28-29
Bush, George 26, 75, 80

Callaghan, James 5
Cambodia 58, 79, 84, 96
Camdessus, Michel 83
Camé, François 84
Canada 3, 5, 13, 15, 32, 35, 37-38, 40, 52, 60, 69-70, 94, 104, 106-108, 113
  Department of Foreign Affairs and International Trade 108
Capital flows 98
Carter, Jimmy 101
Central America 79
Central and Eastern Europe 19, 58-61, 68, 76-77
  assistance for economic restructuring 37
Central banks 4, 13, 32, 35, 37-38, 42-43, 79
Chechnya 93-94
Chemical Action Task Force 36, 42, 85
Chemical weapons 58

Chernobyl nuclear reactor 58, 69, 76
Chernomyrdin, Viktor 25
Child health 62, 82
Chile 29
China 28-32, 42, 58, 76-77 *See also* Tiananmen Square massacre
Chirac, Jacques 25
Chrétien, Jean 79
Clark, Joe 5
Climate change 58, 62-63, 69-70, 97
Clinton, Bill 14, 27, 30, 51, 80
Commonwealth 3
Concert of Europe 2
Conflict prevention 78
Contact Group (former Yugoslavia) 40-41
Costa Rica 29
Counterterrorism Experts' Group 36, 42, 85
Crime 36, 39, 57, 63, 68-70, 77, 84, 97 *See also* Financial crime, High-tech crime, Transnational organised crime
Crisis management 28, 38, 52, 126
Croatia 77, 84
CSCE (Conference on Security and Co-operation in Europe) 4, 61, 77 *See also* OSCE
Customs procedures 83
Cyprus 62, 84
Czechoslovakia 81

Dalhousie University (Halifax) 110
Daniels, Joseph P. 6, 67-69, 103
de Guttry, Andrea 3, 8, 43, 45, 74, 84
de Ménil, Georges 102
Debt 19, 50, 58-59, 63, 68, 70, 73, 96-97
Defarges, Philippe Moreau 2, 73, 75, 94
Democracy 21, 27, 29-30, 32, 47,

58, 61-63, 76-77, 84, 96

Denmark 4

Denver Summit (1997) 14-15, 18, 25-28, 42, 48-49, 62, 68, 70, 74, 95, 106, 108
    documents 48, 74-76, 80, 95-96

Developing countries 21, 28-29, 51, 57-63, 70, 73, 81, 96 *See also* Debt, North- South relations, Sustainable development
    poorest 59, 68

Dhahran terrorist attack 78

Diouf, Abdou 81

Dobson, Wendy 6

Documents *See under* Summits (G7/G8), *under specific summits and specific ministers*

Drugs 20-21, 42, 50, 57-59, 62-63, 69, 76-77, 79, 97

Duisenberg, Willem 37

Earth Summit (1992) 3, 38, 59, 62

East-West relations 70, 73, 76
    economic 57, 68
    security 58-59, 76

Eastern Europe *See* Central and Eastern Europe

EBRD (European Bank for Reconstruction and Development) 8, 37, 42, 46

EC (European Community) 2, 4, 13, 46, 59 *See also* EU

ECB (European Central Bank) 32, 37

Economic development 21, 69-70, 84

Economic growth 20-21, 30-31, 50, 57, 59-63, 67-69, 73, 93, 95-97

Economic issues 26, 43, 57-59, 61-62, 64, 68, 73, 76-77, 79, 83, 125-126 *See also* Financial issues, Macroeconomic issues,

Microeconomic issues

Economic recession 20-21

The Economist 32

Education 47

Egypt 81

Electronic commerce 84

Emerging economies 63

Employment 20, 46, 50, 57, 59-63, 69-70, 97 *See also* Unemployment
    national action plans 83, 97, 116

Employment ministers 36, 38, 63, 97
    documents 82

EMU (Economic and Monetary Union) 32, 37, 62, 96

Energy 20, 36, 39, 57, 63, 67-69, 96 *See also* International Energy Technology Group, Nuclear energy, Oil

Environment 20-21, 57-58, 60-62, 68-70, 73, 77, 84, 93 *See also* Climate change, Global warming

Environment ministers 20, 36, 38, 82
    documents 82

Estonia 81

EU (European Union) 2-3, 25-31, 35, 37, 39, 62, 80, 109, 113, 126 *See also* EC
    Information Society Project Office 82, 109

Euro 37

Euromissiles 15, 58, 68, 76

Europe 25, 28, 32

European Commission 25, 78

European Council 25, 28

Exchange rates 4, 35, 37, 57, 68-69, 73

Expert groups *See* Task forces, working groups and expert

groups
Export controls 58, 86

Fanfani, Amintore 79
FAO (Food and Agriculture
    Organization of the United
    Nations) 48
FATF (Financial Action Task
    Force) 36, 42, 83, 85
Favier, Pierre 84
Finance ministers 4-5, 7-8, 13, 15-
    16, 20, 25, 28, 30, 32, 35-40,
    42-44, 46, 49, 51-52, 58, 68,
    81, 83-84, 101, 113
    documents 44, 49, 53, 78-79, 81,
    83-84, 96-98, 108-109, 113,
    117, 126
Financial crime 83
    Expert Group on 36-42
Financial crisis (1997/98) 13-15, 30,
    37, 51, 64, 126 *See also* Asian
    financial crisis (1997/98)
    impact on poorest 50, 62, 96
Financial issues 26, 36, 64, 83, 85,
    95-97, 109, 126 *See also* New
    financial architecture
Financial Post (Toronto) 114-115,
    121
Financial Times 7, 14, 52, 102
Ford, Gerald 4, 13, 101
Foreign ministers 8, 20, 25, 28, 36-
    40, 43, 49, 84-85, 101, 113
    documents 82-84, 96, 98, 108,
    113, 126
Forests 62, 84 *See also* Tropical
    forests
Former Soviet Union 60 *See also*
    USSR
    newly independent states 59, 77
Former Yugoslavia 77 *See also*
    Bosnia, Croatia, Kosovo,
    Serbia

Contact Group *See* Contact
    Group (former Yugoslavia)
France 4, 13, 15, 21, 25, 32, 40, 51,
    69, 76, 94, 106
    Ministère des Affaires étrangères
    108
Francophonie 3
Free Trade Agreement (Canada-US)
    32
Funabashi, Yoichi 102

Gandhi, Rajiv 81
Garavoglia, Guido 20-21, 93, 95
GATT (General Agreement on
    Tariffs and Trade) 45, 58 *See
    also* Tokyo Round, Uruguay
    Round, WTO
GEF Working Group of Experts 37
Genscher, Hans-Dietrich 4
Germany 4, 8, 13, 15, 25, 29-30,
    32, 38-40, 94, 126
Giscard d' Estaing, Valéry 4-5, 105
Global Information Society 36, 38,
    57, 60-61, 70, 82, 106, 113
Global issues 2, 7, 20-21, 27, 30, 57,
    61-62, 77, 84, 125
Global warming 58
Globalisation 61-62, 98
The Globe and Mail (Toronto) 67
Gorbachev, Mikhail 26, 59, 80-81
Governance 2, 30, 63, 96
Group of Thirty 3
Growth *See* Economic growth
Guadeloupe meeting (1979) 15
G3 29, 32, 36, 38, 126
G5 4, 35-37
G6 special summit (1985) 13
G7 Governance 113, 121
G7/G8 *See also* Summits (G7/G8)
    and international organisations
    45-53, 74
    archives related to 98, 101-102

bodies and meetings 36-37, 42
archives related to 98, 101-102
definition 1-3
documents 73-86, 93-98, 101,
    107-109, 111-112, 115-119,
    125-126
G7-inspired institutions 37, 42
G8 Conference on Growth,
    Employability and Inclusion
    38
internet resources 74, 82, 101,
    106-124, 126
leaders 1, 3-5, 7-8, 14, 16, 25, 35-
    36, 39, 41, 47, 53, 61, 63,
    74-75, 79-80, 93-95, 97-98,
    101, 125
    documents 14, 26, 41, 43-44,
        49, 51, 79-80, 83-84, 96-
        97, 117, 126
members 2, 8, 25-32, 74, 80, 96,
    112, 125-127
ministerial meetings 35-41, 109,
    112-113, 125 *See also* Ad
hoc ministerial meetings,
Employment ministers,
Environment ministers,
Finance ministers, Foreign
ministers, Trade ministers
    documents 81-84, 113, 116-
        119, 121
nongovernmental participation 38
role 5, 7
secretariat, lack of 1, 8, 73, 107,
    111
sherpas *See* Sherpas
SIG (Support Implementation
    Group) 37, 43, 106
system 35-44, 125
    documents 73-86, 102, 123,
        125
Task forces, working groups and
    expert groups *See* Task

forces, working groups and
    expert groups
transparency 126
writings about 98, 101-106, 113-
    114, 121, 126
G8 Bulletin 114, 121
G8 Information Centre *See under*
    University of Toronto
G8 Research Group 67, 70, 111-
    114, 116, 121
G9 (proposed) 32
G10 46, 51
G11 (proposed) 29
G15 28, 81
G16 (proposed) 29
G22 42-43, 85
G24 37, 42, 51

Hajnal, Peter I. 103, 105, 111, 113
Halifax Summit (1995) 3, 7, 14-15,
    20, 38, 42, 46-47, 60-61, 64,
    68, 78, 85, 93-94, 107, 110
    documents 61, 73-75, 77-78
Health 47, 69 *See also* AIDS, Child
    health, " Roll Back Malaria
    2010", WHO
Heath, Edward 105
Henning, C. Randall 20, 32, 102
Herz, Bernhard 103
High-tech crime 63, 97
HIPCs (Heavily Indebted Poor
    Countries) 50, 69-70, 96
Hodges, Michael R. 3, 6, 32, 43, 67,
    74, 80-81, 94
Hong Kong 43, 62
Houston Summit (1990) 14, 42, 46,
    58, 67-68, 85
    documents 75, 80, 94
Human rights 30, 47, 57-58, 61-62,
    70, 76-77, 84
Humanitarian relief 48, 61
Hungary 81

Hurd, Douglas 76, 105

IDA (International Development
   Association) 50, 63, 96
IFAD (International Fund for
   Agricultural Development) 48
Ikenberry, G. John 8, 93
ILO (International Labour
   Organisation) 48, 50, 63, 97
IMF (International Monetary Fund)
   4, 8, 15, 30, 43, 45-47, 49-53,
   61-62, 64, 68, 98, 109
   Enhanced Structural Adjustment
      Facility 50, 63, 96
   Executive Board 53
   GAB (General Arrangements to
      Borrow) 47
   Interim Committee 49, 51
   line of credit 52
   Managing Director 28, 35, 46, 53,
      78, 83-85
   NAB (New Arrangements to
      Borrow) 47
   SDRs (Special Drawing Rights)
      47
   surveillance 49-52, 57-58, 68
   transparency 49, 51-53
India 28-30, 40, 43, 69, 81
   nuclear tests 39, 64, 83, 97
Indochinese refugees 57, 76
Indonesia 28, 38, 43, 64, 69, 97,
   126
Infectious diseases 62, 84 *See also*
   AIDS
Inflation 4, 20, 57, 61, 68-69, 73
Information, economic and
   financial 47
Information Society and
   Development Conference 38
Information highway 20 *See also*
   Global Information Society
Inoguchi, Kuniko 8

Intellectual property 84
Interest rates 52, 59, 68-69, 73
International Energy Technology
   Group 36, 42, 85
International financial institutions
   39, 43, 45, 48, 63, 83, 96-98
   reform 47-49, 60-61, 64, 70
International Nuclear Fuel Cycle
   Evaluation Group 36, 42, 85
International organisations 1, 45-53,
   73-74, 101, 107, 109, 121, 125
   reform 20, 46-47, 61, 68
   transparency 50
International trade *See* Trade
International War Crimes Tribunal
   78
Internet resources 74, 82, 101, 106-
   124, 126
   governmental 106-109, 113-114,
      116
   international organisation
resources 109, 114
   academic 109-124
Investment liberalisation 50, 96
IOSCO (International Organization
   of Securities Commissions) 46
Iran 15, 57, 76, 84
Iran-Iraq war 58, 76
Iraq 62, 77, 84
Ireland 4 *See also* Northern Ireland
Israel 58, 61, 76-77
Italy 13, 15, 32, 35, 37, 40, 52

Japan 2, 4, 13, 15, 21, 25, 28-30,
   32, 35, 37-38, 40, 43, 52, 60,
   69, 76, 103, 107-108, 126
   Ministry of Foreign Affairs 108
Jobs *See* Employment
Jobs Summit *See* Employment
   ministers
Jospin, Lionel 25
"Jubilee 2000" 63, 79, 97

Kinkel, Klaus 77
Kirton, John J. 2, 5-6, 20, 32, 67,
    69-70, 94, 103
Kissinger, Henry 4
Kohl, Helmut 102
Kokotsis, Eleonore 67, 70, 103
Köln Summit (1999) 14, 26
Korea 43, 77, 84 *See also* North
    Korea, South Korea
Kosovo 40, 64, 84, 97
Kyoto Protocol (1997) 63, 70, 97

Land mines 70, 84
Latin America 14, 51, 64, 77
Latvia 81
League of Nations 2
Lebanon 58, 76, 79
Lewis, Flora 8
Library Group 4, 35
Libya 58
Lithuania 81
London Summit (1977) 14, 42, 57,
    68, 85, 101
    documents 73
London Summit (1984) 14, 58, 68
    documents 76
London Summit (1991) 3, 13-14,
    26-28, 59, 67-68
    documents 76, 80-81, 85
London Suppliers' Group on
    Nuclear Materials 37, 42
Louvre Accord (1987) 21, 37
Lyon Group 36, 42, 82, 85, 113
Lyon Summit (1996) 7, 14-15, 17,
    28, 42, 46-48, 61-62, 68, 70,
    119
    documents 47-48, 61, 74, 77-78,
    85, 95

Macroeconomic issues 7, 20-21, 27,
    30, 32, 57, 68-70
Magombe, V. P. 105

Major, John 7, 59, 94-95, 104-105
Malaysia 43
MARIS (Maritime Information
    Society) 109
Market economies 13, 27, 30, 77
Martin-Roland, Michel 84
Maull, Hanns W. 8, 94
Media *See* News media
Mediterranean 77
Merlini, Cesare 2, 5, 93
Mexico 28, 43
Microeconomic issues 20-21, 57, 70
Middle East 46, 58, 62, 64, 70, 77,
    79, 84, 97
Migration 57
Millennium Bug 27, 50, 64, 97
Mitterrand, François 25-26, 28, 79-
    80
Monetary issues 21, 37, 57-61, 68-
    69, 78
Money laundering 20, 42, 58, 60,
    63, 97 *See also* FATF
MTCR (Missile Technology Control
    Regime) 37, 42
Mubarak, Hosni 81
Mulroney, Brian 79
Munich Summit (1992) 14, 26-27,
    38, 67-68
    documents 59, 77, 94
Myanmar 84 Myanmar 84

NAFTA (North American Free
    Trade Agreement) 32
Nagorno-Karabakh region 77
Naples Summit (1994) 2, 7, 14-15,
    26, 46, 60, 67-68, 95
    documents 60, 73-75, 77
NATO (North Atlantic Treaty
    Organization) 27
Netherlands 25, 28
New financial architecture 49, 51,
    53, 68-69, 78-79, 85, 97

The New York Times 73
News media 25, 57, 67, 73, 75, 79-
    80, 94, 98, 101-102, 107, 112,
    115, 126
Nigeria 29-30, 84
Non-aligned movement 28
Non-Proliferation of nuclear,
    biological and chemical
    weapons 58-59, 61-62, 64, 76,
    84, 86, 97
North America 28, 32
North Korea 61, 77
Northern Ireland 64, 97
North-South relations 57, 73 *See
    also* Developing countries
Nuclear energy 27, 36, 57 *See also*
    International Nuclear Fuel
    Cycle Evaluation Group,
    London Suppliers' Group on
    Nuclear Materials
Nuclear safety 57, 59-63, 68-70, 84,
    97 *See also* Chernobyl
    nuclear reactor
Nuclear Safety and Security Summit
    (1996) 13, 28
Nuclear Safety Working Group 36,
    42, 85
Nuclear weapons 58-59, 61-62, 77

OECD (Organisation for Economic
    Co-operation and
    Development) 4, 8, 36, 45-47,
    50, 52, 61, 63, 97, 109
    Jobs study 46
    ministerial meetings 75, 109, 113
Oil 21, 57
OPEC (Organization of the
    Petroleum Exporting
    Countries) 4
OSCE (Organization for Security
    and Co-operation in Europe)
    47

Ostry, Sylvia 29, 103
Ottawa Summit (1981) 14, 35, 57,
    68
    documents 76, 79
Owada, Hisashi 6, 75, 94

Padoan, Pier Carlo 20-21, 93, 95
Pakistan 40
    nuclear tests 39, 83
Palestinians 61, 77
Panama 79
Paris Club 27
Paris Summit (1989) 14, 28, 42, 58,
    67-68, 93
    documents 76, 79-81, 93
Pauly, Louis W. 46
Pérez, Carlos Andrés 81
Peru hostage incident 82
PHARE (Assistance for Economic
    Restructuring in the Countries
    of Central and Eastern Europe)
    37
Plaza Accord (1985) 21, 35, 37
Poland 43, 81
Political issues 7, 21, 27, 57, 61-62,
    73, 76-79, 95, 125
Press *See* News media
Prévert, Jacques 73
Primakov, Yevgeni 80
Putnam, Robert D. 3, 8, 58, 60, 67-
    68, 77, 103
P8 2, 13, 15, 26, 48, 60, 68, 74, 77-
    78, 95

Quadrilateral meetings *See* Trade
    ministers

Rambouillet Summit (1975) 13-14,
    57, 68, 101
    documents 57, 94
Reagan, Ronald 13
Recession *See* Economic recession

Refugees 76, 78 *See also*
Indochinese refugees
Regional development banks 61 *See also* African Development
Bank, Asian Development
Bank
Regional issues 57, 78, 84, 97
Reno, Janet 82
Riis, Nelson 75
"Roll Back Malaria 2010" 50, 63,
96
Ruggiero, Renato 84
Russia 2, 8, 13, 15, 19-20, 25-27,
29-31, 36, 39-40, 43, 48, 59-
62, 64, 68, 70, 74, 77, 81, 83,
93, 95, 125 *See also* USSR
Permanent Working Group on
Assistance to 36
Rwanda 61, 77

Sachs, Jeffrey 29
San Juan Summit (1976) 13-14, 57,
68, 101
Sauvagnargues, Jean 4
Schmidt, Helmut 4-5, 105
Schröder, Gerhard 14
Security issues 21, 30, 57, 60-61,
76-78 *See also* East-West
relations; security issues,
Regional issues
Senegal 81
Serbia 77
Sherpas 7, 25, 35-36, 41, 74-75, 84,
95, 109, 113
documents 74, 77, 84, 95, 113
SIG (Support Implementation
Group) *See under* G7/G8
Singapore 43
Small and medium-sized
enterprises 36, 39, 62, 82, 109
Smuggling of human beings 63, 97
Smyser, W. R. 7, 43

Somalia 84
South Africa 29-30, 43, 58, 79
South Korea 29
South Pacific, French nuclear tests
in 94
Southern Africa 79
Spain 28
Spero, Joan 104
Starbatty, Joachim 103
START (Strategic Arms Reduction
Treaty) 26
Stephens, Philip 105
Structural issues 21, 46, 70
Summit of the Arch *See* Paris
Summit (1989)
Summits (G7/G8) 13-21, 36, 43 *See also* G7/G8 and *specific
summits*
agenda 8, 25, 57-64, 74, 79, 93
archives related to 98, 101-102
chairman's statements 75-78
chairman's summary 7
communiqué 73-77
compliance with commitments
67-71, 121, 125
cycles 19-21, 60, 67
definition 1-3
documents 3, 45, 64, 70, 73-81,
93-98, 107-109, 111-112,
116-119, 125-126
format 8, 25, 43, 96
internet resources 74, 82, 101,
106-124, 126
origins 4-5
outside communications to 80-81
political declarations 75-78
press conferences 79-80, 102,
107, 112, 116, 126
reform 7-8, 69, 94-95, 127
results 62, 67-71
special summits 13, 20, 36
writings about 98, 101-106, 113-

114, 121, 126
Sustainable development 49, 62, 73
Sutherland, Peter 105

Task forces, working groups and
     expert groups 35, 41-42, 113,
     125
   documents 82, 84-86
Taxes 47, 75, 83
Terrorism 21, 36, 39, 57-58, 62, 68,
     70, 76-78, 82, 84-85, 113 *See
     also* Counterterrorism Experts'
     Group
Thailand 43
Thatcher, Margaret 105
Tiananmen Square massacre 58, 76
Tokyo Round 57
Tokyo Summit (1979) 14, 42, 57,
     68, 85, 101
   documents 57, 76
Tokyo Summit (1986) 14, 28, 35,
     58, 68
   documents 76, 83
Tokyo Summit (1993) 3, 14, 16,
     27-28, 35, 39, 43, 46, 59, 67-
     68, 75, 83
   documents 59-60, 77
Toronto Summit (1988) 14, 58, 67-
     68
   documents 79
Toronto terms 58-59
Trade 19-20, 57-63, 67-70, 75
   liberalisation 21, 50, 62, 96
Trade ministers 20, 25, 35-37, 60,
     68
   documents 82
Transnational issues *See* Global
     issues
Transnational organised crime 39,
     50, 60, 62-63, 70, 82
   Senior Experts' Group on 36, 42,
     82, 85, 113, 119

Transparency 49-53, 98, 126
Tropical Forests, Brazil Pilot
     Program on 37
Trudeau, Pierre Elliot 57, 79

Ukraine 20, 28, 36, 39, 60, 82-83,
     96
UN (United Nations) 45, 59, 63, 77,
     84, 97
   Agenda for Development 48
   arms register 59
   Economic and Social Council 47
   General Assembly 38, 62
   International Drug Control
        Programme 50
   peace-keeping 59
   reform 45-50, 61-62, 68, 70, 78
   regional commissions 48
   Secretariat 47
   Secretary-General 28, 78 *See also*
        Annan, Kofi
   Security Council 30
   specialised agencies 49
UN (United Nations) system 2, 6,
     49-50, 61
UNAIDS (United Nations
     Programme on AIDS/HIV) 50,
     63
UNCED *See* Earth Summit
UNCTAD (United Nations
     Conference on Trade and
     Development) 47, 61
UNDP (United Nations
     Development Programme) 48
Unemployment 4, 57, 59, 61, 68, 73
     See also Employment
UNEP (United Nations
     Environment Programme) 45,
     48
Unesco (United Nations
     Educational, Scientific and
     Cultural Organization) 48

UNICEF (United Nations Children's
Fund) 48
UNIDO (United Nations Industrial
Development Organization) 48,
61
United Kingdom 1, 4, 13, 15, 21,
32, 37, 40-41, 43, 52, 63, 95,
104, 106-108
Foreign and Commonwealth
Office 108
United States 4, 13, 15, 21, 25, 28-
29, 32, 35, 38, 40, 43, 52, 58,
60, 69-70, 76, 78, 104-108,
126
Information Agency 108-109
National Archives and Records
Administration 101
Treasury Department 108
Université de Lyon 106, 110
University of Toronto
G8 Information Centre 101, 106,
109-124
indexing and searching 114-
116, 119
site maintenance 115-116
use and users 111-112, 116-
124
G8 Research Group *See* G8
Research Group
Library 111
Uruguay Round 13, 35, 58-60
USSR 2, 13, 15, 19-20, 26, 46, 58-
59, 68, 70, 76, 80-81 *See also*
Former Soviet Union, Russia

Venezuela 81
Venice Summit (1980) 14 , 57, 68
documents 76, 85
Venice Summit (1987) 14, 28, 58,
68
documents 76, 79
Versailles Summit (1982) 14, 28,

57, 68, 85
documents 76
von Furstenberg, George M. 67-69,
103

Weapons of Mass Destruction 64,
86, 97
Group of Experts on 37
Web sites *See* Internet resources
Weston Park 25
WHO (World Health Organization)
48, 50, 63, 96
Whyman, William E. 7-8, 73, 75
Willard Group *See* G22
Williamsburg Summit (1983) 14,
58, 68
documents 58, 73, 76
Wilson, Harold 4
Wolfensohn, James 83
World Bank 4, 8, 15, 30, 43, 46-47,
49-53, 61-62, 64, 98, 109
President 28, 78, 83-85 *See also*
Wolfensohn, James
transparency 51
World Food Programme 48
World War II 58, 76
WTO (World Trade Organization)
27, 45, 48, 50, 60-62, 70, 109
Director- General 28, 78, 84 *See*
also Ruggiero, Renato

Yavlinski, Grigori 80
Yeltsin, Boris 16, 25-26, 79, 94,
102
Yom Kippur War (1973) 4
Yugoslavia *See* Former Yugoslavia